THE PASSAGE

THE PASSAGE

A TRAGEDY OF THE FIRST WORLD WAR

G.A. EBELSHAUSER

Edited by
RICHARD BAUMGARTNER

griffin books

Griffin Books
743 11th Avenue
Huntington, WV 25701 USA

ISBN 0-9604770-2-0

Book design and maps by Richard Baumgartner

Printed in the U.S.A.

Other books edited by Richard Baumgartner

FRITZ — The WWI Memoirs of a German Lieutenant
JOE'S WAR — Memoirs of a Doughboy

For Elfriede

ACKNOWLEDGMENTS

When Gustav Ebelshauser died on February 6, 1961, his manuscript already had lain in a desk drawer for two decades. Twenty more years would pass before it was removed from the drawer, dusted off and sent to me in early 1982 by Ebelshauser's widow, Elfriede, of Liberty Corner, New Jersey. With gracious assistance she also provided many of the photographs found in the book's photo section, as well as details pertaining to the background of her husband and his narrative.

I am further indebted to several others who helped with research related to footnoted aspects of Ebelshauser's account, especially Tony Spagnoly and Peter T. Scott in England, and Dr. Juergen Kraus of the Bavarian Army Museum in Ingolstadt, West Germany. And a special note of thanks is extended to Paul M. Smith of Fairfield, Pennsylvania, and Wade Lucas of Barberton, Ohio, for invaluable services rendered during the book's production.

R.B.

INTRODUCTION

Almost exactly 20 years after his best friend was killed while stringing barbed wire in No Man's Land in 1916, Gustav Ebelshauser began writing the following story.

It begins in 1914 when the author was 16, and ends in early 1920 when he was 21. It is a story of the First World War and how a few of its cataclysmic events grossly effected change and transformation in the life of a teen-age boy — a youth raised in Switzerland who spoke French, but who fought in a Bavarian regiment in the German army.

Born in Lausanne on St. Patrick's Day, March 17, 1898, Ebelshauser had barely outgrown childhood knickers when the war sucked him away from his neutral native land and surreptitiously threw him into a field-gray uniform of the Kaiser's Imperial army. Thus began a series of personal ordeals that was to last nearly half a decade — elucidated vividly in the third-person style of Ebelshauser's account.

However, unlike many First World War accounts by participants it was not Ebelshauser's intention to document every day or week of his experience, especially when writing of events or recalling personal thoughts and conversations with 20 years of retrospection. But his story is much more than a narrative simply describing a "worm's eye" view of battles or trench life in chronological fashion. It also slices into the psyche of the common German soldier during the conflict's midway point when many of those in the fighting lines began questioning the war's purpose among themselves. And, it shows that, despite the differences of language and color of uniform, the German soldier invariably grumbled, joked, prayed to the same God and bled red just like his enemies.

In many ways Ebelshauser's account is reminiscent of two themes so prominently delineated by Erich Maria Remarque in *All Quiet on the Western Front.* The boy is sent off to war and the grist mill of the front (blast furnace, in the author's words) steals his youth and ages him both inwardly and physically far beyond his actual years. In Ebelshauser's case, the latter is illustrated graphically in two of the photographs found elsewhere in this book.

The same themes of lost youth and premature aging were echoed in much of the war literature written and published 10, 15 and 20 years after the final shots were fired, irrespective of the writer's nationality. In one of these accounts another young German, Hans Markmann, felt the acute strain after more than three years of fighting. Shortly before he was killed on the Western Front in February 1918, Markmann wrote to a friend:

"When I imagine that I am 21 years old ... and when I further think about that in peacetime I would be in the university, drinking, doing dumb things, kissing girls and perhaps even studying, at times I am confused. We have gotten very old out here. Just imagine when we return home. We will be terribly old men at the age of 22 or 25."

Ebelshauser's story deals as well with a third theme common to many examples of 1914-1918 personal narratives written between the world wars — disillusionment. But it is not so much his own that receives attention; rather, it is that of many of his German comrades. Even though he was technically a volunteer, the author had never idealized war or soldiering. In fact, it is quite probable that he never thought at all about these things until the summer of 1914.

Disillusionment, argued Eric J. Leed in his book *No Man's Land: Combat & Identity in World War I*, was most often a function of a combatant's social status or, more exactly, of his sense of social contradiction imposed upon him by his social status. Leed wrote that the disillusionment of literate, upper- or middle-class soldiers — often volunteers — invariably came with the apprehension of the industrial, technological character of the war. Cowering within the bowels of the earth in a dimly lit dugout while a bombardment of heavy shells from distant, unseen guns pulverized the trench (and other human beings) into unrecognizable debris only 25 feet above was cause to disillusion anyone if the experience was repeated enough times.

On the Somme in September 1916, Ebelshauser lived through one of the war's most intense artillery barrages as well as the first tank assault in history. As the high explosive and shrapnel rained down on the battlefield's wasteland, there was little resistance he could offer in the confines of a "protective" shell hole reeking of cordite fumes while covering his face or chipping mud from the chamber of an almost useless rifle. Flesh and blood were ground into the soil by an invisible enemy who had disappeared behind a mask of machinery.

Disillusionment with such suppression and the monotony of life and death at the front frequently nurtured the adoption of a fatalistic philosophy, something Ebelshauser writes of in Chapter Eight:

"Two months before in the same sector they had almost drowned in the mud. It had rained in torrents for a whole week without a minute of interruption. Veritable lakes had formed and the trenches were nearly impassable with brown water knee deep. Since then he had become a great exponent of fatalism. He believed that if his hour was at hand he would be catapulted into another dark and unknown world, no matter what he did or where he stood. Of course, one had to be careful just the same, otherwise it was not fatalism anymore but premeditated self-destruction. In many cases, however, it was most difficult to pronounce the final judgment between accidental and self-imposed death."

Yet, despite such thoughts and the physical and spiritual hardships which the war brought him, the author continued to hold out. He did so by clinging to the visions of the faces of his family and the hope of somehow returning one day to Switzerland. "Home" became his driving force, his reason to go on living.

After the war Ebelshauser moved to the United States and was married on Armistice Day in 1931. He completed the manuscript on the eve of the Second World War while living on Long Island, New York, but within a year the typed pages were placed in a desk drawer where they would remain for the next 40 years.

Here, then, is his story.

Richard Baumgartner
June 1984

1

Lausanne, while not as well known internationally as its neighbor, Geneva, is one of the most beautiful and picturesque towns of French Switzerland. Seated on the shore of Lake Leman, its central location affords a magnificent outlook over the Land of Savoy on the other side of the blue waters, with the immaculate snow-capped Alps in the distant background. Closely connected is its harbor, Ouchy. Together they form the pleasant resort of Ouchy-Lausanne, familiarly identified on the travel schedules of many foreigners.

After more than 20 years of living in the same place, the Ebelshausers entertained no intentions of moving. The Rue de la Tour, lying in the center of Lausanne's business district, was ideally suited to their needs. They enjoyed its quiet and restful atmosphere. It was within walking distance of the market and a public school was right around the corner. Easy access to their shoe store also had been taken into consideration. They were fond of their surroundings. The thought of leaving had never entered their minds. Only death could move them to another world.

Christian Ebelshauser was a tall, massive, broad-shouldered man in his fifties. He wore his thin blond hair brushed back, standing on end a la Hindenburg. His large and prominent nose appeared smaller due to a thick growth of brown, wiry hair below it — a mustache of which he was proud. He once had worn it with well-greased, tilted points in the style of the Kaiser. Now it was cut short, "a la mode Anglaise." It made him look younger.

His large blue smiling eyes reflected the innocence of a child. Above all, a strong note of sincerity and frankness was expressed in his features, in his unaffected manners, in all his gestures. His straight, tall stature gave the impression of great physical strength. Everything about his person was a revelation of his German ancestry. Even without these characteristics, his origin was revealed by a typical accent of his German French.

Antoinette Ebelshauser was just the opposite of her husband. Of exceptionally miniature size, the crown of her rich mass of jet black hair barely reached to his armpits. But the woman made good in width what she lacked in height. She was more than stout, appearing from a distance like a large, slow-rolling ball. Diet was a word unknown to her. She always ate to her heart's content what she liked best.

Their children were their everything, the objects of concentrated effort and paramount ambition. They had had nine. Five had died as infants. The surviving four kept them busy almost night and day. But they did not mind the work. No sacrifice was too much for the future of their three boys and daughter.

Elise already was a young lady of 21, and about to be engaged. A tall, well-built girl with blond hair and blue eyes, she had all the traits and characteristics of her father. She was the right hand of her parents. Her skillful assistance at home, at the market and in the family store was greatly appreciated by them.

Gustav, five years younger, had just been confirmed and was getting used to wearing long pants. He was almost a perfect blend of his mother and father. Of the former, he had big brown eyes and dark hair. From his father he acquired a tall stature and a willful chin. His lips and smile were a mixture of both.

After another five years came Albert and Oskar, 11 and 10 years of age, respectively. Like his sister and father, Albert was a fair boy and quite stout for his age. Oskar was more the picture of his mother, except for his slenderness. They were still going to public school for another few years. Albert was a very studious pupil, while Oskar did not care much for textbooks, preferring instead a good detective story, read in secret.

At the end of April 1914, the second year of Gustav's special study had come to a close. His ambition was to enter the employ of the Swiss Federal Railroads. His friend and next door neighbor, Hermann Guether, a year older than himself, had been partly responsible for the choice of his future vocation. On an errand to the villa of the famous pianist Ignace Paderewsky, to whom Hermann was bringing some sheets of music his father had written, they had come to discuss their plans and ambitions of life. Urged by his friend, Gustav had asked his parents' consent to join the same school. To his surprise they readily acceded to his wish, but with the condition that he enroll for the special course of railroading, rather than take up commercial training.

So in the spring of 1912 he entered the same school as his pal. But before he could qualify as a government employee, he had to become a Swiss citizen. Under the law, Gustav was considered a German subject because of the nationality of his father, even though he had been born in Lausanne. His papers were sent for and entrusted to Monsieur Dubois, a lawyer, who was charged with the commission.

It was near vacation time. Everybody was planning and making ready to leave town. Business was in full swing. People were cheerful and happy in anticipation of beautiful days ahead. Lausanne was simply bubbling over. Smiling faces everywhere reflected the joy of living. The great yearly exodus to the country and mountain resorts was about to begin.

Suddenly, in the midst of this peaceful atmosphere, the assassination of Austrian Archduke Franz Ferdinand on June 28, 1914, came like a bombshell. A feeling of great uneasiness rose and darkened the European sky. The most critical point of the situation was reached on July 23, following Austria's ultimatum to Serbia. Five days later Austria declared war on Serbia, and on July 29, Russia began mobilization.

With trembling hearts, the Ebelshausers had watched closely the daily press reports, always hoping against hope to find somewhere a reassuring message. Instead, in rapid succession, events took a turn for the worse, shifting brusquely from discord to open antagonism and enmity. The evil net had been spread. Three days later the climax was reached when the clouds suddenly burst forth in a terrific thunderstorm, and the repercussion was felt all over the world.

On the 1st of August, Switzerland declared general mobilization. Lausanne's population, like the rest of the nation, was thrown into a state of turmoil, anxiety and consternation. By dramatic coincidence, August 1 also was Switzerland's celebration of Independence Day. To Gustav's great disappointment, this date fell on a Saturday. He had planned a party with some of his friends for that day, but the market and his errands stood in the way. To miss the sight of the great bonfires on the surrounding hills while having one of their own in the outskirts of Hermenches was beyond his conception. But perhaps, if he behaved well, his parents might still let him go after five o'clock, the market's official closing time.

To this end, he quickly responded to his mother's many calls for errands. He was the connecting link between market stand and the store. Whenever a certain size shoe was missing, he ran to his father to get the number called for.

Shortly before noon, his mother sent him again to the store. With unusual willingness, Gustav started his short trip at a quick pace. He even had it in mind to beat his previous record established that very morning. Fortunately, his father had no trouble locating the goods. With three boxes under his left arm and the loose model-shoe under his right, he began his run back to the stand.

Then, just as he was reaching the square, he was held up in his course. Before he knew it he found himself closeted in the center of a large crowd with no possibility of escape. The audience was growing rapidly. Pushed from all sides, Gustav could not see what was going on. He was beginning to wonder about it when he heard the beating of a drum. Lifting himself on his toes, he caught a glimpse of one of the ancient uniforms of the Swiss Guard. The tall man wearing it also wore the old military three-cornered hat. With a big drum hanging slightly to one side, the figure certainly was making an impressive spectacle. A voluminous, long mustache accentuated the severity of his martial bearing. The drum suddenly ceased. Following a short and tense silence, the man began shouting, though Gustav only caught a few words of great significance.

"... Germany has declared war on Russia ... In view of the grave political situation in Europe ... Switzerland must be on guard and is calling her men for a general mobilization ..."

"It's war, war, WAR!"

It looked as if the people suddenly had lost their senses. The scream of "war" was taken up on all sides. The crowd kept milling around in a mad turmoil without breaking up or getting anywhere. Like the drummer, Gustav had a tough time getting himself untangled, but patiently and with all his strength he managed to work his way through and began to run the short remaining distance to his mother.

"War has been declared! Germany against Russia! Switzerland is mobilizing!"

Out of breath, Gustav paused for a moment. "They say France is going to go against Germany, too."

"Yes, I heard about it. It's all over town. News, especially bad news, travels fast. Did you get all I wanted? Here you are, young lady. Sorry you had to wait so long. How do you like this shoe? Isn't it horrible about this war?"

His mother was a bit excited in spite of her outwardly calm appearance. In the same breath she mixed business with war. She could not quite concentrate on her sale. Thoughts of impending trouble and danger flooded through her mind. Her naturally pessimistic instincts were responding to a dark foreboding in her sensitive and anxious heart.

For the next two days Switzerland, in an attitude of cautious silence, adhered strictly to her principles of neutrality. When France declared war on Germany on August 3, however, a raving wave of French fanaticism suddenly took hold of Lausanne's population, throwing the city into a veritable turmoil. Nourished with French propaganda, it seemed as if Lausanne's citizenry had only been waiting for this signal in order to give free play to its real sentiment and opinion.

A day later, when Great Britain threw in her lot with the French, Lausanne went wild with joy and uncontrolled enthusiasm. Had it not been for an official order of restraint on the part of the authorities, the city would have been ready to join forces on the side of their admired friends. In their excessive frenzy it would have taken very little persuasion to have them turn against their own country. Of course, the violation of Belgium's neutrality also had done a great deal to sway Lausanne's public opinion.

Under these lamentable circumstances it became increasingly difficult for the Ebelshausers to remain unaffected. Dark, sinister clouds were massing and obscuring their sky. They looked at the future with great apprehension and uncertainty. They had felt all along a moderate decrease in their business, but it was not until the war's first Christmas and the New Year holidays that they began to grow alarmed. A good number of old and faithful customers they had served for the past 20 years suddenly, and without motive, dropped from sight. Others kept coming, but only rarely, and with smaller orders than usual. There was scarcely any hope for new and steady patrons.

It was after supper. The family still sat around the table discussing the situation. Gustav had come home bleeding. He had been in a fight. A bunch of boys had provoked him, railing at his German nationality. After a hail of stones, he had been hit and taken to flight. He wore a bandage hiding the scar on his forehead.

"Now listen," said his father angrily. "I don't want any of our boys getting mixed up in street fighting. And you, Gustav, should be the first one to keep out of it and set an example. You should be ashamed of yourself, a big ..."

"I couldn't help it," Gustav defended himself. "They had been watching for me around the corner. They began to call me names like 'sale boche' and 'cochon d'Allemand.' When they couldn't get hold of me, they began to throw stones."

"It was the same thing with us last week," Oskar said.

"Yes, we got the best of them after a while. We had Maudruz and Gaulat cornered and gave them a good beating. Those two won't make trouble anymore." Albert was boasting about their achievement.

"Well, don't pay any attention to them," warned his father. "Just go your own way and pass them up as if you hadn't heard anything."

"What if they jump us and ..."

"Then, of course, you must defend yourselves," father said, giving Albert no time to finish his sentence. "But don't any of you ever give the pretext for something to start. Understand?"

"It's terrible!" mother exclaimed. "As Germans we don't feel safe to go out of the house."

"Don't take it so tragically, mother," Elise remarked. "These are just harmless street broils between boys. There's no danger for us."

"I wouldn't say that so loud if I were you," she retorted petulantly. "When they tear down the flag at the German embassy and the police have to intervene, it seems to me that this should be a warning for us to watch our steps, don't you think?"

"Ach, you know who did it," Elise replied. "Just a bunch of extreme fanatics, and French students were among them. That explains everything."

"I'll admit that," her mother agreed, "but suppose we should fall into the hands of such a crazy bunch, what then? And why did they have to summon a detachment of troops from Morge when Wille, as chief of the Swiss Army, came to pay a visit to Lausanne? It wasn't in his honor but for his protection. Who knows what's going to happen next?"

"You make it worse with your pessimism, mother," her husband said. "If I were ..."

"That's not pessimism, it's reality," snapped Mrs. Ebelshauser. "Why play blind when you can see what's going on around us? What became of Paches, Belomey, Jordan and all the rest? And take a peek at the market some day. You'd think I had the pest! They avoid me whenever they can. Count all the old customers we've lost already and more are leaving week after week. Do you still think I am a pessimist?"

"Don't worry about them," father said bravely. "They'll all come back again. Just a passing fancy..."

"I wish you were right, father. I hope we haven't lost our business by the time they decide to come back, because we'll soon have to close up if this boycott keeps on."

"I think we'll get along all right, if it doesn't get worse," Elise remarked calmly, always prone to side with her father. "We may have lost a few French patrons, but we've gained some new German ones. We almost balance, I believe. We'll have to compare once, sometime next month, just for curiosity."

"Have you seen Dubois?" inquired mother, changing the subject. "You shouldn't wait any longer. Gustav must have his papers before he finishes school, and April will be at the door before you know it."

For more than a month following the first announcement in their daily newspaper, the Ebelshausers had planned to go down to the train station and take part in the general welcome of the German crippled and wounded. The French and German governments had reached an agreement concerning the exchange and repatriation of unfit soldiers so badly injured or mutilated as to be of no further service to their respective countries. The Swiss officials had given their approval and authorization for these convoys to cross the border and pass in transit through their territory.

Fifteen minutes before midnight they came to the station square.

"My goodness, look at that crowd! We'll never make it. Come, let's go back home. We can come another time."

Trailing slightly behind her tall husband, Mrs. Ebelshauser loathed the thought of having to push her way through the throng. She had no patience either, and the realization of having to wait for a long time before getting to the platform made her wish she had stayed home.

"Now, don't you get impatient," replied her husband in his low, deep voice. "We'll soon get by when they open the gate."

"Why don't they open it now?" inquired Oskar, always desirous to know the reason for everything.

"They're waiting for the trains to come in first to prevent accidents."

"It's nice to see so many people," Elise said. "I never thought there were so many left on our side."

"And don't you fool yourself," father responded, "they're not all here yet."

"See, papa, they've thrown up a double cordon of policemen," Gustav observed.

"Yes, I know. They have to since last week when a bunch of young fellows began to riot, throwing stones at the soldiers."

"It's a shame," said Mrs. Ebelshauser. "The poor soldiers, it's not their fault, and these young fools don't know any better. But wait until their turn comes. They'll think differently then."

"They're coming in now."

Two long drawn whistles were heard, bringing the vast crowd to a sudden silence. Conversations were resumed immediately, but in hushed tones.

"Please don't push, you'll get there," said a rough voice.

"I'm sorry," answered Mr. Ebelshauser, heading for the building with his family holding on behind him in single file. There was pushing and scrambling of feet. Inch by inch, the people slowly were moving forward. Once on the platform they remained gazing at the long train in amazement, not knowing exactly what to do next. And, what was the meaning of the row of dark, unlit cars?

"They're blind," someone said, and all around understood.

"Sorry, you can't get in," said a guard barring the entrance to one of the cars. "No one is allowed to see them."

"Don't they get anything at all?" asked Mr. Ebelshauser.

"They get everything they want and ask for. If you have something for them, leave it here and I'll take care of it."

Without further word, Mr. Ebelshauser left one of his bags with the guard. Then the family proceeded toward the lighted cars.

"Look, father, here is one watching us from his cot. Poor man, he seems unable to move." Following Mrs. Ebelshauser they all moved toward the car.

"How are you? Isn't it good to go back home?"

Mr. Ebelshauser pushed his head through the open window to take a look inside while he talked to the man to whom he gave another bag.

"Yes," the wounded man smiled sadly. "I hope to get there in time for my burial. I used to be a man, but they won't recognize me. I'm just about ready for the grave. It's the end, but I'll rest on home ground."

"Don't despair. You'll be all right again. Just don't give up hope. Best of luck to you."

Moved to tears by the spectacle of tragedy, Mr. Ebelshauser drew back from the window. He had tried to shake hands with the man but had found him tightly bundled up. The soldier kept looking in their direction, but the smile had faded from his lips. His pale face of skin and bone wore an expression of intense suffering. He was clenching his teeth in a visible effort to overcome the pain.

"Come, let's go further up." Mr. Ebelshauser could no longer stand the sight of the soldier's face. "It's terrible to see these men on beds of affliction without being able to help them or do something to relieve their torments."

By this time the platform had become so crowded that Mr. Ebelshauser realized immediately the impossibility of holding his family together. They all would have to go their own ways individually. At her insistence, he took his wife home on the next trolley car. She was too tired and overcome by the crowd and so much misery.

Meanwhile, Gustav had forced his way through and managed to get in front of the line. Large splotches of blood on the window panes and sides of the cars had attracted his attention. He lifted himself on his toes to take a peek. Upper and lower berths were both occupied. But a great amount of bandages hid the faces. A bit of neck in the open collar of a uniform, slightly protruding from under the covers, was all he could see. It was enough. The blood-stained bedsheets were telling something of the stark drama of war. Every one of the covered and bandaged bodies was bearing witness to the cruel massacre the nations were waging against each other, adding the bitterness of reality to many of the sad stories he had heard and read about.

"Oh children, oh children!" a woman addressed the youngsters. "I'm so glad you're under age. You can be thankful for that."

Suddenly, just as if this woman's call had been a signal, a volley of stones came hurtling over the platform and against the cars. The next minute the whole station was thrown into a terrific pandemonium. Police whistles intermingled with clangs of breaking glass, shrieks of pain and calls for help. For his own protection Gustav disappeared inside a car. At the very instant he opened the door of the compartment, a brick came crashing through a window pane and struck a wounded soldier on the jaw. A scream of pain shot through the car, then the man began to sob aloud. Blood ran down his cheeks and out of his mouth. A nurse hurried up to him and began to wash his fresh wound. Two teeth were broken and he spit them out. Gustav had just enough time to jump down as the train was preparing to leave, earlier than usual. With the exception of several policemen and detectives, the platform looked deserted. Once home, he told his father he had seen a man who was not a man anymore. With both arms and legs missing, blind and insane, the wretched creature had been bundled up in a basket. It had been an awful sight.

"And to think of these ruffians throwing stones at such poor fellows," Mrs. Ebelshauser said. "They should be made to pay for that."

No one replied to her sad remark.

"At Last The Truth About The Belgians" ... "Teutons' Behavior During Belgium's Invasion" ... "Pillaging and Massacring on a Grand Scale" ... "Convince Yourself of the Barbarians' Atrocities" ... "Arrival of Belgian Refugees, Mutilated Women and Children at Lausanne" ...

So many announcements in the press could not fail in their purpose, even more so as the most exaggerated and dreadful accounts about the Germans were contained in each article. According to these fantastic reports, the Germans had behaved worse than beasts. Plundering and ransacking homes in Belgian villages seemed to be their only objective.

The bombastic stories had done their work well. To Gustav it looked as if the whole town had come down to the station for the reception of the poor mutilated Belgians. A large number of people must have been there since early in the morning with a view to secure the best places of observation. There were quite a few strangers, too — suburbanites and even

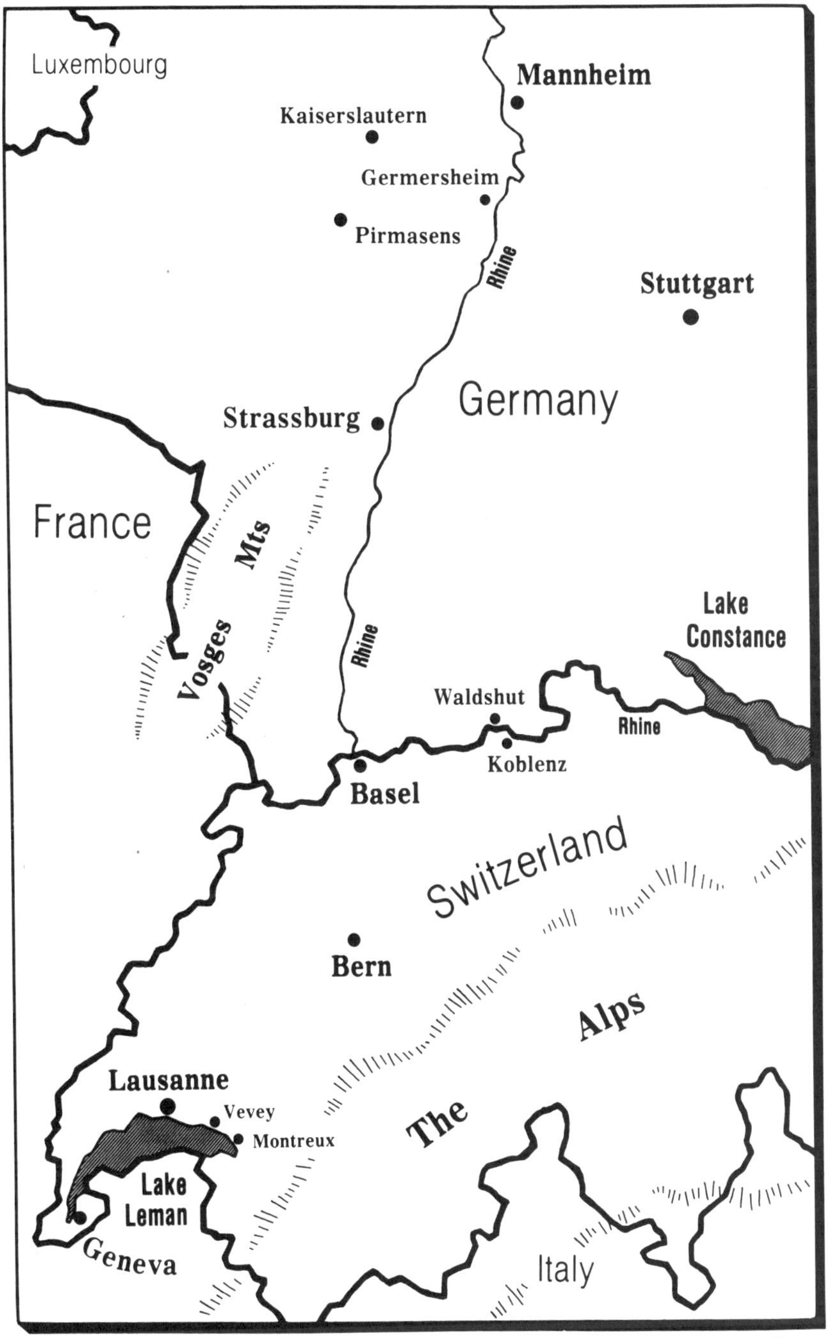

Map illustrates pre-1918 borders

some who had come from distant quarters for the great occasion.

The station had been trimmed and flagged for the ceremony. The authorities were doing their best to make the refugees feel at home. It was a clear and beautiful day. A radiating sun was playing its part as a sympathetic host. Gazing at the large clock on the station building, people impatiently were pacing to and fro on the square. They were waiting for the big moment with great anticipation, preparing to offer their pity, love and assistance to those in need. Suddenly, the conversations ceased when word passed from mouth to mouth that the train had just pulled in. Desperate efforts were made by those in the back to gain access to the front line. Some began climbing lamp posts which were scattered about the place.

"Bring out the mutilated Belgians!"

"We want to see the Belgians!"

One after another they began to yell with impatience for the big show to begin. After all the promises made by the press it was now impossible to disappoint the mass. They all had come to see something that was supposed to be unusual.

At last, a military band appeared. There is nothing like music to appease a crowd. The band blared out the Belgian national anthem, immediately followed by the Swiss. It was the first official gesture opening the ceremony.

"Vive la Belgique!"

"A bas les sales Boches!"

"Vive la France!"

Slowly, four by four, the Belgian refugees were passing through the gate. The band struck up the martial tune of "Sambre et Meuse" while the crowd yelled and shouted its greetings. With bright, smiling faces, the Belgians responded by waving. The procession was in progress. They were in no apparent hurry, and seemed to greatly enjoy the scrutinizing looks of the great mass of people. They seemed touched by such a display of interest and sympathy. Modestly and unaffected, they passed between the lines of spectators. A bright spirit of gaiety prevailed among the youngsters. The women wore serious expressions; yet, they were all smiling and looking around with admiration. Old men followed in the same mood. They looked lean and undernourished, but there was no trace of any so-called mutilations to be found anywhere. No better proof could have been furnished to the public. After witnessing this parade they all knew the real value of the press' lying reports. The Belgian procession worked as a boomerang for the French.

Lausanne's first reaction was to begin showing some respect and recognition to its German minority. At the same time, people became wiser and more suspicious of the daily press. Fantastic reports about the Germans were, for a time, completely ignored. However, this change was only to be of short duration. Early French propaganda had done its work well, stamping the general trend of people's opinions. The wave of fanaticism slowly returned, grabbing anew a hold on the population. The printed stories soon were taken up again. According to them, the Germans had instigated this cruel and insane butchery and were, therefore, "barbarians," "Huns" and "boches" just the same. This was the accepted verdict in almost everyone's opinion.

It was March of 1915 and spring was in the air. Gustav was preparing for his final examination when the unexpected blow came to him in the form of an official announcement. It was brief and clear, but to him the words meant more than mere abandonment of a career. They meant the renunciation of a beautiful dream. Was it really possible? Was it true? He went over the lines again, reading to himself aloud —

"Effective immediately all applications for Swiss citizenship are suspended until further notice. No new applicants will be taken during the war."

Monsieur Dubois had failed, and no amount of pleading could have moved him to take any action. The case was lost. Gustav was neither German nor Swiss for the moment. He had but one choice. Returning his papers to the German consulate, he was thus registered as a German. Nevertheless, even though he could not hope to become Swiss, he went through the strenuous final examination with great success. His would have been among the best reports had it not been for his terrible low mark in "behavior and deportment." With the usual carelessness of youth, it always had proved to be too much for him to be serious for a whole hour. Full of harmless mischief, he constantly was inventing new tricks, resulting in disturbances in the classroom. On many occasions some of his machinations had caused his comrades to be seized with a sudden spell of contagious hilarity, much to the consternation and vexation of his teachers. Gustav's trouble was his honesty. His innocent face always betrayed him. Every time he was caught as the culprit. Still, Gustav seemed incorrigible. His parents often had prevailed upon him, and for a short time everything would go fine until he felt the urge for a practical joke come upon him. It was his second nature. Now that school had come to an end, the seriousness of the situation in which he found himself brought a radical change in his life. His eyes and lips ceased smiling altogether. After so much studying and hard work, the prospect of unemployment was more than he could stand.

"Nothing again." Dejected, Gustav almost tore the papers in folding them up.

"You might still get a reply to one of your applications," his mother consoled him gently. "Don't give up hope so quickly."

"I'm not, but it looks bad for me just the same. You've got to admit it."

"Oh, I know it's not going to be easy for you to break through, but I'm sure you'll get your chance some day."

"Some day! Some day! How long will that be, I wonder?"

"Don't lose patience, son. Perhaps father will be able to find you something."

"I thought so, too. But all his friends seem to be in the same boat."

"Well, kicking and grumbling won't do you any good."

"Damn war!"

"Yes, it's terrible. A soldier looks like the only job to be had nowadays. They don't care who you are and what you speak, as long as you show fighting spirit. Disgusting! I hope they don't get you for the trenches."

Any conversation with his mother led to this topic. She just hated the thought of it, but the war could not be avoided.

"I'll still be here for a good while. The shooting will be over by the time I come of age."

"Don't say that so loud. If it lasts too long they'll drag you in."

"Ha! They couldn't get me out of here. I don't care what Elise says, I'm not Theo."

"Shhh ...! Don't talk like that. Poor Elise, she's all fire and flame for her fatherland. She is very brave just the same."

"I hope she'll never feel sorry for what she did," Gustav thought, keeping silent. "She might never see Theo again. If that happens, she'll only have herself to blame for it."

His sister had been on the point of moving heaven and earth to induce her sweetheart to leave for Germany to join the army. That was more than he could understand. After such a long courtship it had not been easy for Theo to make his decision. He would have stayed in Switzerland regardless of what people would think and say about him. He had yielded to Elise's pleading, taking the step in spite of himself. Because Elise wanted him to be a man instead of a coward, as folks would have tagged him had he remained in Lausanne, Theo had made up his mind to go. For her sake he was now being trained to be a soldier at Kaiserslautern.

The sudden departure from his drab and despairing existence came to Gustav as a great surprise. Unknown to him, his father had answered an advertisement in the "Bund," a German newspaper from Bern to which he was a regular subscriber. An important Swiss concern desired the services of an intelligent young man to assist its technical department manager. There was good opportunity for advancement and to learn the trade. With his letter Mr. Ebelshauser had sent a photograph of his son. A very promising reply came by telegram, nearly upsetting the whole family. It was a request for Gustav to meet a Mr. Riegel at the Hotel Zur Post in the small Rhine town of Koblenz at the company's expense. Gustav whistled and sang for joy. Work was in sight at last. Since they were being so generous, it certainly looked like a splendid opportunity.

Gustav was amused by Riegel's visible efforts to converse in French.

With the peculiar manner characterizing the German, his ways were calm, although each of his moves assumed capital importance — be it the careful filing of the letter he had just taken out of his desk, the writing of a short note, the closing of a drawer or the readjustment of a pince-nez on his long, thin nose. Removing his glasses, as Gustav soon discovered, was just a habit with Riegel. His pince-nez actually was so tightly fastened there was no possibility of its falling off.

His luxuriant blond hair, impeccably groomed and shiny, was parted in the middle. A short trimmed mustache of a slightly darker shade gave his face a martial appearance. The dark gray sport coat lent to his general allure a note of vivacity, underlining a good physical structure. To complete the picture, Riegel wore a pair of knickers, golf hose and high shoes with double soles. Opening his shirt collar, he motioned to Gustav to follow his example as the day was unusually hot.

"Let's go and see Mr. Dammel, the director," Riegel announced after another glance at his watch.

Following a narrow path across bare fields, in less than 20 minutes they reached the embankment of the Rhine which Gustav already had sighted from his hotel. Riegel could not fail to notice the puzzled expression on his face as they neared the river. He felt it his duty to furnish the uninitiated applicant some explanation.

"Lonza's main office is at Basel," he said. "They have a branch at Viege. Now they are constructing a new plant just across the Rhine, for which they obtained a concession from the German government. But it is a Swiss concern. All the employees, with only a few exceptions, are residing in Switzerland, most of them right here in Koblenz. If you are interested, and if Mr. Dammel decides to hire your services, you could live at the hotel with me and many others from the firm. Of course, it will be necessary for you to have a passport to cross back and forth across the Rhine. Today I will take you along under my custody. Mr. Dammel will give you some more information about that."

They had no trouble passing inspection before being permitted on the small ferry boat. The Swiss guards were even jovial, taking Riegel's word about him without question. The German inspectors took their task more seriously. Gustav had to have his name registered and was given a special slip to be presented upon his return. Even his clothes and pockets were investigated before the two were allowed to proceed to their destination.

Gustav felt overcome by a strange feeling to be standing on German soil. He was seized by an unexplainable fear of looming danger. But his alarm soon was dispelled.

"You'll find plenty of company among the employees doing the crossing," Riegel assured him. "It's just a matter of getting used to it. I'm sure you'll come to like the rides after a while."

Gustav did what any lad would have done under the circumstances. He began to dream and build castles in the air while waiting. Riegel had left him at the gate with a promise to return within a minute or two. Gustav was impressed by the gigantic size of the establishment. The long office building looked as if it had just been completed. The gray walls still retained a bright polish and an immaculate cleanness, revealing their recent erection.

Glancing through a covered hallway into the vast fenced area, he saw various groups of masons diligently at work constructing a series of buildings of original shapes and dimensions. The whole place presented a picture of feverish activity. If hired, he soon would learn about the uses of all these queer structures. At any rate, he was interested as well as curious. Perhaps this was his opportunity for a splendid future.

"If only I knew the bigshot," he sighed aloud. "I wonder what he's going to think of me."

Riegel returned a few minutes later. "Mr. Dammel is too busy and won't be able to see you." He handed the young man's certificate back to him.

Gustav was about to put on a face of bitter disappointment. Instead, he brightened up again and was overjoyed to hear Riegel conclude his message.

"But you're hired for the job."

His diploma and Riegel's good word had done the trick. He had not expected such luck. All he had to do was to bring home the good news, pack his things and return. He literally ran all the way back to the ferry.

The ease with which he crossed the border took away the last shadow of fear and danger which had been persistent in his mind. The inspection was performed as a matter of routine, and without any risk of arrest or complication as he first had suspected. He would be able to reassure his parents, should they raise the question.

2

For the first time in his life Gustav was enjoying his newly acquired independence. To dispose of his time after work according to his own pleasure made him appreciate his position all the more. To show his family right from the start that he was able to stand on his own two feet filled his heart with pride and satisfaction. At last, luck had come his way.

It had taken him almost two weeks to get settled and used to his new surroundings. Riegel, very obligingly, had made all the arrangements, persuading Mr. Maurer, owner of the Hotel Zur Post, to place a very nice room at his disposal. The large double window on the northern facade gave a wonderful view of the Rhine Valley. In the foreground just across the Rhine he could watch the towering chimneys of the plant he was working for. He often would let his glance sweep over German territory as he wondered about the many events of war which must be taking place in that country. From this distance there was nothing abnormal to be detected. The whole countryside looked quiet and peaceful. It was almost impossible to believe that Germany actually was in a state of war.

At night, the sparkling, rolling waters of the river reflected the moonlight, scintillating like so many stars under the glare of electric lamps. Many an evening Gustav already had spent sitting at his window, lost in the contemplation of this nocturnal scene. Still, more than once since his arrival he had strangely missed the incomparable sight of Lake Leman and the Alps. Then his thoughts unconsciously would turn to fond recollections and memories of home.

His long trial month finally came to an end. Mr. Dammel was satisfied. Gustav was now on Lonza's list of regular employees. He was delighted for, not only did he regard this enrollment as a promotion, he saw it as the beginning of a bright and promising future.

But three weeks later, on July 15, 1915, Gustav instinctively sensed danger when he was summoned to the main office. The director was waiting for him, but this time there was no smile in his greeting.

"Listen, Mr. Ebelshauser, you are residing in Koblenz at the Hotel Zur Post, aren't you?" Dammel wore a serious expression.

"Yes, sir," Gustav replied without the slightest suspicion.

"You're crossing the Rhine daily on a German passport, aren't you Mr. Ebelshauser?" Dammel's big cigar was moving up and down, following the movement of his lips while he jotted down the replies.

"Yes, sir," Gustav said again, wondering at the question.

"Just as I thought, Mr. Ebelshauser. A new regulation has just been issued by the German government. It calls for a little change in all German passports held by our employees residing across the Rhine. Just a formality."

For the first time Dammel looked straight in his face.

"Let me see your passport, Mr. Ebelshauser."

"It's in my locker, Mr. Dammel."

"All right, go and get it." It was a demand spoken in a commanding tone.

"Yes, sir."

A strange sensation, an unexplained feeling of fear crept into Gustav's chest. What was the matter with his passport all of a sudden? He returned to the office.

"Hmmm, I see. Hmmm!" Examining the booklet, Dammel murmured a couple of times to himself. Then, addressing him in a louder voice, he said, "I don't think the change affects your passport. You're only seventeen. But I'd better make sure about it. I'm going to the city hall anyway. I'll be back this afternoon before closing time. Tell Schneider to take you along at noon. You can have your lunch at Waldshut for once. I'll call for you as soon as I am back."

"All right, sir. But I'll need my passport for tonight, Mr. Dammel."

"Don't worry, you'll get it long before that. Just leave it to me. I don't even think that a change is necessary for you."

"Very well, sir." With an almost imperceptible bow, Gustav turned on his heels and went out.

Until five o'clock he managed to divert his thoughts. But then, as he watched the hands of the big office clock advance slowly though inevitably toward six, he became anxious and impatient. His alarm grew from minute to minute as there seemed to be no sign of Dammel's return. Through the open windows he restlessly watched for Dammel's car to come shooting by. At the sound of a motor his eyes would turn in the direction. But it was one disappointment after another. What was he going to do if Dammel did not show up? He held to the hope that he might still come at the last minute.

Deprived of his passport, Gustav had seen himself compelled to go to Waldshut, the nearest small German border town, where he spent a sleepless night. After a hurried breakfast he felt relieved to step out into the fresh morning breeze. He was eager to get to the plant and learn what Dammel had to say. Two hours elapsed in terrible anxiety before he was called to Dammel's private office at ten.

"Did Mr. Schneider take care of you? How was your first night's sleep in Germany? Good? Wasn't it a big surprise?" Dammel appeared in his best mood. At his last question he burst out into loud and unrestrained laughter.

"Yes, sir," he replied,"but the night would have been much better at my hotel."

"I'm sorry, they simply refused to give me back your passport. They want you to appear in person ..."

"Why?" Gustav interrupted, losing his temper. "What seems to be the trouble? Where am I supposed to get it?"

"Keep your shirt on, young man. If you give me a chance I'll tell you what you'll have to do ..."

"I'm sorry, Mr. Dammel, but I'm terribly upset. I don't understand the whole business."

"Well, to be frank with you, neither do I, although I suspect the war has something to do with that new regulation. Anyway, they are waiting for you at the city hall. It's on the second floor, window 22 or 24, I don't remember exactly. You can leave now and you'll just be on time. The appointment is for 11 o'clock. It won't take you more than a short half-hour walk. Stay there for lunch and come to see me when you get back. I am anxious to know how you made out."

"All right, sir."

With these words, spoken in an almost inaudible voice, Gustav left the office with distress in his heart.

At exactly 11 o'clock he entered the large city hall building of Waldshut, taking the two flights of stairs on the run. Finding all the windows closed he began to pace the floor, not knowing what to do. He was profoundly disgusted. "Too bad I gave it away so lightly," he thought to himself. "This would have been a warning. I should have gone across and stayed there. What a fool I was!"

Alone in the large hall, he had the impression of being in the wrong place. After 20 long minutes of waiting he was about to go down to the lower floor when window 24 snapped open. He came back and stepped up to it, casting a swift glance inside. He saw nothing but a group of clerks comfortably seated around empty tables, each holding and reading a newspaper. Two men were standing farther back, leisurely filing some notes or correspondence in various small wooden cases. Gustav stood at the window watching. No one seemed to take notice of him. Finally, after several minutes, he took a coin from his pocket and began to rap on the window board to attract someone's attention.

"Yes, sir, what is it you want?" called out one of the clerks without lifting his eyes from his paper.

"I was to be here at 11 o'clock for my passport," he replied in a raised voice.

"Passport? To the ground floor, window 17."

Angry and nervous, Gustav hurried down to the ground floor.

"Yes, what is it?" asked the man at window 17.

"Gustav Ebelshauser is my name. I'm calling for my passport."

"What name did you say? How do you spell it?" The man opened a drawer and after going through the file, added, "It's not here. When did you leave it?"

"Mr. Dammel brought it here for me yesterday."

"You mean Mr. Dammel from the Lonza Werke? Are you one of his employees?"

"Yes, sir," Gustav said, somewhat relieved at the thought of being served.

"Just go up those stairs over there. It's window 24 on the second floor."

"What do you mean? I just came from there and they sent me down here."

"They did, heh? Maybe the man didn't know you were with the Lonza Werke. Did you tell him that? Or did you expect him to smell it?"

Gustav literally was boiling within as he went back to window 24. He saw the same fellows still reading complacently without being stirred a bit by his approach. After another few minutes of waiting, one of the men put down his paper on the empty table and in a very dignified way, rose and stepped up to wait on him.

"I was here before for my passport, but was told to go down to window 17 on the ground floor. They sent me here again. My name is Ebelshauser, Gustav Ebelshauser, an employee of the Lonza Werke."

He had recited his story in one long breath, not permitting any interruption. His face was slightly flushed with wrath.

"So what!" the man said. "Who told you to come here?"

"My God," Gustav exclaimed, "I just explained it. Mr. Dammel also said I should come here."

"Dammel? Dammel? Who is he?" Before he could give a reply, the clerk already was adding, "Oh yes, Lonza's director, of course."

"Yes, sir!"

Once more Gustav noticed the change in attitude at the mention of this name. Dammel seemed to be a password among the clerks for reverence, politeness, a showy display of courtesy, as if to make one forget the tone of arrogance used before.

"Yes, yes, I believe I remember now. Mr. Dammel was here yesterday for you, wasn't he? I see, well ... there has been a change of departments around here since last night. So you go down to the first floor and knock at window 9. Ask for Mr. Eggner who is now in charge of the passport division. Sorry, sir, but it can't be helped."

"Mr. Eggner, please?" Gustav asked the man standing at window 9.

"What can I do for you, sir? I'm the man you are looking for."

"Oh, er, Ebelshauser. Gustav Ebelshauser is my name. I've come for my passport. Mr. Dammel of the Lonza Werke left it here for me yesterday."

"Here, just write down your name on this piece of paper." The clerk took the slip, examined the handwriting for a second and continued, "I'll be right with you, Mr. Ebelssshauser."

Eggner disappeared behind a high partition, then came back with the passport and some other papers in his hand. From another drawer he removed a blank form which Gustav recognized as a questionnaire.

"Mr. Gussstav Ebelssshauser!" The man pronounced his name with a resounding accent and a prolonged roll of the 's.'

"You are German, Mr. Ebelssshauser, aren't you?"

"Well, I was born at Lausanne ..."

"I'm not interested to know where you were born. Just reply to my questions."

"I consider myself Swiss ..."

"Now, Mr. Ebelssshauser," Eggner interrupted again, "I don't give a hang about your consideration. You have here a German passport, consequently you are a German subject."

"Through my father, yes, but I ..."

"Will you please stop trying to tell me stories. Father or no father, I have the evidence of your nationality right here in my hand. So please confine yourself to straight replies to the questions I have to fill out for you.

"Adolf is your middle name?"

"Yes, sir."

Patiently, Gustav submitted to the long examination involving his whole family. For a moment he was tempted to seize the passport and flee. Instead he remained, trying his best to hide his agitation and inner excitement. He forced a faint smile to his lips. Two or three more questions, he thought, and then he would be free to go. But when, at last, the bottom line of the long questionnaire was filled, he received the greatest shock of his life.

"I'm sorry, Mr. Ebelssshauser, but according to a new regulation issued by the government which was put in force last week, no German subject is permitted to reside outside of his country if working within its boundaries. Furthermore, German subjects residing at present in Germany are not to be granted passports or special permission to cross the Swiss border. You see, Mr. Ebelssshauser, either one of these regulations can be applied in your case. Of course, this concerns only men over 16 and under 60 years of age. But your age being seventeen, you happen to belong to this category."

It took Gustav quite a while to recover his breath. "But I must, I have to go back to Koblenz. I have all my things there, and my parents are at Lausanne. I can't be cut off just like that without saying goodbye. What am I going to do with my room at the hotel? I'm telling you, I must be allowed to go back and pack and move over here, since it is the law. This is ..."

"I regret it, young man, but orders are orders and you have to submit to the law like anybody else. Don't worry about your room in Koblenz. Everything will be well taken care of. Here, take this card. It's the address where you are to go tonight to get yourself a fine room. Frau Luette has been notified and is awaiting you."

"But what about all my personal things I have ..."

"We'll send someone along tomorrow to help you. Meanwhile, just forget about it and go back to work."

Gustav had the impression Eggner told him this just to get rid of him. At the same time he realized how useless it would have been to argue about the issue. The man simply would stick to the regulations. There was absolutely nothing he could do about it. After leaving the city hall building he went straight back to the plant. On his way he had to pinch himself a couple of times to make sure he was not dreaming. The day's events were more than he could comprehend.

Frau Luette was a woman in her forties. Her hair had turned prematurely white since the disappearance of her husband who had been one of the first victims of the war. Eggner had been right. Gustav found the woman waiting for him, seated at the entrance of a little three-story house at No. 14 Moltkestrasse. The well prepared plan for his capture had worked according to schedule. Apparently, the woman had even been furnished with a detailed description of his appearance because, as he still was looking for the correct house number, he saw her rise and walk toward him. In her greeting was a distinct note of recognition.

"How do you do, young man," she said, looking him straight in the face. "I am sure you are Mr. Ebelshauser for whom I have been waiting."

"Yes, but how did you know?" he asked with visible astonishment.

"They came yesterday to see my place and told me to expect you around this time. I am Frau Luette, the widow they told you about."

"Oh, they did! I see," Gustav replied, thinking to himself that these rascals certainly were sure of themselves.

Two days later, on Saturday, he got another shocking surprise. Coming in at noon he found his open trunk standing in the middle of the room. All his belongings had been neatly packed and shipped to his new quarters.

"If there should be anything missing," reported Frau Luette, "notify the police."

Nothing was missing. In fact, they had included a little picture — property of the hotel — which he decided to keep as a remembrance of his short stay there.

With his effects still in Koblenz, Gustav had continued to hope to return there. Now he knew! He was not only cut off from Koblenz, but from Switzerland, Lausanne and his home as well. He found himself trapped without any loopholes or possibilities of escape. The action had been so swift he had not been able to foresee or prevent it. He was now in Germany to stay.

Could he really suspect Dammel of having had a hand in this fantastic and cunning scheme? The more he thought about it the more he became convinced of Dammel's guilt. He just could not figure out how such a trick had been worked on him. He probably never would be able to solve the puzzle. If only he had known better, but it was too late now. He was in Germany, the country of his father, a prisoner of state, unable to get out. It was not hard for him to surmise the meaning of his position. It was the war. The WAR! Only that could be a plausible explanation. Perhaps the time was not very far off when young men of his age would be called and drafted to defend the blood-drained fatherland.

3

Hitting him right in the eyes, a ray of sunshine was disturbing Gustav's morning sleep. He began to stir under the covers. He turned on his right side, then on his left, but all to no avail. Unable to continue his interrupted dream, he finally decided to lie on his back for a while. It was no use. Sleep refused to come back. He rubbed his eyes and yawned loudly. For another few minutes he listened attentively to the melodious pealing of the bells. Having grown accustomed to their sounds, he understood each of their voices and signals.

Every tone had its own special meaning. For once the bells did not seem to be echoing another victory. He could tell because the deep basses of the larger bells were missing. This was a simple ringing announcing the various church services. On such a beautiful morning the war did not seem to exist. The mere thought of it was unreal and absurd. But Gustav could not control his imagination. Visualizing the trenches on the fighting fronts, he could not help wondering: When would all the bells mix their voices for the joyous and happy celebration of the return of peace?

Though detained against his will, he rather quickly had reconciled himself to the inevitable reality of the situation. In fact, after only the short space of one week he even had forgotten about the purpose of his transfer to Waldshut, and had become blind to the possible danger of his being drawn into the great world conflict. Yet, somehow, a subconscious, strange and undefined feeling of fear seemed to invade his mind, body and soul.

What would he do today? How would he pass this Sunday? In Koblenz he had strolled for hours along the Rhine. But there he had felt safe. Just as picturesque and inspiring was the savage beauty of the river from the German shore, except for the presence of so many uniforms. Stern-faced guards were met at every step. They eyed civilians with suspicion, especially men, and one felt an instinctive restraint in every move. Germany was a gigantic fortress whose borders were closely watched. The whole country had been transformed into a vast arsenal. Militarism had the upper hand and was reaching the zenith of its power. Field gray uniforms appeared everywhere like a multitude of tiny dust clouds. And enthusiasm still ran high among the people. Men, young and old, dreamed of one thing only — to become soldiers. In every city, town and village, military parades were held ceaselessly to the wild acclamations of the populace.

"Good morning! This sure looks like a splendid day!" Cheerfully, Gustav responded to his landlady's greeting. "But why are you so sad? What's the matter, Frau Luette?"

She looked at him with tears in her eyes as he sat down for his breakfast. At her insistence he had agreed to take Sunday morning meals in the kitchen.

"Musterung!" she said. "They are recruiting boys of the classes '96, '97 and '98. You'll have to register."

"Since when? Who told you?" There was anxiety in his voice.

"It's all over town. Everybody is talking about it."

"So, my turn has come ..."

"Oh, not yet. They only register you in case ..."

"Yes, yes, I see! No wonder they were in such a hurry to catch me."

Frau Luette did not reply and Gustav was too absorbed to talk. Silently, he drank his coffee and ate two slices of brown bread. He was glad to see the woman go to her room, for he already had feared she would start her often repeated story of the tragic disappearance of her husband. It was an obsession with her. Time and again she would show him the postcard from the government with its laconic message: "Rupert Luette lost on the Russian front." After almost a year of hopeful waiting she had now given up the thought of ever seeing him again. Though he felt genuine pity and compassion for her, he could stand her crying no longer. She was getting on his nerves. Even with no place to go he preferred being out rather than having to listen to her lamenting. She was just feeding on his sympathy.

He finished eating and made haste to get dressed. He was impatient to get outside in the sunshine and find first-hand information about the latest decree. He did not have far to go to learn all about it.

Overnight, cities, towns and villages all over Germany had literally been plastered with placards. Their flashing colors could be seen everywhere. It was an order from the government. The fatherland was requesting the immediate registration of the classes of 1896, 1897 and 1898. The nation was appealing to its young generation for the restrengthening of its manpower. Young blood was needed to fill the innumerable gaps left by those who were no more.

Two days later Germany was thrown anew into a state of pandemonium. Waldshut went wild in the general uproar, celebrating the latest victory. Warsaw had fallen. German troops were occupying the great Polish city. Once more the country was being swept off its feet by a wave of frenzied and uncontrollable patriotism. It looked as if the entire population suddenly had gone crazy. People yelled themselves hoarse in loud, vociferous acclaims. "Victory! Victory! We've done it again! Warsaw is ours! We'll soon have them all on their knees!"

Passions were flaming high. The people were losing their heads, singing and crying out for more victory. Common sense was gone, the war seemed to have smothered all reasoning power. Raw, beast-like instinct appeared to be man's sole remaining faculty and guiding force.

What did they care about their own losses as long as "victory" was theirs? Perhaps thousands of men had lost their lives, immolated in the struggle, but only one thing counted for them at the moment. Warsaw, the great city, had fallen. Was such a victory not worth celebrating? Only yesterday their hearts had grieved because 16 men drowned aboard a sunken fishing boat. Only yesterday they had been moved to tears after learning a ship with two thousand passengers had been swallowed up by the ocean after striking a mighty iceberg. How different was the picture today. Today they were shouting endless hurrahs at the sinking of ships and the loss of thousands of human lives. Today a message that the enemy had suffered countless dead was glad tidings to their ears and cause for great rejoicing. War! The word was on everyone's lips, serving as an answer to this state of madness.

Gustav wandered about like a lost soul. He felt sick at the sight of the demented crowd. "You fools! You blind fools!" he would have liked to shout, but he remained silent. He dared not express his feelings. No one would have understood. They would have taken him for a traitor. How could he expect anyone to share his distasteful reaction to all of this?

For two days a question weighed on his mind. Now that he was in Germany he would have to register and pass the examination before the end of the week. Failure to do so meant punishment — a fine or jail he did not know. He had not been able to work properly at the plant, and at night sleep had refused to come. Still, he had to decide. Would they agree? The only way to find out was to try.

On the evening of the third day his mind was made up. He went to the recruiting station to register and pass the medical test. This task accomplished, he went courageously to one of the officers and said, "I would like to volunteer, provided you can have me transferred as an interpreter to a camp of French prisoners."

Bravely, Gustav looked up at the towering officer, but the man's face was impassible. His words seemed to have had no effect at all. Perhaps such a request should not have been made? He was about to turn and go when the officer ordered him to stay and wait. Gustav saw him disappear into one of the consulting rooms from which he soon emerged.

"Yes, that can easily be done, but first you must join the army. You only speak French? Yes, I am making a special note of this on your registration card. All you have to do is wait until you are called." With a clicking of his heels the officer had closed the interview.

Gustav went out relieved, smiling with satisfaction. He had dared and he had won. But would they keep their promise? This remained to be seen.

On the morning of September 15, 1915, he was on his way to Germersheim, the garrison to which he had been assigned and where he was to start a new life as a soldier. There were about 60 men, young and old, bound for the same destination. After a long journey the phalanx of new recruits alighted and glanced around with alert curiosity. Gustav took a look at the men. They, in turn, were gazing at each other, some of them getting acquainted. A few faces wore faint and somewhat cynical smiles, as if to say, "Here we are, where will we go from here? How long will it be and how many of us will be back again?" Yet, no one spoke his thoughts aloud.

It was a queer assortment of men from all walks of life. Peasants and factory workers formed the majority of the group. The rest was made up of white-collar men, apprentices and students.

Assigned to the same barrack, they proceeded like sheep pushed forward in one direction by a mighty but invisible hand. Men of all statures and countenances. Each had been taken away from his home for the defense of the fatherland. Gustav was the only one enrolling as a volunteer, but for a purpose none of his companions needed to know.

Despite their common destination, they remained strangers to one another. They moved forward in silence, each man with his thoughts wandering back home.

4

Tramp! Tramp! Tramp!

The heavy hobnailed boots hit the pavement. Daylight was fighting the last remaining shadows of the night, though the soldiers already had long before begun their tasks. They were marching through the silent, deserted streets of the small garrison town. They could have found their way blindfolded. The marching always went in the same direction to the vast training ground. People no longer appeared at their windows to watch them pass. The great excitement of earlier days at the sight of uniforms had died away. Indifference had replaced curiosity.

Darkness still clung to the earth, unwilling to go. Heavy clouds hung low, and there was not much chance for the weak rays of an October sun to break through the thick envelope. The far end of the drill field was not yet discernible.

"What a cloudy sky this morning! The air feels more like snow than rain." Ebelshauser was concerned about the weather. The prospect of another drill in mud and rain was not very pleasant.

Hans Rueger, "wise Hans" as he was nicknamed, looked up with circumspection. With his usual prudence he replied, "Maybe rain, maybe snow. I'll let you know tonight. I'm a very poor prophet. I never forecast the weather, much less the mood of our captain. Those kinds of guys always have two faces and one never knows which is which.

Rueger was a little taller than Ebelshauser, but only a fraction of an inch. He stood high in esteem among the men owing to his age and wide knowledge of the world. A retired architect, he had travelled extensively in many countries. It was always a pleasure to listen to him telling stories of his many experiences. He was 48, but appeared much younger. Broad-shouldered and heavy set, his stature was that of a prize fighter. Two puffy pink jowls and smiling blue-gray eyes gave him an air of gaiety. His blond hair had thinned out and at the sides was a touch of silver. He was clean shaven, having no use for a mustache hanging "in the soup," as he would say. Congenial, he was always ready with a good clean joke.

It was a matter of routine to pass the first hour on the training ground in mass formation drills. Miles and miles were covered in criss-crossing, marching back and forth, running, turning, forward, backward, sideways. The whole show came to a finish with the famous goose-step parade. By that time every inch of the vast place had been tramped upon. Legs and feet were played out before the real test of group and individual exercises had even begun. A few men already had dropped from the ranks and were dismissed. Their feet were badly swollen from ill-fitting boots which caused painful, burning blisters. They had retired to a small wood lining the west side of the grounds.

"He is furious," Ebelshauser whispered to his pal. "Look how mad the captain rides about. Wouldn't it be funny if he fell off his mare!"

"That never happens to those fellows," Rueger replied. "They have more luck than brains."

"There's 'pea soup' in the air, and it's only the start," Jaeger remarked from behind. "Wait 'til we get home."

"Too bad that nothing can be done about it," Ebelshauser sighed.

"That's an old story, my friend," Jaeger retorted. "It could be done if we held together, but we're a bunch of saps. What good is one of us alone?"

"You might as well give up the idea," Rueger suggested. "That will never do. The best is to take it on the chin and like it."

The company came to a stop. Corporals and sergeants immediately converged toward the captain to receive instructions. Plans were being laid out for the further program of the day. For 15 minutes the men were dismissed. They joined their suffering brothers already squatting under the pine trees. The soil was moist and cold, but unable to stand they had pulled off their boots to soothe the pain. Their comrades swarmed around trying to help them, each claiming to know the best remedy for tender feet.

The assembly signal came much too soon to suit their tired limbs. At the first trumpet call the men stepped forward from under the trees. Officers and underlings took their assigned places. During the short rest period the men almost had forgotten about life and its obligations. Suddenly summoned back to reality, their first reaction was to feel again the cold dampness of the mist still permeating the atmosphere. They had not given any thought to it while talking in the wood with their hands in their pockets. Demurely they responded to the trumpet, testing their superiors to the limits of patience with deliberate slowness. A sensation of impotence and helplessness made them inwardly rebel against the military code.

Times had changed as Ebelshauser soon found out. Only three months ago he had volunteered only because of a promise obtained. What an illusion! What folly to have entertained such a hope! He should have known they would not hold their part of the bargain. A uniform was made for a soldier, and a soldier he had to remain. Life in the army had changed something else as well. His first name was only used now by his closest comrades.

The bells continued to ring now and then, announcing other victorious advances of the troops. Germany still had many enthusiastic souls responding to the call to arms. But how quickly did their enthusiasm completely vanish once thrown into uniforms? As soldiers they soon learned the real meaning of such victories. Each one of them was achieved at the cost of countless human lives. How many thousands had been mowed down — their bodies riddled with bullets from an all-devouring machine-gun — just for the gain of so many yards of ground? How many heroes were falling, perhaps at this very moment? Pressing forward in desperation they found themselves powerless against death. Swept off their feet they fell, biting the dust of the blood-thirsty soil. Small wonder that the melodious pealing of the bells had lost its meaning, so far as they were concerned. Such thoughts crept into Ebelshauser's mind as he stood there ready to resume another intolerable and senseless drill.

"Goose-stepping and saluting is all they teach you in order to get killed." Jaeger could not help expressing his disgust.

"Why don't you take your pill like a man," Rueger replied. "You think the others like it any better? So shut up for once."

"Company ... Attention!"

The command came like thunder. Once more they were made to cross the place in all its length and width. Turning in groups in march column, four abreast, then eight, then sixteen, the company eventually found itself again in the same formation as at the start, following a series of arduous circles and complicated detours. Then came the subdivision into platoons and sections of eight men, each under the supervision of their respective corporals.

"I hope we get the right guy." With these few words, Rheinhard expressed the thought of all those belonging to Ebelshauser's group.

"Why?" asked Heimer. "Isn't Wetzel here today?"

"Yes, but not for us," Rueger said. "He got his assignment already. They like to make changes once in a while."

"Again? Not Schmitz, I hope. I hate that guy." Ebelshauser looked worried about such a possibility.

"That's probably just the fellow we're going to get," Rheinhard answered. "Just watch. See him coming in our direction? Damn it, what luck, and with this weather, too!"

There was no room left for guessing. As they saw the corporal approaching they instinctively put themselves on the defensive, observing dead silence.

"Well, my friends, we meet again. I hope we'll have a good time together." Schmitz greeted his section and the tone accompanying his words left no one in doubt as to his devilish intentions. A sardonic grin on his tight lips, a sharp, critical look from the corners of his eyes, and a twist of the points of his brown mustache told the soldiers the design of the man they were facing again.

Since his recent ascent to the "super" rank of corporal, Schmitz took the greatest delight in the ceaseless drilling and chastizing of his victims. It was his merciless treatment that had won him his first promotion. He was cursed by the men who regarded him as a thorn in their flesh. They fled his presence whenever they could. But Schmitz did not pay the slightest attention to his soldiers' feelings. He did not care about any man's opinion, and went on mistreating his inferiors as if to satisfy a thirst for revenge for an occurance which happened not long before. He had caused the death of one of his men by kicking him in the pit of the stomach. The exhausted recruit so brutally hit had fallen to the ground in a faint. With groans of acute pain he had been borne from the field by his comrades to a quickly summoned ambulance. But he died on the way to the military hospital without regaining consciousness. In spite of all the testimony against him when his case came to trial, Schmitz, through ingenious manipulation of hidden threads connected to a gigantic web of red tape, had been found guiltless in this act of utter savagery, and consequently acquitted.

The whole man's attitude, gestures, deportment, stature and features were the picture of limitless impertinence and self-esteem personified. Even more striking was the over-sized monocle he kept screwed over his left eye. This superficial adornment gave him an air of insolence, doing nothing to hide his deceitful blue eyes. Whether on or off duty, his body stood erect like a steel post. His walk was somewhat stiff due to the tight corset he wore. At all times his chest was thrown out and pretentiously exposed. All in all, whatever his former social station in life had been, Schmitz was a born soldier. He was a man whose sole ambition was to aspire to the highest military honors. Germany literally was infested with thousands of such Schmitz creatures, rendering life miserable and causing discord in the ranks. Any patriotism a soldier might still have harbored in his heart turned to cynicism under the cruel treatment he had to endure at the hands of men of this type. It was just such a hated individual the group of eight men was now facing.

Ebelshauser was the most downhearted. The very sight of the corporal made him conscious of the imminence of another harrowing day. He knew himself to be helpless. Past experience already had taught him that. Why had he volunteered? With hope of a change he had been quite willing at the start. Now he was fed up and disgusted, but found himself compelled to go on with the show whether he liked it or not. Besides, the stage was all set. It was up to him to act and react until he was completely exhausted.

Schmitz lost no time in showing them that he meant earnest business and no play. After a long series of strenuous exercises he made them take up their rifles. The tiresome goose-steps were then practiced for more than an hour. Each man had to pace rigidly back and forth until their leg muscles began to ache. Saluting, too, was one of Schmitz's pet hobbies. How he enjoyed to be saluted and looked upon as a bigshot was manifested strikingly in his expressions and the various poses he assumed. He simply could not get enough of it.

According to Schmitz, none of his men was doing the goose-step properly. This was no surprise, for he was constantly displeased. He seemed to love raking them over the coals without appearing too partial. But he soon betrayed himself by casting his abuse on only one in the group, as if the poor soldier was responsible for the discipline and good behavior of everyone.

"Ebelshauser, step forward!" It was not the first time he had heard Schmitz bellow out his name.

"You rascal! You dirty face of a yellow Frenchman!" The corporal began admonishing him in a low voice with a pinched smile full of contemptuous sarcasm. Then, raising his tone to a yell and accompanied by all kinds of facial gesticulations, he lost control over himself and burst out in a rage.

"Put your heels together when spoken to by a superior, you damn fool! Out with your chest! Head and chin higher! Higher! Stand straight, not like a question mark! There! Now pull in your fat belly! That's a little better!"

Ebelshauser stood at attention while Schmitz, like a photographer about to take a picture, corrected the position to suit his idea of perfection. He began anew to rebuke his mute victim.

"I'm going to teach you what it means to open your pig's ears. When I give a command I expect faultless execution of my order. Who gave you the idea that you may enjoy the privilege of coming half an hour after your comrades ..."

"But I did not underst ..."

"Shut your big trap! Did I give you permission to talk? Don't you know that a soldier is to keep his mouth shut unless he is asked? I don't give a damn about your explanation. Laziness, that's what's the matter with you. But I'm going to drive that out of your system if I have to break every bone in your body."

"But I did not understand your order," Ebelshauser replied, taking advantage of the short pause. He felt an imperative need of defending himself against so unjust an accusation. By saying he had not understood was stating the truth of his personal position. He had no trouble getting along with his comrades, but to grasp the various inarticulate German commands yelled from a distance was another story. Whenever he could not make out what had been said his only chance was to copy and follow his comrades, resulting in a trifling delay on his part which could not be prevented.

"Haha, haha, haha!" Schmitz took his time to laugh at him in a grotesque manner. "That's a good one. So, you don't understand? You dirty swine! I don't speak German good enough for you, is that what you're trying to tell me? You lazy dog ..."

"Nein, Herr Unteroffizier, I did not mean ..."

"Quiet! Close your trap! You said enough, you monkey, but I'll teach you a lesson yet. You asked for it and you're going to get it, too.

"Hinlegen! Auf! Hinlegen! Auf!"

It went on like that in rapid succession. Ebelshauser could barely follow, so fast were the shouted orders. He had to go down, up, down, up, without the slightest hesitation. Out of breath and dripping with perspiration, he was desperately holding on. How long would he be able to do so? He felt himself rapidly growing weak.

"Poor Gustav! That son-of-a-bitch has it in for him," Rueger remarked to his comrades who stood there idly watching the show.

"And how!" replied Heimer. "Too bad he didn't pick on me. I could stand it better."

"That rat will get his reward in time," said another. "One of these days he's going to find himself in hell with his body blown to pieces."

"Boy, oh boy," exclaimed a fourth voice, "if that guy ever gets out to the front I hope to meet him. And when I do there'll be one Schmitz less in the army, you can bet your sweet life on that. And I won't give him time for a prayer either."

Meanwhile, Schmitz pitilessly continued his practice. There seemed to be no limit to his ferocity. Once more Ebelshauser was made to run across the field, lie down and get up, at even quicker paces than before. Then followed the abhorred creeping. The place chosen for this exercise was particularly dirty, wet and full of mud. In the space of 10 minutes Ebelshauser's uniform was soaked and so plastered with dirt there was no trace of its original color.

To satisfy his inner craving, Schmitz ordered the remaining seven to join in the demonstration. He needed the whole group for a real spectacle. To make them realize what he expected, he camped himself in front of the men, stretching his body out on a dry spot and started to explain in his most amiable way the art of crawling.

"Suppose you were suddenly caught in open and uncovered ground, or you wanted to surprise the enemy in his trench about 10 meters in front of you. What, in this case, would be the most sensible way to approach the foe without being seen or arousing suspicion? The only way would be to crawl forward, but very slowly so as to prevent your movements being discerned from such a short distance. Now, watch for the command. I want you to show me what you can do. Ready? One, two, three ... Crawl!"

Schmitz had given the order and rose to his feet to watch. It took the men almost an hour to cover the 10 meters. Several times they were made to go back and start all over again. Some of the men had made an insignificant detour in order to avoid holes and puddles filled with mud and dirty water. This was contrary to Schmitz's ideas. He wanted to see the eight go through the mud or there would have been no fun for him.

At last they had done it. A new command brought them to their feet again. The uniforms were dripping and mud and water filled their boots. They looked as if they had just been retrieved from a shallow pond. Even their faces were covered with filth and grime. And now, standing once more at attention while awaiting further instructions, they were getting cold and beginning to shiver. But the corporal was not through with them yet. For another two hours Schmitz went on with his commands, yelling himself hoarse but showing no signs of relaxing. Finally, the welcome sound of the assembly bugle brought the men relief. The company was reassembled under its captain and once more the collective mass exercise was gone through as a matter of routine. After crossing the parade ground the company fell in marching order, stepping over to the road which took it back to the soldiers' quarters. Another gruelling day had come to an end.

For Ebelshauser, German military discipline soon became an obsession, something to be feared. One never knew when and where the unexpected was bound to turn up. More than anyone else he knew at Germersheim, he felt he had good reason to be so uneasy, so downhearted, so depressed. He did not know why, but he was the one always picked on. There seemed to be no end to his personal persecution.

During the evening of another terrible day with Corporal Schmitz, the thought of a possible escape from his intolerable drudgery suddenly came to mind. Once the idea had taken root it left him no peace and rest. He passed most of the night thinking about it, and the morning found him desperately tired, though with some hope of success. The more he reflected, the more confused he became as to the feasibility of his scheme. But the vision of fleeing his torture remained anchored in his thoughts and followed him night and day.

After a week had gone by he wrote to his parents for money. He did not yet know exactly how he would proceed, but he figured that 150 francs would cover his needs. With the greatest impatience he waited for their reply. When three weeks had passed without bringing the desired answer, he decided on immediate action. He would have to get along with the little cash he now had. He could endure it no longer.

For a while he weighed the sagacity of writing his brother-in-law about the attempt he had in mind, but soon discarded the idea as ridiculous. It was up to him and him alone.

Ebelshauser had counted on taking advantage of a weekend furlough, but there again he found himself frustrated in his expectations. He had been registered for a two-day leave, though for some unexplained reason when his turn came, his name had been removed from the list. A leave would have given him a good chance to depart from the barrack unnoticed. In two days he could have made his way to the border and by the time anyone became suspicious of his absence, he would have landed somehow, somewhere in Switzerland, beyond the reach of lawful German apprehension. With the ground of his native land under his feet he could consider himself in safety.

In spite of the bitter disappointment in all his anticipations — lack of sufficient funds and denial of a furlough — he nevertheless was determined to proceed without further delay. According to his own conception, the long-prepared escape could not fail to be a success. True, there were still many dark points to be elucidated, but he was depending on good luck and his power of initiative. Everything else would take care of itself at the right moment and place.

The last Saturday of November 1915 would remain for him one of the most unforgettable dates of his military career. He asked to be excused from the singing hour because of a splitting headache. Yet, shortly after five o'clock he was on his way out. With measured steps he walked through the long corridors of the barrack and down the four flights of stairs. Then came a second of premonition and hesitancy before he crossed the yard, already plunged in darkness. Motionless, he stood there for a moment and listened to the voices coming from above.

His comrades were singing loudly, completely forgetting themselves. Gone were the torturing tribulations of the day before. Singing had a meaning for them. It was an hour of rest and oblivion during which soldiers became men again, conscious of their own souls instead of just living automatons.

To Ebelshauser the singing sounded like a good omen, a farewell. Before he had time to weaken he stepped swiftly across the yard, passed with self-assurance the two sentries at the main gate, and disappeared quickly through the streets. The weather seemed willing to enter into the conspiracy. Dark, heavy clouds hung low in the sky. It was already pitch black. The rain had stopped but the earth was still wet. As if looking for a cheerful ray of hope, he lifted his eyes to scrutinize the heavens. Not a single star was visible and the moon was hidden behind an inky veil of pregnant clouds. The atmosphere was chilly, filled with permeating dampness. It made him wish for his overcoat which he intentionally had left behind as undesirable for the purpose at hand.

After a few skillful detours to avoid recognition, he reached the store where he made the purchase of the necessary apparel for his disguise. To the suspicious shopkeeper he explained that he was going on furlough and wanted to give the suit to his cousin, an auto repairman. It consisted of a mechanic's blue overalls with coat to match and included a collar, tie and cap. Satisfied with his bargain, Ebelshauser left with the bundle under his arm and immediately struck out for the open road which was to lead him to freedom and safety. The west exit of the garrison was quite familiar to him. It was the connecting link between the barrack and the training ground. To be walking on this very same road in the dark of night by himself gave him a strange feeling of unreality. It was like an imaginary dream too beautiful and intoxicating to be true.

He stopped for a few minutes on a small bridge which crossed a narrow but deep ditch, the last remnant of age-old fortifications. Though the rampart had long since been demolished, parts of its wall served as a support and bridgehead. With a pounding heart he took a last glance at the town he was about to leave with the hope of never returning. Inwardly he prided himself on the cleverness of his calculations. To have bought a ticket and entrain at Germersheim would have attracted undue attention. To avert suspicion he had decided to proceed on foot to the next station. He was too smart to get caught so easily this time. He was so excited at the prospect of success that he paid little notice to the light drizzle that began to fall as he reached the main road. In another 10 minutes the lighted windows of the last house of the garrison would disappear from sight.

He headed in a straight line for a patch of woodland that came next along the road. He had chosen this spot to put on the disguise, and from the wood a good stretch of road could be travelled in total darkness. At the fork he had to go left instead of right, the route usually taken by the company. There was no possibility of missing the directional post.

"So far, so good," he thought. Taking the roadside ditch with a light jump he quickly climbed the slope and vanished into the wood. Water came dripping from the lower branches as he cut his way through the densely growing pines. For fear of being drenched he refrained from going any further. Besides, there was no time to lose; the minutes were too precious. Having abruptly stopped he immediately began the process of his transformation. Not only did he deem it unwise to discard his uniform, but he would have been too cold without it. The change, therefore, was comparatively easy. All he had to do was slip the overalls and jacket over his uniform, put on the collar, tie and cap and, presto, the soldier was converted into a first-class mechanic. The only difference, so far as he could judge in the dark, was a sensation of tightness. Damn, he thought, the whole outfit should have been at least two or three sizes larger. The only thing that seemed to fit perfectly was the tie.

But for all his swiftness, Ebelshauser had been overtaken by nature. The drizzle of a moment before had ceased and in its place a thick, impenetrable fog had filled the atmosphere. From his vantage point he could not even distinguish the road below. Groping around, he traced back his steps. Just as he was about to jump again he caught sight of two shadows. He ducked into the ditch, stretching himself into the mud. With a trembling heart he watched the forms approach, holding his breath until they had passed by. It had been a close shave. The short moment of tension had seemed like an hour. He waited another minute or two. Nothing could be seen or heard. Reassured by the silence and convinced of his safety, he cautiously ventured out of the ditch and on to the road.

Suddenly, in his attempt to gain the other side of the highway, he nearly collided with two other persons who emerged from the fog like ghosts. His heart jumped to his throat. Unable to retreat in time he thought it unavoidable to apologize in order to clear himself. But the right words did not come to mind. Instead, he blurted out an innocent query about directions.

"Excuse me, please, which is the way to Sondernheim?"

Had he kept his tongue it was likely that nothing would have happened. But with his insecure and stuttering voice he already had given himself away.

The simple question, the manner in which it was said, the construction of the sentence and the strong, revealing French accent all were more than sufficient to arouse immediate suspicion. However, the blunder had been made and it was too late to correct himself. He realized the absurdity of his question as soon as he had spoken. The die was cast and he could only blame himself for the consequences. He trembled when, instead of replying, one of the two forms began to question him.

"Where do you come from?" a man's voice asked with severity.

"Germersheim," Ebelshauser answered softly.

"Germersheim?" repeated the man suspiciously. "And you mean to tell me that you don't know the way to Sondernheim?" There was a note of anger as well as sarcasm in his tone.

Ebelshauser did not reply. A short silence followed, then he made a motion to leave when the man shouted a command.

"Stop! Not a step further, understand?"

Ebelshauser stood there as if suddenly nailed to the ground. He did not dare to move. While ordering his companion to retreat the man came a step nearer and his accusation bluntly rang out into the foggy silence.

"A prisoner attempting to escape, hey? A Russian?"

"No, sir," came the frantic reply.

"Then you're a Frenchman."

"No, sir, no Frenchman either."

"Well, well," the man resumed. "You don't say! We'll soon find out. Let's go down to the light by the bridge. I would like to take a good look at you. No, you go first, and don't step aside either."

The man then produced a revolver. "No running or I'll shoot. Go on now, forward!"

For Ebelshauser everything went black. He had gambled and was again losing the game. It was as if everything was crashing down over his head like a house of cards. What was going to happen to him now? His imagination began to run wild. What would be his punishment? He saw himself in jail, then he thought of home and his parents. They would never learn what he had done. Maybe they were going to beat him. His mind was haunted by all kinds of grotesque pictures. His dream of liberty was turning into a nightmare of gloom and fear. He felt paralyzed as he walked automatically with half-closed eyes toward the bridge. For half an hour he had breathed the sweet perfume that only freedom can give to a prisoner. Now he was being snatched away and about to be put behind bars, not unlike a butterfly bagged by a collector during its very first day of life.

"Halt!" shouted the man from behind. Ebelshauser stopped short directly under the glare of one of the arc lights at the head of the bridge.

"Turn around!" came the next command.

Ebelshauser came face to face with his captor. With wild astonishment he beheld the chief physician of the regimental staff. With him was a woman, probably his wife. She stood at a distance and frowned at him.

At the first sight of his prisoner the officer burst out laughing, unable to restrain himself. Ebelshauser was startled. The spell of laughter seemed contagious for the woman also began to smile. He was in no mood to respond, and unable to understand the reason for this sudden outburst he flushed at the thought of being so brazenly ridiculed. But the officer soon became serious again. It was no time for Ebelshauser to show any evidence of anger.

In spite of the light he could not see the officer's face. Only the protruding point of his nose, the gray, waxed mustache and a potent chin were the parts that came into full view. His eyes were hidden by the deep-set visor of his cap.

"Well, well, by jove! This is the kind of fellow you turn out to be! You ought to be ashamed of yourself. Can you beat that, Anna, to have men like this bird in the ranks!" The woman made no reply.

"Come along," the officer ordered. "We'll get your number at the next station."

When they arrived there they entered the guardhouse and the men exploded into a roar of riotous laughter. He had felt miserable at first but could not help laughing, too, as soon as he finally caught sight of himself. No wonder he had been detected and recognized. His absurd disguise was enough to give anybody the jinx. Even though the mechanic's outfit had proven a tight fit, he had felt himself at ease. But in the dark and rush of escape he had failed to notice the poor fit of the garment. The legs of the overalls as well as the sleeves of the coat were much too short. His uniform stuck out from beneath the thin blue covering in all four directions. Even through the open front of the jacket his field-gray tunic was plainly visible, and the flimsy tie clearly looked like it did not belong there. He had to admit that his was the most grotesque picture of a man he could imagine.

Ebelshauser spent two intolerable weeks in virtual solitary confinement while awaiting trial. During the first few days he tried repeatedly to tempt his guard into conversation. But no matter what he said the guard seemed immune and could not be moved to respond. In maintaining strict silence his keeper was only conforming to special instructions. He would stare at his prisoner and then suddenly turn away with a helpless shrug of the shoulders.

The case obviously appeared more serious than he at first thought. Did they really suspect the actual objective of his evasion? If so, what on earth was going to happen to him? Had he told conflicting stories? He could not recall all the answers he had given his interrogators. To be regarded and treated as a dangerous character certainly was a bad omen. His nervous thoughts perplexed him and he pondered over the possible outcome of the impending trial.

In such a feverish state of mind he saw himself die, his body riddled with bullets from a firing squad. This nightmarish scene soon became an obsession. It made him afraid to fall asleep for fear that he would wake up shortly afterward, his shivering limbs bathed in cold perspiration. Ghastly visions haunted his brain and forced bouts of shaking. More than once he was frightened at the sight of his own shadow. His incarceration and lack of sleep were beginning to tell on his face, and he wished the whole rotten business would be over with soon.

At last, on the first day of the third week, Ebelshauser was led haggard and terror-stricken from his cell. Although warned about the proceeding the evening before, he found himself utterly unprepared for the ordeal. He was in a terrible state of excitement, his face emaciated and pale, his eyes bloodshot and heavily underlined. With head bowed in shame he walked through the streets of Germersheim like a machine. He felt the curious gaze of civilians who paused on the sidewalks to watch him pass by, but with unbearable humiliation he could not bring himself to look at them. An hour later he was ushered into the large courtroom, filled to capacity. At his appearance the flow of conversation subsided immediately. Somewhat dazzled by the flood of light he stepped forward quickly between his guards. Walking through the center of the room he mounted a specially-built platform and took his place on the prisoner's bench. He felt himself the target of dozens of scrutinizing, malevolent eyes, and it gave him the impression of being surrounded by enemies. He glanced at the floor, reluctant to face the crowd.

When he finally did he was flushed with visible embarrassment. He naturally had expected a packed courtroom, but he had not counted on the presence of all the high-ranking officers. Never before had he seen so many military celebrities gathered together in one spot. A more perfect exhibition of medals and colorful, resplendant uniforms was unthinkable. It also left him with the impression that the higher the military rank, the worse the eyesight, for nearly every one of the upper crust was wearing the traditional, but mostly useless, monocle — the infallible symbol of the aristocracy.

As far as he could make out, not a single man of his rank was present. Neither could he find a familiar face among the officers. There seemed to be no one there from his own company. This brief survey of the courtroom made him lose confidence and filled his heart with apprehension. He began to despair of the ultimate verdict. What would his fate be? Could he possibly succeed in convincing his judges of his innocence? But there was no doubt in his mind that they already were prejudiced against him. That would make it twice as hard for him to speak in his own defense.

His thoughts were beginning to wander back home when he was ordered to stand for the reading of the accusation. Hesitatingly, he rose to his feet and waited. The array of brilliant uniforms still arrested his attention, and one by one he inspected the monocled faces. Then he turned to look at the solemn countenance of the reader. For the benefit of the audience the clerk was giving out the facts in their succession as recorded. In a monotonous voice he read at length a series of depositions made against the prisoner by the arresting officer. Then came a detailed report from Inspector Benz which painted a minute and complete analysis of his investigation. From the latter, Ebelshauser was quite surprised to learn of the suspicion he had aroused.

Proceeding first on the assumption that he was a French spy, his whole outfit, including a pair of double-soled shoes his father had given him before he left Lausanne, had been cut to pieces in the expectation of discovering some kind of revealing notes. Very definitely, the protocol went on to state, nothing to this effect had been found and therefore, while he was guilty of desertion, no evidence had been uncovered to warrant the accusation of spying. At the end of the reading the clerk folded the long document and laid it aside very carefully.

Ebelshauser was glad of the opportunity to sit down again. Asked if he had anything to say he merely replied that he had not, accompanying his answer with a negative move of the head. He reflected that it was useless for him to speak now, hoping for a better chance to clear himself when called to relate his own story.

A short pause followed during which he felt himself growing hot and cold at the same time. He tried to prepare what he was going to say. He realized at the outset that his poor knowledge of German would be a terrible handicap. On the other hand, he counted on the questions from the state's prosecutor to save him from this difficulty. It would be easier for him to say yes or no, adding a few words here and there instead of getting confused and groping for some correct word or expression in the middle of a long, drawn narrative.

"Will the accused, Ebelshauser, take the stand!"

Roused from his meditations, he got up and walked down the few steps to the box, taking his seat within the enclosure.

"As briefly as possible, will you tell the court what prompted your desertion?

In a second Ebelshauser was on his feet again. But when he glanced at the audience he became shy and unassuming. For a moment his first words seemed to stick in his throat. He closed his eyes in a strenuous effort to overcome the terrible sensation of impotence. He had finally prepared a short speech; yet, as he stood there he could barely concentrate his thoughts and find anything to say.

"I would like it to be understood first of all," he began to stutter at last, "that I never ... entertained ... any intention of deserting ..."

At the sight of the gallery's grinning faces he paused. It was obvious that he could find no sympathetic or believing souls in the audience. He was lost with them before he had even started.

"All I wanted was a chance to go to Pirmasens to visit my relatives and show myself there as a soldier. I would have been back early Monday morning, figuring that my absence would have remained unnoticed. Three times I was supposed to go on leave, and three times I was refused permission to go. I could wait no longer and made up my mind to take a chance the way I did."

He had resumed and concluded the tale of his adventure in one breath. Had he been allowed to speak the truth without fear of retaliation or incriminating himself, he could have told a good mouthful to his listeners. Why had they constantly pestered and persecuted him because of his faulty understanding of German? Was all the misery and mistreatment regarded as necessary as a compensation for his having enlisted as a volunteer? Why hadn't they kept their promise to him? If only he could speak his mind! But what did these high military officials care about his personal feelings? It was beside the point and had no bearing upon the case. They no doubt had no regard whatsoever for the opinion of a man of his rank.

Conscious of the prevailing attitudes he perceived around him, he was resolved to stick to the story he had just told. He had realized immediately after his arrest that telling the truth would have sealed his own verdict of guilt. Both the chief physician and Inspector Benz had done their best in a vain attempt to make him change his version. But he had kept steadfast to his only line of safety, feigning ignorance of any other design but a visit to his father's home town. Here again, as twice before, he fully sensed the incredulity of his listeners. He had the impression that, perhaps, his tale was too simple to be true.

At the request of the judge, the state's prosecutor stepped forward. Within a few minutes a stiff examination was underway.

"Accused Ebelshauser," said the prosecutor, "you have sworn before the court to tell nothing but the truth. Therefore, I warn you that any false testimony on your part will be regarded as a confession of your guilt." After a short pause he brought up the first question.

"Now tell me, Ebelshauser, what exactly was your premeditated destination when you left the barrack on the evening of November 27th?"

"Pirmasens," the prisoner replied without hesitation, looking directly into the face of his questioner.

"Are you sure you're not mistaken?"

"No, sir, I'm not."

"Was then Pirmasens really the only place you wanted to go to? Answer yes or no."

"Yes, sir."

"Your only objective was to pay a visit to your relatives, is that it?"

"Yes, sir."

"And who are the relatives you wanted to see so badly?"

"Uncles and aunts, all brothers of my father."

"You mean the aunts are the wives of your father's brothers?"

"Yes, sir, of course."

Someone was heard laughing in the gallery. Apparently he was not the only one who found this last question rather ridiculous and out of place. But Ebelshauser remained imperturbably calm and serious. He suspected either a trap or the desire of the prosecutor to test his wit and patience. The man's small, piercing eyes were not pleasant to look at and much too cunning to inspire trust and confidence. As the accused he would have been unwise to take the last inquiry as an innocent joke. He kept on his guard for he had everything to lose.

"Now, Ebelshauser, you intimate that you wanted to go to Pirmasens to visit some relatives, but you also have a relative in Kaiserslautern, haven't you?" The attack was now being made, just as anticipated.

"Yes, sir, I have."

"So why should you have chosen Pirmasens instead of Kaiserslautern as your destination?"

"I don't know."

"So, you don't know! How would you like me to refresh your memory a bit? Had you not a much farther place in mind than Pirmasens? Answer yes or no."

"No, sir."

"Isn't it a fact that Theodor Frech, as a brother-in-law, stands nearer to you than all the other relatives you have in Pirmasens?"

"Perhaps." He could not be too positive about that, afraid to involve himself deeper in a position that promised no issue. At the same time he could not help wondering how and where the man had gotten hold of all this information. Had Theo written to him while he languished in his cell? Had a message revealing his relationships come from home? What had transpired during the two weeks he had been shut off from the outside world? He dared not guess and in his ignorance he decided to manage keeping on the defensive.

"I will not tolerate so evasive a reply!" thundered the prosecutor in a visible rage. "Aren't you more intimately acquainted with Theo Frech at Kaiserslautern than with the rest of your relatives at Pirmasens? Yes or no?"

"Yes, sir."

"Then again, why Pirmasens and not Kaiserslautern? Are you not on the best of terms with your brother-in-law?"

"Yes, sir."

"Answer my question, why go to Pirmasens then?"

"I don't know," replied Ebelshauser desperately. Would this fellow never stop pounding away at the same question? What was his motive? What kind of a trick was he up to? He just could not figure out the tactics the prosecutor was pursuing. But there was something uncanny about his ways and expressions. Undoubtedly, he was preparing the ground for another assault on his memory, perhaps even on his character.

In religious silence those in the audience strained their ears and eyes so as not to miss a word or move. The officers sat stiff and motionless, focusing on the accuser, then on the accused. Their looks were severe, cold, critical and devoid of sympathy. Only a few appeared bored with the slowness of the procedure.

"You still don't know? All right then, but you had 16.75 marks in your pockets when arrested. How much did you figure for the fare?"

"Oh, about 10 marks for a round trip ticket," he answered with very little conviction.

"Ten marks, heh? Very interesting! Gentlemen of the court, I want you to note this reply." The prosecutor turned back to Ebelshauser.

"Now, if this is your estimate of the cost of a round trip ticket to Pirmasens, how is it that you so urgently requested your parents at Lausanne to send you 150 francs?"

"I, er ... I thought to myself ...I had it in mind to buy a few presents and wanted to make sure I would have enough money with me."

The question had come like a bombshell. He sat for a few minutes, gasping. He could see through the prosecutor's game now. But this revelation was of no help to him. Quite the contrary, it looked like a very damaging piece of evidence against which he could not effectively defend himself. He felt the implication sealing his doom.

"You expect us to believe that? Had you not planned to escape for good, making your way to Lausanne?"

"No, sir," cried Ebelshauser vehemently. "I did not."

"Your negation sounds as loud as an affirmation. However, I'll leave it to the judge to decide the case. In the meantime I am returning you to your bench where you're to await the decision of the court."

Dejectedly, he resumed his place between the two sentries. There was no hope for him. He was already anticipating a stiff sentence. On the other hand, he did find some consolation in the thought that after two or three years in prison the war might be over. He surely would be safer behind bars than he could expect to be in the frontline trenches. After all, a long jail sentence would, in the end, prove to be his own protection against being killed in action, thus insuring his ultimate and safe return home.

"Take out the prisoner!"

Now that the ordeal was over he felt relieved. In a short time he would learn the price to be paid for his adventure. They would find him ready to take his pill bravely, for he counted on no more than three years of imprisonment, probably less. In spite of all the symptoms to the contrary, he even dared to hope for a possible acquittal.

Like two deaf and dumb creatures, his guards kept their lips pressed tight as clamped oysters. Not a sound came from either one of them since they had gone on duty. Watchful as dogs, they stared at him, observing at close range each of his moves and reactions. They were sullen and sinister company.

From outside the courtroom he heard the gavel followed by the guttural voice of the officiating judge calling the gallery to order. A profound silence fell over the crowd as he reentered the great hall. Somehow, the scene brought back to mind forgotten memories of not so long ago. How many times had he appeared before the austere galaxy of the school board to face the various complaints of his professors, all because of his uncontrollable tendency toward mischief? So far as he could recall it seemed that proper conduct and deportment always had been two of life's toughest problems for him. The latest escapade was but an outgrowth of his unsettled youth, a characteristic of his nature. Of course, he was ready to admit that this unfortunate affair had been a big blunder on his part, but nothing else. He could not understand why so much fuss was being made about it except, perhaps, for the sake of a show and to keep up traditional military prestige.

The very moment he took the stand again he realized that all his meditations had been vain attempts at consolation. His former fright began increasing by the minute. The frigid face of the judge was far from reassuring, while those of his entourage were equally sombre and menacing.

Suddenly the judge rose to his feet. Ebelshauser felt himself growing weak, but summoned all his energy and courage to remain standing. His hour had come. A few more minutes of excruciating tension and he would know his fate. He looked at the judge with an air of despair, waiting for him to speak and pronounce the verdict.

"In view of the depositions made against the accused, Gustav Ebelshauser, by the arresting officer, Chief Physician Heinrich Ludwig Langer, and Inspector Rudolf Benz, backed by evidence and ..."

A long recital followed. He could hardly wait for the end of the protocol, burning to learn his fate.

"... therefore, following a fair trial extended to the accused, the prisoner Gustav Ebelshauser has been found guilty of desertion. Consequently, after due deliberation and in accordance with articles ... of the military penal code, the prisoner is hereby condemned to death, to be executed at sunrise by a firing squad at a date to be determined within the next two weeks."

At the word death, Ebelshauser's face turned white. It struck him numb, as if he suddenly had been deprived of all his senses. For the first few seconds he thought he had gone insane. He heard the word but could not believe it to be true. Execution by firing squad at sunrise had finished his illusion of having misunderstood.

With a supreme effort he stayed on his feet, leaning heavily against the small enclosure. His legs wavered under a trembling body. For a moment he had the impression of falling, then again of being blown up into the air. The blood ran hot and cold through his veins, his heart beating fast to the point of bursting, and yet, seeming to stand still. He gasped. Cold perspiration came to his forehead. Then he fainted.

He lost consciousness for a minute or two, and when he was revived the court was still in session. He could hear someone speaking as the guards helped him back to his seat. Looking in the direction of the voice an expression of astonishment came over his face when he recognized Captain Geyer, his company commander, as the speaker. Standing in one of the last two rows, the captain was asking the judge for permission to address the assembly. Was his case not yet concluded? Having obtained the court's consent, Captain Geyer made, perhaps, one of the shortest but most memorable speeches of his career.

"May it please the court to pay attention to the following. With a sense of justice and impartiality on my part, I move that the capital punishment pronounced against the accused be set aside or commuted to a lighter sentence. The sole reason for my request is that this man cannot be found guilty of desertion since he has not yet sworn allegiance to the flag and the colors. Thank you."

"You mean to say the prisoner here present has not yet taken the oath and pledged honor and obedience to the flag?" inquired the judge in a thunderous voice.

"Exactly, your honor," Captain Geyer replied courteously and calmly.

"Then why was this not reported to me before?" The judge's round face was reddening with anger and he obviously was making quite an effort to hold his bursting temper under control.

"Had I been asked," the captain said, "I would have told you, but apparently I was not supposed to interfere. No one came to me for advice. I learned of the impending trial at the last minute, that's why I am here ..."

"It's enough, Captain Geyer," the judge interrupted. "Please be seated."

At this point a cacophony of discord broke loose in the courtroom. In his state of bewilderment Ebelshauser could not exactly make out what was going on. From the few words he caught he perceived that his audience was now divided into two camps as a direct result of Geyer's belated deposition in his favor. Some were siding with the captain for acquittal while others staunchly opposed a reversal of the death sentence. A number of the officers left their seats to walk down the aisle for a few words with the judge. He could not hear what was being whispered. The ghastly scene of his imminent execution was haunting his mind and he could not comprehend that, after so terrible a shock, his brain still seemed to function normally even though he felt himself on the verge of insanity. Even his heart had regained its steady, regular beat, just as if nothing had happened.

"Volunteer Gustav Ebelshauser!"

He heard his name called by the judge, but in an entirely different tone. The title of volunteer struck him as funny, yet promising. If the word "prisoner" suddenly was dropped as part of his name, there must be a good reason for it. As he rose he lifted his eyes. To his surprise he beheld the same justice with a sympathetic if not smiling face.

"Considering ..." the judge began, launching into another long statement of legal verbosity, "... the court has declared in favor of a suitable compromise, whereby the death sentence pronounced against you is revoked, to be replaced by the merited punishment of three days of barrack confinement."

Ebelshauser looked around in amazement, tears draining from his eyes. In the next instant he was sobbing aloud, unable to restrain himself any longer. The guards led him crying like a child out of the courtroom.

He had escaped with his life on a mere technicality.

5

"Dear brethren and friends!

"Reunited as we are today in this venerable house of worship, we praise God, our Lord, for all the tangible proof He has given us in the fulfillment of our conquests and great victories. We thank our heavenly Father for His infallible guidance through the stormy sea of world evolution and revolution and for having helped our great country, the German people, to resist the forces of our enemies ..."

The padre had prepared a patriotic address rather than a sermon, to which there seemed to be no end. His audience, mostly soldiers from the garrison, was sitting on hot coals, losing patience. This preaching about the beloved fatherland was getting on their nerves. They had heard too much of it already. If there really was a merciful God, why did he not put an end to the world massacre? Many soldiers pondered this question and it was the most frequent argument for a loss or abandonment of faith. If they were in church that day it was simply to keep up the age-old German custom at Christmas. Moreover, in attending the service they had a good chance to escape other duties at the barrack. It was a welcome outing, a variation from daily routine. There also was the possibility of a chance meeting with a skirt and the birth of an unexpected romance. The thought of God was quite remote in their minds.

"Let us all look now to God in prayer," the pastor concluded.

"It's about time he finished," Heimer whispered. Ebelshauser smiled at his friend's remark.

"Let's beat it." Schwarz already was up and urging his comrades to follow.

"We'll be out in a few minutes," Rueger said, remaining seated. "Be patient!"

The usual return to the barrack in formation had been dropped for the day. On their way out the four were joined by Strauss and Ferder, and the little group went for a stroll through the streets.

"Since we're off we might as well make the best of it for the day," Heimer proposed as they stopped at a corner. "What do you say, fellows?"

The response was unanimous. They all were eager to get started and have their own way for once.

"Well, boys, make up your minds." Heimer was in good humor and seemed to be willing to take the lead. "What do you propose after that cold shower in church?"

"A cold shower all right," Schwarz readily agreed. "They ought to send those padres and fat-belly priests to the trenches. Maybe they would soon form a different opinion about 'Gott mit uns.' "

Strauss, a Jew, took up the complaint. "They give me a pain in the ass. Some of these black-robed dandies are really crazy with their 'Gott mit uns.' What about the French, the English, the Italians and all the rest? Don't you think God is with them, too?"

"I hate to discuss the matter on the streets," Heimer said, "but you are right about those 'black crows.' One is worth less than the next. And don't forget, most of them do it because they've found it to be the best way out of the war. I wish I could preach. I wouldn't mind being one of them just to save my neck."

"Some of them are all right, I believe," remarked Ebelshauser.

"You would side with them," the implacable Heimer coldly retorted. "Of course, I don't blame you for not knowing what you're talking about. You're not dry behind the ears yet."

"Wait a minute," Rueger interjected. "I must side with Gustav. Sure there are some crazy fanatics among them, but in the majority these pastors are okay. I know some of them personally. They hate war just as much as we do. You can't make them responsible for the world's condition. If men have become insane you can't blame God for it, can you?"

Oh, let's drop the question and quit arguing," Ferder suggested. "Let's go somewhere for a good time. After all, it's Christmas."

In the warm atmosphere of a nearby pub decorated for the occasion they enjoyed a substantial meal and joined with others singing carols and popular songs. Physically and mentally refreshed, after several hours they went back to their quarters in a happy mood.

"Kompagnie ... stillgestanden! Achtung! Augen ... rechts!"

The close of another maneuvers was at hand. On this occasion a regimental inspection — the nightmare of every German soldier — was scheduled to take place. Such a ceremony was bad enough in favorable weather conditions, but in the middle of winter with snow and subfreezing temperatures, the very thought of it was unbearable. For weeks in advance each company, each section, each individual had been put into action from early morning until nightfall. Special drills and exercises had been devised and run through in view of the coming great event.

From General Headquarters orders would travel through the regular military channels, descending degree by degree until reaching the lowest step of the ladder, the Unteroffizier. However, from one step to the next each command underwent a slight change. By the time a command was imparted to the man of ordinary rank the same message was almost unrecognizable from the original.

On this day — as a result of the following typical example — the whole regiment already stood at attention waiting for the colonel commanding to show up. But the men found themselves on the parade ground much too carly.

Said the major to the captain: "Have your company ready for inspection tomorrow afternoon at three o'clock sharp. There will be a mass formation of the entire regiment. I want our 'Herr Oberst' to get a favorable impression of your men. They are to be completely equipped and in irreproachable form. Please give your orders accordingly."

Said the captain to the lieutenant: "Orders from headquarters. Have the company ready tomorrow at two o'clock sharp. The men are to be fully equipped with 'sack and pack.' There will be a regimental inspection led by the colonel and I want him to be impressed by the impeccable form of our company."

Finally, said the corporal to his men: "Orders from headquarters. The company is to march out to the training ground tomorrow morning at eleven o'clock sharp. We are to assemble fully equipped with the whole regiment for inspection and parade shortly after one. I expect every one of you to be in perfect form. Any mishap will be severely reprimanded and punishment will be sure to follow. Everything must be ship-shape. So get busy cleaning your kits. I don't want to see a speck of dirt showing on your uniforms. Remember, the colonel and his staff are to lead the review. I want to be proud of you so let me see what you can do."

Thus were the instructions on the eve of the great event. Hours had been passed in cleaning and shining. All were anxious to look their best. They knew only too well what it meant to be caught and fall into disgrace because of a missing button or tarnished buckle.

The companies were lined up in straight double rows. Each soldier stood erect, rooted and frozen to the snow-covered ground as if carved out of stone. From a distance the huge gathering took the form of a vast and mighty, but calm and immovable human sea. Like all inspections of this nature, it constituted a living monument, an impression of realism, a vivid example of well known German soldiery. For such special occasions Germans were trained not only to be soldiers but, if need be, to be able to ignore their own bodies, forgetting that they were made of flesh and blood. Each man, whether in individual, group or mass exercises and drills, was taxed to the maximum of his physical strength and power of resistance. No one was spared. They all were getting a chance to go through the mill.

"Kompagnie ... stillgestanden! Achtung! Augen ...rechts!"

All through the deep lines the command to stand at attention with eyes right again was vociferously shouted. The formidable crushing unit of human power and concentration of energy formed an invisible link between each statue-like soldier. For more than five hours they had been held on the same spot, waiting for 'Herr Oberst' to show up. It was approaching five o'clock and still there was no indication that the inspection was about to begin.

A sharp, frosty wind was blowing from the north. It swept the sky, chasing away the snow-laden clouds. Every now and then the sun was given a chance to cast its rays on the earth's immaculate white carpet which extended for miles in front of the troops. But nature's grandiose creation did not — could not — mean much to the thousands of cycs clustered on the parade ground's square.

"I wish it was summer," someone whispered behind Ebelshauser.

"Shut up," came a hushed answer from another fellow.

Silence was restored at the approach of an officer who paced up and down the line. The long, endless waiting continued, every passing minute adding new agonies to the immobile creatures. Frozen ears listened to the turmoil going on within themselves. At last, surrounded by his usual array of satellites, advisers and consorts, the Oberst appeared and approached very slowly.

"That low-down bum is finally showing up," said the same voice as before. "Maybe he needs a good watch."

"Shut up, you dumbbell, are you crazy? Do you know what it means to get caught talking like that?"

"Both of you shut up," came someone else's command.

The colonel seemed to have made up his mind to begin the inspection. Sitting on top of his horse it might have been that he himself was starting to feel the cold and was unwilling to risk further exposure for the sake of the regiment. The final test was at hand. A deep sigh of relief escaped from the ranks. "Present arms!" was the prelude to the ceremony as well as the salute of honor to the approaching dignitaries. With a nonchalant gesture the colonel acknowledged the greeting and the soldiers returned to their former position of attention. The long awaited and much feared inspection actually was underway.

"All this fuss for a guy like that!"

Once again Ebelshauser heard the same voice. "If only he would keep quiet," he thought, "for if he gets caught we'll all be in for a tough time."

Fortunately, no observation was made. Laughing and joking among themselves, the officers passed one row of uniforms after the other, hardly looking at the faces. The regimental band played "The Salute to the Flag" while they rode through the ranks. Careless as they seemed, however, they were very quick to discover the slightest mistake. Woe to the man who would compromise the otherwise successful exhibition of his company. There would be no end to his disgrace. The officers paused here and there, amused and laughing at the funny position of this or that soldier, or at the sight of an unusual expression, or at some other striking feature. The man in question not only had to swallow the sardonic, insulting remarks, but he was supposed to be filled with endless gratitude for having been noticed by these high-ranking chieftains.

It had taken hours, days, weeks of merciless training to bring about this masterful and majestic show. Yet, the actual regimental inspection was completed in less than 15 minutes — and for what purpose? Perhaps for nothing else than to subject the German soldier to blind obedience and discipline. This abnormal test was to teach him supreme physical endurance, patience, sacrifice and self-denial which were to be his qualifications representing the crowning glory of the Kaiser's Imperial Army.

On a sunny and balmy March morning in 1916, the Third Company of the 17th Bavarian Infantry Regiment assembled promptly in the barrack yard. Corporals were making the rounds of their respective groups. Everything seemed to be in perfect form and condition. The military students of last September had been graduated into master soldiers. The amateurs had become experts. Gone were the haggard and frightened looks in the men's faces. Almost seven months of daily army routine had hardened them. They had matured under the constant vigilance and guidance of their proud, but tyrannical, guardians, and were now ripe for the firing lines.

It was long after sunrise. The place literally was packed full with a mixture of soldiers and civilians. It was hard to figure where all these strange people had come from. Many a uniform was surrounded by a group of relatives and friends, and the whole scene took the appearance of a festival. But at close range one quickly became aware of the tragedy actually taking place.

"You'll be careful, son. You're the only one I have left." A sad-faced, middle-aged woman garbed in black exhorted her son in a mild and soft voice. "I don't expect you to be a coward. Do your duty and I'll be praying to God for your safe return."

"Don't worry, mother. I'll soon be back, you can bet on that." The young man comforted her, smiled broadly and added, "Besides, we aren't going to the front. We'll be behind the lines for a long time before coming to the trenches."

"Yes, I know, son. Father said the same thing when he left a year ago. Where is he now? He's been missing for eight months. If he were alive I'm sure we would have heard from him."

"Please, mother, it won't help you to cry. Dry your tears and look at me with a smile."

Both fell silent. There was no use talking anymore. Had they not said all there was to say? What else could they do but wait for the final signal in order to fall into each other's arms for a last, painful embrace? There were hundreds of similar scenes that day.

"So there you are, Weber. I've been looking all over for you."

Ebelshauser approached a group of comrades who, because no one had come to see them off, were forming a circle for themselves in a far-off corner near the fence.

"Hello, Gustav! What are you doing with your cigarettes? Let's have a treat before you have them crumbled up in your pockets. What do you say?"

Weber was in a most jovial mood. He did not seem to have a care in the world. In fact, he was one among the few who actually looked forward to leaving for the field as the start of a great adventure. The word "fear" was not in his vocabulary.

"Too bad, big boy, but you're too late. I only have one or two left. I gave the others to Hans."

"Hans! Hans! You would! Don't you think that guy is getting enough? Take a look. See him? Over there, more to the left by the side entrance."

"Yeah, I see him. It looks as if the whole town has come to bid him goodbye."

"I'm telling you, he won't be able to take everything along. Believe me, those peasants are better off with all this food than us poor city dwellers. But I suggest we move over there, we might get something, too."

"There you go again," Ebelshauser said, laughing. "Better leave them alone. We'll get our share somehow. The cigarettes I gave him may prove a good investment at that."

"Right you are, Gustav. Why go begging? What do we care, after all? Hans and all the rest of them can't make us jealous. They all have but one belly each and once it is full they've got to stop eating, or burst if they don't."

"I know. We're just as well off as the others no matter how many people have come to see them off. In an hour we'll all be by ourselves. Everything will be over."

"Nice outfit, isn't it?" Weber pointed sarcastically at himself. "I hope these boots don't give me too much trouble like the last ones I had. And just take a look at this little toy in case I have to play the butcher." He displayed a long-handled dagger which he kept in the shaft of his left boot.

"That's a beauty! How much did you pay?" Ebelshauser pulled out his own which was somewhat smaller. They both held the weapons in their right fists in a mock fight of jumping at each other's throats. The blades glittered and flashed in the sunlight.

"Mine is at least an inch longer," remarked Weber proudly. "It'll make it easier to reach the heart if it comes down to that. I want those Tommies to know the difference between a Bavarian and a Prussian."

"Are we really the only ones to carry daggers in our boots?" inquired Ebelshauser as both replaced the knives in their hiding places.

"I never heard otherwise. Besides, the Prussians haven't got the guts. They do all the talking while we Bavarians are the ones who really act. That's the difference between us but it means a lot."

"What time have you got? We'll be moving soon."

"Yeah, it won't be long now. The place will be empty in half an hour. Some of the officers are already on the spot just waiting for orders."

"Did you see Schwarz in his new outfit? It's a peach of a uniform."

"Anything special?"

"Just wait. Take a look at him when we fall in. You can't help laughing and at the same time feel sorry for the poor bugger. His whole body could disappear in his pants and the tunic could hold three fellows of his size.

It's a shame the way they're going to send him out to the field."

"Well, it's more or less a matter of luck. Those quartermasters are always trying to put one over on you. I had to go back four times just to get a helmet that fit. It doesn't really matter to them. That's why so many of us look more like clowns in a circus than soldiers about to fight on a battlefield. Schwarz is no exception."

The excitement came to a climax when the company's commander put in an appearance. It meant only a few more minutes of respite. Soldiers and civilians fell into each other's arms in long embraces. Mothers, wives and sweethearts could hardly let go of their men — in some cases even refusing to set them free, so infuriated were they at the compulsory separation.

Captain Geyer paced up and down the yard. Upon reaching the main gate he signalled his orderly and the latter assisted his master into the saddle of his white mare. The decisive moment had arrived. Everyone knew the meaning of this preparation. Suddenly, dominating and compelling, came the command:

"FALL IN!"

For the next few minutes there was a tumult and scramble beyond description. But thanks to the efficiency of German militarism all talking came promptly to an end and order was reestablished. The soldiers lined up in their usual formation with "sacks and packs." A last minute inspection was made.

"Forward, MARCH!"

The band struck up the martial air of "Fredericus Rex." The men began their last parade in the homeland and marched off toward the station followed by all the civilians who had remained. The streets were lined with spectators in a bid of farewell. The residents of Germersheim always knew about such convoys for the soldiers had become a part of their population. Handkerchiefs flew in the air but many were used to dry uncontrollable tears. Boisterous and shrieking youngsters ran in front of the band and on both sides of the column.

Immediately upon disbanding at the station a mad and frantic rush took place on the small platform. Each soldier sought out one of his own in the crowd. It became a most difficult task for the officers to divide their men equally among the cars. They began to grow angry when their police whistles brought no instantaneous response. And when their shouted commands remained just as ineffective they lost their tempers altogether and started to go after the delinquents. Such insubordination could not be tolerated. Like flying dragoons the officers fell on each embracing party, seized and dragged the men back with them. The growing indignation of the civilians left them cold. War was an excuse for everything.

A few moments later the long, shrill whistle of the first engine ripped the air, followed by the shorter blast from a second machine. Very slowly the long train began to move. A forest of waving arms rose from the car windows and on the platform. Shouts and screams filled the air. The train rapidly gained speed and in two minutes the show was over. Heavy and tense, silence returned. The men hung to their own thoughts, registering in their minds the fleeting scenes of a few moments before. They were leaving with the hope of returning. But how many of them would actually come back?

The front was their destination. They knew that much. The exact name of their landing place did not matter. They only had to follow their leaders. On the map of the General Staff their road was already traced. Sooner or later they would face the implaccable enemy. What would be their fate then? With this question mark etched on their foreheads the men in field-gray were on their way to the Western Front, gliding along the rails to the line of battle somewhere in France. It was a beautiful day in March of 1916, a day which heralded the imminent return of spring.

Shortly before midnight the following day they alighted at Lille and were lined up in the dark in front of the station. The assignment to their respective billets took an endless time. Tired from lack of sleep, excitement and anticipation, they barely paid attention to their new surroundings. They were conscious of only one thing: having left the fatherland far behind they could no longer feel certain about their safety. Soon after crossing into Belgium the rhythmical, muffled sounds of artillery had become discernible in the distance. The cannonade had grown louder and more distinct as they rolled to the west, and at night the reddish color of the front line had been plainly visible from the train. Now, standing in France, the thunderous voices of the guns were not only heard but felt as well. Following each loud report the ground vibrated under their feet.

Other clues of their proximity to the danger zone were the hushed tone in which all the commands were given and a sharp contrast in the attitude of the officers. They seemed much more concerned now about forging harmony and closer understanding with their men. Not a single harsh word was heard.

Ten days had been more than sufficient for the newcomers to give the town the once-over. Contrary to what they had expected, they soon found that there was little difference between barrack life and the present existence behind the lines. Hopes for a welcome change in military duties so far had failed to materialize.

During the evening of another strenuous day, Ebelshauser and his friend Fritz Thaler held a discussion with their comrades. They had just finished dinner and felt in a mood for talk. Birnbaum gave vent to the prevailing resentment.

"It doesn't seem to matter where, when and how we are, there is always a place for drills and exercises. We'll have to drill in hell, too, I suppose."

"Pretty soon they'll have us practice goose-stepping right in the front lines," Thaler piped in. "If fighting and killing is our job, then why this silliness about parade ground marching and saluting?"

"You said it," Schwarz agreed. "They make me sick with their stupid drills. I wonder what kind of new orders Apfel is going to bring back tonight?"

"It's strange that Apfel should be summoned instead of the orderly. I wonder what's behind the secret meeting they're holding at such an hour?" Thaler asked.

"What's so strange about it?" Ebelshauser said. "One of those higher-ups is having a birthday, or maybe they're just holding a party — you know, something really special."

"Is that so?" Thaler's face expressed doubt. "I don't know why but I have a hunch that we'd better get ready for bad news. I met one of those messengers two days ago. He was on his way to headquarters. I didn't get the name of the place but it's not far from here. He was in a great hurry. Those guys always are, you know, but a flat tire stopped him. I talked to him while he was fixing his machine."

"How far are we from the front?" Loewenstein intervened. "That's what I would like to know."

"Keep your mouth shut for a while, will you?" Ebelshauser was anxious to hear the rest. "Give Fritz a chance to finish."

"As I was saying," Thaler continued, "I was facing a tough egg. This messenger took a good look at me, grinned and finally said, 'A greenhorn, heh? How long have you been out here? Just arrived, I guess, otherwise you'd know better and stop asking questions.' "

"These guys are all the same," Heimer said as Thaler paused. "They really give me a pain in the neck. The way they act with their 'important news' you'd think they were the Kaiser himself."

Thaler resumed. " 'Ten days,' I told him. 'Wait 'til you're here 10 months,' he answered. 'You'll be initiated then and know how to keep your mouth shut.' He started laughing at his own reply. For a moment I thought he was having a fit. But he soon became serious again, righted his cycle and started the motor before installing himself in the saddle. Just as he was taking off he looked back and yelled, 'Good luck! You'll need it the way things are going out there.' And the next minute he was gone."

Thaler's last words took effect in a foreboding manner. A long silence ensued. Looking at each other, the men clung to their own thoughts. The rhythmical ticking of an alarm clock on the room's mantelpiece — one of the few remnants of the former occupants — was the only audible sound to be heard for a while. No one seemed willing to speak first.

In the meantime, twilight had turned into complete darkness. Every now and then a sudden gust of wind caused some of the dislocated windows to rattle in their frames. The air was heavy and hot, full of moisture. Though they did not exactly miss him, the continued absence of their corporal that night somehow made them feel very uneasy. Perhaps it was their imaginations, but the noise of artillery fire reaching them from the front sounded much louder and the ground's vibrations seemed to increase in number and intensity. Fear crept into their hearts.

Oskar Pechthold, who until now had kept quiet, suddenly rose and began pacing the floor. Nearing the table around which they sat, he finally exploded, "Wouldn't it be swell for us to be deaf! At least we couldn't hear all the silly messages that are carried around in the army. When it comes to the point, half of it is pure invention."

Pechthold then turned to Thaler and added, "I'll bet my boots that fellow wanted to make an impression and scare you. And from the way you told the story, he almost succeeded."

"Hello, boys," said Apfel jovially, closing the door behind him. The corporal took off his cap, flung it on a bed, unhooked his belt and opened his tunic. Although in his forties, the man appeared much younger, especially with a fresh haircut and shave. He had just come from the barber. The few reddish hairs under his nose had been left untouched because of his desire to raise a mustache that simply refused to grow. His cheeks, blown up like little balloons, gave his face a striking roundness. While well fed, he ate very little. Apparently, war and food had had no effect on his body yet. His blond hair was combed flat, parted almost in the middle. Glossy, it was held in position with a lotion of a peculiar smell.

For a head of its size, his ears were unusually small but well formed, like those of a lady. An equally small nose must have felt out of place on his broad face. His deep blue eyes almost disappeared beneath a bushy forest of eyebrows, giving him at times a look of great severity. But Apfel was modest and unassuming. Therefore, his promotion to corporal had been the surprise of his life. He was one among few who dared take a stand on behalf of his men. To them he acted more like a father.

All eyes turned to him as he slowly stepped toward the table. He was smiling, Yet, there was something in his face, in his glance, in his behavior that betrayed a hidden thought which he seemed reluctant to reveal.

"Planning an excursion?" he said. "Where to?"

"Just trying to get located," Thaler replied without lifting his eyes from the map spread out in front of them. "See, that round spot in red there is where we are now. But where about is the front line?"

Apfel bent closer over the map, straightened up again and said, "To be exact, I don't know myself, but it's somewhere just west of here. Anyway, we'll have a good chance to find out the correct answer tomorrow. We're to relieve two regiments of Prussians, supplying barbed wire and ammunition up to the first line.

"I thought so!" exploded Schwarz. "They would pick us for the dirty job. I would rather be sent to the trenches than play second fiddle and be used as a mule."

"Well, Schwarz, if I had my choice I'd rather go home," retorted Apfel. "That's how I feel about the whole business anyway."

"Oh, I know it's not your fault," Schwarz said as if wanting to apologize.

"What time are we to start, corporal?"

"Boys, you better jump into the feathers after getting everything ready for tomorrow morning. We're to join the Second Company at the south-east entrance of the town at four o'clock and then proceed immediately to the depot for loading. Half of the men will carry two boxes each of hand grenades or a spool of wire. We're to start from the depot no later than five. Half an hour later we'll bump into the 'Berliner Grossschnautzen' whom we're to relieve. From there we'll be led by an officer from the Prussians. I don't know about the return trip, but we're supposed to be back at eight."

A minute later the men were up preparing for the morning's adventure. It was going to be their first trip to the front, their first real test. As soon as they were done they silently undressed and went to bed. Many that night could not find sleep.

A light drizzle was falling the next morning as they walked to the depot. Apfel had sounded the alarm at 2:30 to have them ready on time. With heavy eyes they had crawled slowly and reluctantly from their beds. No one was in a mood to joke or laugh so they proceeded silently through the dark and deserted streets. Only a few dim lights were burning to protect the town from total obscurity. Every now and then a gust of wind blew the rain directly into their faces, forcing them to slow up. The poor visibility was increased by onrushing low clouds which moved around like black smoke. In many places on the outskirts of the town they had to march two abreast, the others following closely in their footsteps. No matter how careful they meant to be, all of them came to stumble along the way. Loud swearing and wild imprecations escaped from the men in trouble. Once on their feet again they would warn their followers: "Watch out! Big hole! Step aside to the left. Step aside to the right." The ground on which they were penetrating had been badly shot to pieces. The road resembled a mountain path after the passage of an avalanche. Large rocks were strewn about and deep holes, revealing the eloquent language of explosive shells and mines, became more and more frequent. Aside from a slight difference in color — easily lost sight of — the road and surrounding fields were one mass of earth and bore the horrors of secret and silent suffering.

"Just in time, Apfel," came the greeting from Lieutenant Hartmann, the officer in charge of the night expedition. "We're about to start. Get your men loaded and let me know when you're ready."

"At your service, Herr Leutnant," responded the corporal. "Where are the wire rolls? We won't be long. It's only a quarter-to and we were not supposed to meet here anyhow. In fact, we'd still be waiting for you down below, according to the order. But seeing nobody there I took it on my own responsibility to go ahead.

"I thought you'd use your head and I'm glad you did," Hartmann said. "There was a slight misunderstanding. As for the wire, it's back there behind the ammunition."

The lieutenant spoke softly and with a cunning smile. He towered a head taller than the corporal, having to bend his lean body forward while in conversation with Apfel. He was the type of man that had found in the army a real career and vocation. But in opposition to many of his fellow officers Hartmann was neither a roughneck nor a high-hat. When it came to the point of being of assistance to the enlisted man, he was quite a sport.

"Here, follow the line," Apfel said to his men. "You'll find the supplies in the back. I'll be with you in a minute." Before they left they heard him say to the lieutenant, "This is disgusting weather for their first venture."

"Why, Apfel, I'm surprised," Hartmann replied. "On the contrary, this is just as fine as could be. A splendid conspiracy between us and the sky. Better to get a few raindrops in the eyes than a rain of steel bullets, don't you think? You better tell your men about it. They ought to be thankful for all these clouds. It's the best protection for their skin. Now, hurry up. We want to be back before daybreak."

Four abreast they quit the depot and marched out through open fields across country. The weight of their loads, increasing with every hazardous step, made the advance more difficult. They had barely been on their way for 20 minutes when Hartmann gave the command to file in a single row. The lieutenant took the lead while Apfel closed up the rear.

The entire landscape appeared calm as if plunged into a deep slumber. Even the heavy artillery was taking time out for a short breathing spell. The usual yellow line of fire had disappeared at the horizon. Instead, earth and sky looked like a cohesive mass made from only one element — blackness impenetrable. Noiselessly, the men seemed to glide over the ground like phantoms. No one said a word.

As they approached their goal the air was permeated with a strong smell of powder similar to that of burning sulphur. A short while back they had left the open field to enter the first trench. It was the connecting link between the front and rear lines, between the actual fighting forces and the various headquarters directing operations from distant points of safety. Later they would learn that such "communication" trenches often proved to be the most important of all other trenches. Disregard for their maintenance resulted in the loss of many precious lives. Like the main tributaries of a river, so were the connecting ditches to be considered. For obvious reasons their lines were never straight. There were many unexpected turns and more than once the tired men bumped against the trench's dirty walls. They also passed numerous other openings and corridors, some leading to other sectors, some ending in a cul-de-sac. The men had to keep close together.

Everything had gone fine. They had reached the first line without mishap and not even a flare or starshell had interrupted their march forward. The rain had abated somewhat when the long column came to a halt and awaited further orders for the disposal of their supplies. No one seemed to know exactly what to do. Apfel joined Hartmann to ask for his viewpoint.

"Maybe we're a bit too early," the lieutenant said while looking at his watch, "or else they didn't expect us so soon." He gave the man nearest him the order to unload. Then turning again to Apfel, he said, "Stay here, I'll try to find the company's commander."

He had hardly disappeared behind the next bend of the trench when he came back with a captain. The latter praised him for the quick work and told him to have the men dispose of their wire rolls and grenades along the line, one load every five meters. Then he asked the lieutenant to have a drink and Hartmann readily accepted.

Reassured by the reigning silence, the tension of fear under which the men had been laboring suddenly was abandoned and they moved more freely in the execution of their task. Tongues loosened and the frightening moments just passed were quickly forgotten.

"If it continues as quiet as this the war will last for another 10 years," Schwarz said.

"That's true," replied Pechthold. "It really doesn't seem possible that one might get killed at a moment's notice."

"If this is supposed to be the fighting line, then I wouldn't mind staying right here instead of going back for more drills," remarked Heimer.

"Imagination and reality are two different pictures," Birnbaum agreed.

Ebelshauser and Thaler also were finished with their job and started to walk back to their point of departure. Before leaving, Thaler stopped at one of the posts and queried the lookout peering across No Man's Land.

"Hello, there! How are tricks? How does it look?" Without changing position the man turned his head. The expression on his face was one of surprise. He did not seem to have understood so Thaler repeated his questions.

"The Tommies are behaving all right tonight," the soldier said, "but something tells me they're preparing for some kind of surprise. I like it quiet, but when it's too quiet there's something wrong someplace, I'm telling you."

"Any casualties lately?" questioned Thaler further.

"Five badly wounded and 14 dead, plenty for five days."

"Going to be relieved tomorrow night, heh?"

"Yeah, thank God. Getting sick of it. Nothing in the belly for the last three days. Damn guys, too lazy to bring out everything."

The lookout took up his post again. Turning away, his eyes scanned the wide space between the German and English trenches. Seeing nothing suspicious in the darkness he resumed his talk.

"You just arrived I heard. Well, how is it going at home? How is the spirit? Have they still something to eat and wear? Is there really going to be a revolution? Where do you come from?"

"Germersheim, if you know where that is," replied Thaler. "Of course, the people are bitter and suffering from all kinds of privations, but one can feel in their hearts a grim determination to hold out as long as necessary. Revolution? Don't be silly. No thought of it."

Thaler spoke the last few words with emphasis and great conviction.

"Germersheim? No, never been there," the soldier said. "Ever been to Berlin? That's the place I come from. Some city! Wish I could go there in the morning. Been out here since the beginning. Haven't missed a single day. Hope they'll soon send me home for a couple of weeks ..."

He was interrupted by a hushed voice. "Come on, boys! Hartmann is already waiting for you. He's impatient to get back."

Day was breaking when they reached their quarters. The excitement was over. Nothing had happened to keep their minds awake this time. Their fearful anticipation and expectations of their first trip up to the line had proven far worse than reality. They could laugh now. But they knew that the unusual lack of activity at the front on this occasion was due mainly to a stroke of luck, a coincidence over which they had no control. That their expedition might have turned into a bloody affair did not occur to them. So far as they were concerned they now had been in the first line, and that was all that mattered. They could speak now about their own experience to those who would come after them. They felt qualified and, therefore, not deserving of the title "greenhorns" any longer. The realization that they were still far from an advanced stage of experience came to them three days later when the whole sector, into which they had moved without a scratch, was literally blown up by a severe attack. The English artillery had spoken. The slight tremors of the past few days to which they had grown accustomed became veritable earthquakes, following each other in rapid succession. Orders came that they would have to hold themselves ready for any emergency. Everything was packed in great haste. To play it safe, their quarters were moved from the ground floor to the cellar.

The disaster wrought by the heavy guns was tremendous. The whole town was in a panic. But the most lamentable picture was that of old, helpless civilians and children who seemed to be losing their heads not knowing what to do or where to run for protection. Many of them were so frightened they could barely move. A few were killed by shellfire. Most, however, piled what little remained of their valuables in carts and fled toward Belgium.

The soldiers alone seemed immune, though the bombardment caused quite a number of casualties. Two days after the attack Apfel and his men, along with the Third Company, were transferred to a different sector more to the west near La Bassée.

6

Biting his lips, Ebelshauser marched along at the side of his friend, Thaler. The two had become inseparable. He immediately had felt inwardly drawn to Thaler whom he judged to be a man of sense, sincerity and open views. At first Thaler had appeared to him rather bold, but on close examination Ebelshauser had been pleased with the charm of his impetuous personality. Thaler, he thought, had something apart, something unusual, something that distinguished him from the average type of soldier he had met, with the exception of Hans Rueger. Thaler's high forehead indicated a person of intellect and education. His traits were refined. Put into a different company he easily could have taken the place of an officer. A chiseled nose, together with his firm lips, denoted a strong character. Blue-gray eyes were the reflection of his heart and soul, emotional and passionate, yet full of devotion and tenderness.

Immediately on their heels followed Heimer and Schwarz, then Birnbaum and Loewenstein and finally Pechthold and Rueger. The rest of the company hung after them like a long train hangs on its engine.

Hampered by the deep blackness of the night the long file advanced slowly, not unlike a serpent crawling lazily through the jungle. The only difference was that the poisonous reptile had been replaced by more dangerous human beings called soldiers, and that the jungle was then called, in the better language of high civilization, "No Man's Land." The most ferocious beasts of the jungle could not hope to compete in cruelty. The wounds inflicted by man were far worse and deadlier. In the jungle, hunters tracked the beasts. In the modern European wilderness of No Man's Land, men used all sorts of cunning and awe-inspiring devices in chasing and tracking their own flesh and blood. Compared with this field of bloodshed and carnage the jungle appeared like a peaceful abode, a place of escape, a desirable refuge.

One could not help marvelling at the rapidity with which the senses reacted in the darkness. They had been here only once. And yet, it already seemed like an old habit. The difference was their inward struggle between fear and stability. Tension and nervousness grew the closer they came to their new position. Stoically, they plugged along, ever forward, simply because they had no other choice.

"Obstacles ahead! Clearing the way!"

The mouth-to-mouth message worked like balsam on their overexcited spirits. Calmness reappeared on their faces. They immediately felt the ground for a spot to squat or lie down while waiting for the column to move again.

"Some cactus," remarked Thaler.

Ebelshauser's group was shovelling hard to clear the way. Back to the open field flew the mass of earth which had caused the unexpected congestion.

"That sure was a heavy landing," Ebelshauser said, lowering his voice to a whisper.

"Boys, a cake of this type on the head and you're gone. A painless passing and a free ticket to the other side." Schwarz wiped the sweat from his forehead with the back of his hand.

"Rather this than left a cripple for the rest of my days," murmured Loewenstein.

"Come on, come on, get busy!" The officer leading them grabbed a spade to hurry things along. "We can't stay here the whole night holding up the detachment. Let's cut through here, just enough for one man to pass."

The dirt sailed over the top on both sides of the trench.

"Try it now, I think we can get through," came the order. "It will do for the moment. They'll have more time to improve the passage when they come back if they feel like it."

"Shall I give the signal to go forward?" asked Ebelshauser.

"Just a minute." The officer gave the work a final examination. "All right, forward march! Pass the word."

The long human serpent began moving again. One by one the men passed through the small opening.

"Hold to the right! Big hole!" came the next warning. But the march proceeded with more assurance and acceleration as they approached their goal. Each man was eager to get down into his assigned dugout where he would feel far more secure. But safety could be found nowhere. Even the deepest concrete-built dugout could be blown up or collapse. But then, death came so quick! In such cases life simply was snuffed out, as one blew the vacillating flame of a candle.

Still, a soldier preferred the dugouts to the open. There was not much difference between man and the beast. The deeper the hole, the safer both felt. Daylight had become dangerous for man — he could only move about at night in the darkness of a moonless sky. And this was supposed to be the outcome of a so-called modern and progressive civilization.

"Anything special to report?" Thaler, the first to hold watch, questioned the man he was relieving.

"No, very quiet tonight. In fact, too quiet to suit me. They may be up to something. You'd better keep a sharp eye out. You can't trust any of them, especially the Tommies. Well, so long, chap, and good luck to you."

His comrades, already waiting in a crumpled bunch, once more became animated the minute he joined them. They were going back for three days of rest. Meanwhile, Apfel and his men were occupying the dugout which was to be their new home for the next six days.

First the cots — crude wooden frames and wire netting — were taken possession of. They reminded them of their installation as new recruits back home. The difference was in the material and the location. The atmosphere itself was altogether different, but soldiers got used to everything very quickly. Since it had become their lot to live under the earth they had developed considerable talent in making their subterranean habitations as comfortable as possible.

"Next time let's bring some hay," Loewenstein said. "It keeps you warmer." Comfort and caution against the cold were his constant worries.

"Maybe there'll be no next time for us." Birnbaum, his friend, was no help in cheering him up.

"In that case we won't need anything and we'll sleep better than ever."

"Ebelshauser, you're next to go on watch," Apfel said. "Before you go out see that the stove is burning. Tell Thaler to look after it before he goes to sleep. It's terribly damp in here. The walls are all wet."

"All right," he replied. "First let me take a good nap while I can."

He slid into his cot. Some were already snoring away. For the next two hours there were no disturbances. The flickering flame of a candle burned peacefully, the only light illuminating the dugout's interior. A multitude of noises penetrated from the outside world, but he was too tired to hear much of anything. Besides, he had become used to them.

Life in the dugouts would not have been so bad had it not been for the fearful rodents. The beasts not only had become intolerable but even dangerous. They always traveled in large groups. The rats, in some cases, even attained the size of cats. They were so voracious that any attempt to chase them away usually resulted in their collective attack on the men. The only way to temporarily get rid of them was to lure them with food. A watch would be set up. While the rats fed on the meager portions of bait the men made ready to kill them on the spot with sharpened spades. It was too bad if their blows did not take effect because, infuriated by the sudden attack, the rats leaped at their enemies and a fearful battle was on.

The mice, however, were easy to frighten away. The slightest move and ... zzzt ... zzzt ... they were gone. The men had no chance to lay hands on them. They seemed more cunning in their schemes to rob them of their rations. Much smaller than the rats, they found no difficulty in making their way into the men's bread bags. To ward off the invaders they had struck on the idea of hanging the bags on a string in the middle of the dugout where the rodents could not reach them so easily. But even then they were fooled more often than they would have liked to admit.

Other pests which rendered life miserable for the dugout dwellers was the formidable propagation of vermin. Once they had infested a certain section it was impossible to get rid of them. Many were the sleepless nights caused by these parasites, feeding and sucking the blood of their victims. When hostilities outside seemed suspended for a while, noiselessly but just as tenaciously another war constantly was being waged beneath the surface between man and all sorts of animals. It was an endless fight for daily food and self-preservation. Since men had invaded their territory the animals were rebelling, waging a continuous battle against the intruders. Added to all this was the cold dampness of the subterranean abodes. Wood was not always available to keep the stove fires burning. The awful humidity worked on the men's systems. It did not take long for rheumatism to develop, causing severe pains.

"Why and for whom?"

Squatting on the wooden duckboards on the bottom of the trench, Apfel's men were having a heated argument over the reasons for their being here instead of at home. Schwarz had brought up the question to which he thought better to give his own reply.

"We're out here fighting just for the sake of two cousins who can't stand each other. It's nothing more than a dirty family affair, but millions of people must suffer, bleed and die for those bastards. One guy gets shot and killed and the rest of the world must suffer the consequences of his assassination. Do you call that justice? It's a shame, I'm telling you."

"I agree," said Thaler. "If Franz and Wilhelm had any grievances against the president of France, George or Nicholas, why didn't they fight it out with each other? Why should the people always do the fighting and dying in their places? Wouldn't you call that fair?"

"That's what I say," approved Birnbaum, "and believe me, I'm speaking for everybody. Anyway, if they did the war would have been over long ago and we'd still be enjoying peace at home."

Loewenstein was quick to back up his friend, adding, "Had it been one of us who'd gotten shot, you can bet your sweet life that nobody would have cared. Just because it happened to be a duke here we are, shooting and killing men we haven't ever seen or heard of."

"Too bad," responded Rueger, "but all this talking won't change matters. We're just powerless, lead soldiers in the hands of an overgrown wild child who loves to play battle with them. He doesn't care a whoop what happens to his toys. We're here against our will, pushed forward by exhortations and commands. All we know is 'submit and obey.' Our personal feelings don't count. Try to express your own opinion and see where you land ..."

"Why get so excited about it?" Thaler interrupted. "It's nothing new. If we spoke French, Russian, Italian or English our enemies would turn out to be our friends. They aren't any better off than we. Just like us, the only thing they've been told is to kill in order not to be killed themselves."

"To me," said Ebelshauser, "it's nothing but jealousy, rivalry and the

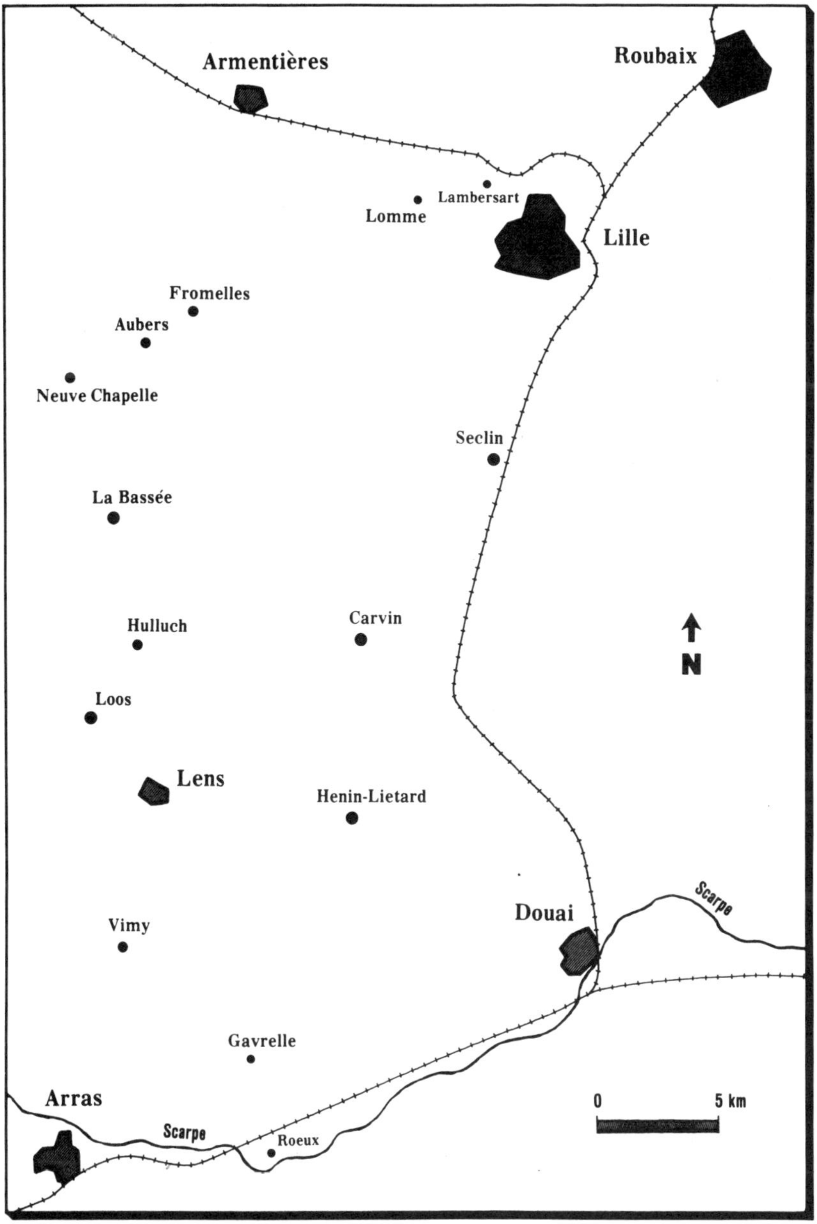

battle for supremacy between races and nationalities. Each nation wants to impose its language, its laws and its customs on its neighbors, and vice versa."

"No doubt about that," Rueger said excitedly, "but I'll bet you won't find one man in a thousand who is able to tell you why or what he is fighting for. The average man simply believes what he is told by his own government, and his opinion, without suspecting it, is formed by the news items found in his daily paper which is controlled and owned by the very same government."

"What difference does it make," roared Heimer. "Whether we know the truth or not we're here to stay just the same. Read history. Whenever something happens in a country, no matter where, who is to blame, who has to pay and who has to suffer the consequences? Tell me, you wise guys, who the hell gets his throat cut? Who if not we, the poor people!"

"You had better not shriek so loud," came the warning from Pechthold. "They might take you for a revolutionary, even though we well know how right you are. Still, what can we do about it all? Hell, one goes nuts thinking about it."

The fierce controversy was rising to a pitch of bitter dispute. Tempers were growing hot and excited. The discussion was a direct result of their momentary inaction. Each one was eager to express his personal opinion in a burst of irritated and incensed feeling. Once more they realized their utter helplessness and nihilistic existence.

Although they had predicted and feared it, the sudden bombardment took them by surprise and the argument came to a brusque conclusion. With their instinct of self-preservation they scurried away to safety, hiding in the depths of their dugout just as rats and mice creep back to their holes when attacked.

The ground began to shake. It felt like an earthquake. With each explosive tremor they had the impression that one more shock would bring about their complete destruction. Will it hold out? Would they escape this time? The expressions on their faces were pathetic. Motionless, nailed to the spot by terror, they stared at the roof of the dugout, then at each other, without a word. They were trying to hide from oncoming death. Young or old, none of them wanted to die.

"Let's be on the lookout," Apfel yelled, breaking the strain. "It's their old favorite trick. They have all their batteries centered on the first line trying to kill and wipe out all resistance. They're trying to tear our wire to pieces."

Apfel appeared calm and impassible. He stood among them like a teacher, speaking softly to dispel their fright. He knew how to help his men regain their temporarily lost self-confidence. No one made a remark. In silence they listened to the bombardment going on outside.

"You see," Apfel continued, "thinking the coast sufficiently clear, the enemy's artillery barrage is then slowly raised in an attempt to cut us off from the rear. Then it's zero hour when they go over the top. That's the time for us to catch them! They'll attack under cover of their own fire. Just wait and see. Of course, since we got wise to their strategy they don't do it all the time. I wouldn't mind getting fooled that way for a change. At any rate, they aren't going to catch us sleeping!"

Apfel's expectations were not disappointed. Courage and temerity returned to his group. All of them were slowly recovering from their first shock. Without a word, Thaler and Ebelshauser mounted the steep stairway. Long minutes went by before they had reached the top. A few more seconds and they deliberately emerged into the trench, holding fast to each other.

"Watch out, Fritz, a mine!" Ebelshauser ran for a hole in the wall.

Thaler dropped flat, waiting. The explosion was terrific. Hearing a stifled cry of despair, Thaler jumped to his feet just in time to see his friend swallowed up. Ebelshauser lay buried in the excavation. Under the impact of the mine's detonation the thick, muddy clay roof of his refuge had given way, crashing down over his head.

Everything went black. He saw himself irrevocably lost. In his fall his helmet had slipped over his face, keeping his mouth free. But he could only breathe faintly. He tried to move. It was impossible. A rock was crushing his belly and the pressure was increasing. He was suffocating. Perspiration moistened his entire body. A stupor came over him. Was he dreaming or losing his senses? He tried to yell but no sound passed his lips. He was still conscious. Muffled noises of spades and picks came to his ears. Would he come out of this alive? His thoughts became confused. Memories were fading. Was there really a God? He had miraculously escaped the firing squad. Now he was about to die of suffocation. Lausanne, Montreux, Vevey, Ouchy, the Alps, Lake Leman — the pictures shooting by were not clear. Then he was gone.

When he came to, Thaler was sitting by his cot in the dugout, holding his hand.

"My God, I thought you'd never wake up, Gustav. How is it?"

Ebelshauser smiled faintly at the sight of his comrade. "You saved my life, Fritz ..."

"Oh, come on! They all helped. But tell me how you feel."

"I don't know. Terribly tired, as if I had been beaten ..."

"Small wonder the way we went to work on you to bring back your breath," Thaler interrupted him again. "Don't talk now. Drink this and rest. You'll be better in the morning."

He took a sip, shook his head and spat. "What is that?" he asked.

"Heavens, don't spill it! It's too precious. We got it from the next group over. A hot grog with rum. Gulp it down, it'll do you good and put hair on your chest."

"But it's so bitter."

"We couldn't get any sugar, so be a man. It'll warm you up."

Ebelshauser drained the cup to the last drop. Having wiped his lips his head fell back on the improvised straw cushion. He fell asleep, exhausted.

"We'll be back in an hour. Going back to the dump for more ammunition and barbed wire."

Thaler turned around, disturbed in his macabre thoughts. Apfel stood with his men, ready to go.

"How about Ebelshauser?"

"Don't worry about him. We gave him a good dose. He'll sleep the whole night through."

"Suppose something happens — the trench is empty!" Thaler did not like the idea of their going.

"We'll be back soon," replied Apfel jovially and confidently.

"All right by me, corporal. You must know what you're doing."

"It's not a matter of knowing, Thaler. We got the order to get the supplies."

Apfel left with his men and Thaler was alone. An hour is quickly passed, he thought, especially for Gustav.

The sun had disappeared and the sky's colors were darkening. Daylight still persisted, though, unwilling to give up the fight against the invading shadows. A stiff breeze blew in Thaler's face bringing smells of rotting flesh from No Man's Land. It looked as if the English were willing to keep peace for the night. Everything was quiet. In the distance the sudden flares of cannon could be seen. The detonations followed like thunder follows the lightning of an approaching storm. Floating in the air the acrid fumes of powder stung the tongue. Tears came to his burning eyes, impairing his vision. Thaler moistened his handkerchief with saliva and began to rub his eyelids. He blinked a couple of times but felt the irritation increasing. He soon found himself crying for no reason at all. His sight was failing him. Something was wrong. Dipping his handkerchief in a puddle he applied it to his eyes. It did him good for a moment but objects still appeared blurred. Could it be that the surrounding mist contained something else than smoke and powder? He could not decide and remained waiting for the atmosphere to clear.

"Gas! Gas! GAS!" A man ran through the trench shouting his warning. Thaler cleared his throat before putting on his gas mask. Having never made use of it, it took him quite a while to adjust and make it fit tightly to his face. Now he understood the tears. He took a deep breath and found the mask was functioning all right. How quickly darkness had come! For a moment he thought the ground was disappearing from beneath his feet. He had absorbed some of the dangerous poison. He steadied himself and looked over the trench, but he could not see anything beyond two meters. The mask's goggles were perspiring and the fumes had become an impenetrable fog.

"Gustav! Gustav! GAS! Put on your mask and come out! Gustav!"

Thaler kept shouting and listened for a reply. When he did not hear anything he readjusted his mask and went down the dugout's stairs as quickly as he could. He found his friend lying on the floor, choking, his gas mask under his right arm. He seized the instrument, but it was no easy task to fit it properly. He tried to lift him but had to give up. The body was too heavy. He ran out to get Rueger. Together they managed to carry Ebelshauser out of the dugout. Upon reaching the trench they met with Apfel and his men.

All of them helped to heave the body clear over the top. It was the highest spot they could think of. If Ebelshauser was still breathing this was the best place for him. Heavier than air, the gas always crept low to the ground, descending and sinking into the trenches and dugouts. It was the second time Thaler had saved him from certain death. Very slowly but steadily, Ebelshauser felt his respirations becoming clearer. Eventually the wind shifted to another direction. Soon all traces of the gas disappeared and it was safe to take off the masks. The men lifted Ebelshauser back into the trench. In his weakened condition he could not stand on his feet. Dizziness came over him. In a trance, he suddenly burst out in loud and uncontrollable sobbing. The crisis had passed. He was definitely out of danger.

Dark clouds kept the sun away and daybreak was very slow in coming. The air was heavy, full of humidity, but no rain fell. The watery clouds, transporting their burden from one place to another, moved almost invisibly through a breezeless atmosphere. Men and earth were somnolent, hard to rouse from their lethargic sleep. The watch posts felt their eyes droop and close in spite of themselves. Even the enemy's line appeared motionless as if they, too, had fallen into a state of drowsiness. It was their sixth day out and the relief was scheduled for that night. All was quiet, but one could feel the pulse of human life in its ceaseless breathing. Instinctively, one felt a constant watchfulness of one's every move, an awareness of surrounding danger. The food carriers were expected with the morning coffee. Except for the first day when the carriers had been late because of constant firing, the men had no kick coming. True, the portions could have been larger. One grew very hungry during a long day. The ersatz coffee was getting weaker and weaker and was too cold by the time it reached them. But the carriers could not be blamed for that.

"What's new? Any mail yet?" Invariably, these were the first two questions asked when the carriers came into sight.

"Mail is here!" one of them announced while waving a small parcel and a handful of letters and postcards. At the same time his right hand held the heavy coffee kettle in balance. He was careful not to spill a single drop for, regardless of its taste and concoction, the liquid was most appreciated as an eye-opener. It woke them up.

"Let me have the bag! I'll play the mailman this morning!"

Small as he was, Schwarz came running out of the dugout like a mouse out of a trap and grabbed the little bundle from the man's hand. As the others got ready with their mess tins, Schwarz ran back to the dugout and called down the stairs, "Hey, boys, get out of your hole if you care for coffee and ... MAIL!"

He shouted the last word at the top of his lungs. In no time the men assembled around Schwarz, the diminutive shrimp who, with a cunning smile, gave himself an air of importance. He was getting a great kick out of keeping his entourage in suspense before starting to read off the names to whom the letters, cards and package were addressed.

"Come on, Albert, make it snappy," snarled Pechthold who did not like the joke. "If you can't make out the handwriting then let me have the job."

"Patience!" replied Schwarz in a softer tone than usual. "Keep your shirt on. Children must behave. Don't worry, Oskar, you'll get what's coming to you. A couple of minutes more or less, what's the difference? All right now, close your eyes and open your ears. Here goes!"

Schwarz played his role well, doing a splendid imitation of the notorious training officer Schmitz, stories of whom had circulated all along the trench. He brought his right hand to his eye as if to place a monocle, and then passed his thumb and index finger over his lips, twisting each side of an imaginary mustache.

"To the winner of the first ticket ..." He started reading at last.

"Hermann Winterhof!"

When no answer came Schwarz himself gave the reply. "Moved. Checked out of hotel without paying for his room or leaving a forwarding address. Residence unknown. Return to sender. Next!

"Gustav Tiede ... two houses below, around the next corner.

"Ludwig Kurtzweg ... out of town at present. To be left in care of the porter.

"August Kniese ... on vacation. Back to sender.

"Karl Fortzmann ... new address, heaven or hell, we'll find out later."

The men greeted each of Schwarz's remarks with roars of laughter and applause, adding some of their own wisecracks. At the same time they waited with expectation for their own names to be called.

"Max Huber ... hospital.

"Fritz Thaler ..."

"Here!" shouted Thaler, stepping forward to take hold of a letter. He immediately inspected the envelope on both sides, studying the graceful handwriting while trying to weigh the news it contained.

"What have you got there, Fritz?" Ebelshauser inquired. Without giving a reply Thaler retired to the tranquility of the dugout to be alone. Ebelshauser watched him disappear.

"And now let's see to whom this little package belongs ...Wilhelm Hoefer ... Second Company. Transferred ...that's all!"

As if to hide their disappointment the men started to tell stories. There soon followed an endless series of funny tales and jokes. Smiling lips and laughter returned. The mail was quickly forgotten. Such was life in the front line.

Instead of clearing up, the sky had grown darker and darker. Shortly after midday the heavy clouds broke forth in a stormy, torrential rain. A limitless sea fell from the heavens accompanied by the flashes of lightning and the crashes of thunder. Gusts of wind travelling at terrific velocity blew from every direction. The air was charged with electricity. The heaviest guns would have sounded like toy pistols compared to the deafening cracks of the thunderstorm. It seemed as if nature itself wanted to express its contempt, its utter disgust with man at large, and annihilate them all at once. The fury of the elements made the men in the trenches gasp in awe. It brought back to them the irrefutable realization of their own nothingness when chastized by the mighty hand of their creator.

Apfel and his men were finishing their meager evening meal. No ration carriers were expected that night. Food would be given out upon return to their billets in the rear. No hour had been fixed because a new oufit, unacquainted with the sector, was to relieve them. The company's cook had orders to hold everything in readiness and keep the kettle boiling.

"Group leader Apfel?" inquired an unexpected visitor when he reached the bottom of the dugout's steps. His face could hardly be seen in the dim candle light.

"Here, what's up?" Reluctantly, Apfel rose as he recognized the orderly from regimental headquarters.

"I need one man from each group for repair work. That damn storm is responsible for quite a lot of damage. The whole length of our trench has collapsed on one side."

"But we are to be relieved tonight, don't you know."

"Headquarters is well aware of the schedule, but it can't be helped. The trench has to be fixed before the new troops move in."

The two men stood rigid, face to face. Apfel had a scorching reply on the tip of his tongue and was about to forget himself. He opened his mouth to speak but the words stuck in his throat. His face turned red. Considering that they were to be relieved that very night this last-minute request was burning him up. Inwardly he was boiling, fighting with himself to keep his temper under control. He would not have minded any other time, but not that night.

"Have that man ready when I come back from calling on the last two groups," the orderly said. Without waiting for a reply he saluted and disappeared.

Apfel seemed unable to make up his mind. He glanced around as if to fix his choice. How well he could read the thoughts in the men's tired faces. Six days out was long enough for any one of them. They were glad to get back without having to do some extra work. Desiring to be fair, he finally resorted to asking instead of ordering.

"Who wants to go?"

When no one came forward he continued, as if talking to himself. "Well, someone will have to go. Orders are orders."

As silence persisted he gradually felt embarrassed. He could simply order the man, but he was reluctant to do so, hoping for someone to volunteer without compulsion. Yet, the minutes were passing quickly and the orderly soon would return. Apfel began to pace up and down like a lion in his den. He suddenly stopped short, apparently struck by an idea.

"Come on, boys!" he said in a pleading tone. "You know how I hate to send anyone against his will. Is there nobody to take this responsibility off my shoulders?"

One by one he looked each of his men straight in the face. Apfel could well understand their feelings. But he had not given up yet. He fervently appealed to their manhood, their honor and their spirit of comradeship.

"Don't forget why we are here. It's not for our pleasure, certainly not, but in defense of our loved ones at home. Do not fail in your duty after pledging your word of honor in the maintenance of discipline and obedience. I would like to see one more tangible proof of that old spirit of brotherhood that has existed among our valorous soldiers ever since Germany became a nation. It is thanks to her army and navy that Germany has today become the greatest power on earth, and you owe it to your ancestors to serve in a like manner, worthy of their approval."

He paused for a moment as if to judge what effect his little speech had made. At the same time he consulted his watch, another indication that it soon would become inevitable for him to stop haranguing and make a decision.

"Two more minutes, boys ... Come on, make up your minds. I tell you what, the one who volunteers will be off duty all day tomorrow to do as he pleases. Who says the word? One more minute and I'll have ..."

"Will I have to report back here after the job?"

"Shake, Pechthold, old boy, that's the spirit!" His eyes shining with gratitude, Apfel stretched both hands forward and clasped the volunteer's right hand vigorously.

"Oh, there's nothing to it," Pechthold said, his face reddening. "And damn it, it took me long enough."

"Yes, I expect you back. We can't leave before you return, even if the relief is already here. But I don't think they will be. It's only seven and your job won't last more than two hours, maybe less. We'll wait for you here. So long and take care of yourself."

"Okay, corporal," Pechthold grinned as he started up the dugout's steps. "If they're here before I get back, take my kit along. Bye, bye, see you soon!"

Barely 10 minutes had elapsed after Pechthold's departure when another visitor made his entrance.

"I want to see the group leader."

"Here!" came Apfel's response as he rose once more to approach the man. The latter, after showing Apfel a piece of paper which the men took to be his credentials, assumed a more acid air.

"A minute inspection shows a gap of about 15 meters at the left flank of our sector where the barbed wire has been completely destroyed and torn to pieces. The staff commander wants to know why this has remained unreported."

"It was hardly possible to see anything today during that terrible storm," Apfel retorted with animation. "Besides, is it not possible that the soaked ground ..."

"Never mind the possibility you may think of, it won't change the evidence," snapped the intruder, cutting short Apfel's tentative explanation. "What's important and what concerns you and your men, as well as the group next to you, is that the missing wire must be put up at once."

"But ..."

"Orders from staff! There is no 'but.' If there is any objection you'll have to consult headquarters."

"I make no objection," Apfel replied in a meek voice, "only we are to be relieved tonight."

"Oh!" exclaimed the factotum. "That's where the shoe hurts!" His next words came like a series of thunderclaps. "Please bear in mind that the staff is perfectly aware of the expected relief. But it has given orders for the wire to be erected and fixed before the relief comes. If necessary the hour of its arrival will be postponed."

"At your service," Apfel said, realizing the futility of an excuse or a possible exemption. However, he added, "One man has just been taken for repair work in your vicinity and there are only seven left."

"I have the situation well in hand and you won't need so many. Leave three men here for watch duty and take four along with you. I'll bring you four more from the next group."

"Do we have to get the wire rolls, too?"

"Not necessary. They have already been ordered and ought to be here at any moment. The respective posts also have been advised about you going out. Don't let your men step beyond the restricted limits of your sector if you want to insure their safe return. In case of unexpected difficulties which may force your men out of the way, 'Emden' is the password. Make sure that they know it. You won't have to report back to the staff, but relief or not, don't quit the trench before finishing the job. I'm holding you responsible for excellent work. Now go to it. I'll get you the other four men."

He saluted, clicked his heels and turned away, leaving Apfel and his men stunned at the new development. Had they known this, how eager each one of them would have been to respond to Apfel's first offer and take Pechthold's place. On the other hand, having more or less experienced that life was, after all, nothing but a series of 'ifs,' they found no difficulty in becoming reconciled to their fate. Besides, they well knew that it was not a matter of choice but a command which had to be executed regardless of their own feelings.

Appalled by the prospect in store for them, the men sat as if rooted to their benches. Apfel was beside himself, almost ready to set an example of open rebellion. He had not moved since the staff officer had left. His attitude of submission changed to that of defiant protest. He gave vent to his anger by swearing and cursing heaven and earth. Then, having exhausted his breath as well as his vocabulary, he recovered his usual calm composure.

"What's the use! All the cursing in the world won't help." He turned and faced his group. "Orders are orders, I've said the same thing before. We have no time to lose if we want to be ready to go back when the relief comes. Who are the three on post duty for tonight?"

"Ebelshauser, Loewenstein and Birnbaum, according to the schedule," Thaler replied, handing a sheet of paper to Apfel for his inspection.

"Is that correct?" he inquired all around.

"Yes," came the unanimous answer.

"I made this sheet up," Thaler explained, "so that each one would know his turn without any possible misunderstanding or confusion ..."

"Splendid, Thaler, a very good idea," Apfel commented.

"In 10 minutes Schwarz and Rueger will be through with their watch. I guess we can wait for them and take them along," Thaler suggested.

"That will be all right."

Writing down the names in a small pocketbook, Apfel called them out again: "Thaler, Heimer, Schwarz and Rueger — our four men. I'll get the names of the others when we leave."

"I want to go with Thaler," Ebelshauser said.

"Don't be absurd, why expose and risk your life for my sake? Besides, you aren't well enough yet."

"You leave that to me if it can be arranged. Rueger will have no objection to changing with me."

The deal was made to the satisfaction of everyone concerned, although Thaler still could not see why Ebelshauser wanted to go along. This mark of attachment and comradeship moved him deeply.

"Let's toss the rolls over, it'll be easier," proposed Schwarz.

"Stop this nonsense," Apfel intervened. "You do just as I tell you and follow the others."

Having reached the outstanding post from which the work was to be started, they held a lookout for a while before attempting to climb over the top. Fortunately, it was a moonless night. Only small groups of stars were discernible here and there in the dark sky. Such obscurity would be very favorable for their work.

In spite of the burden they found it easy enough to reach the emplacement in No Man's Land. Right from the start it promised to be an easy job. The work progressed rapidly. Five rolls of wire already had been spread out and tightened. Suddenly, the first of a long series of star shells came up from the enemy's line, shedding light all over the field.

"Lie down!" Apfel gave the command in a hushed voice. "Don't move and wait a while."

With their corporal in the center, the nine men were lying on their bellies with their faces touching the thick, slimy ground into which they were gradually sinking. The day's torrential rain had made a swamp of the whole area. Getting up again after the first alarm they had to pull themselves out of the sticky slime. But only a few minutes had passed when a second, third and fourth star shell shot up into the sky. The bright lights, sustained by small parachutes, danced overhead. Motionless, like so many dead bodies, the soldiers once more forced themselves into the mud, hiding and holding on for their lives.

"Let's not move for 10 minutes at least," Apfel whispered. "It looks as if they smell something. Maybe they can see our moving shadows. We'll have to be more careful and try to remain on our knees to finish the job."

"You aren't mad at me, Gustav, are you?" Thaler had crept over to his friend.

"Why, what's the matter, Fritz? Why should I be mad at you?"

"Oh, nothing. Only ... I thought ... you know ... about that letter."

"Never mind the letter. Just forget about it. I shouldn't have asked anyway. It was none of my business, even so I didn't mean to be nosy."

"That's just it! I should have shown you more confidence instead of keeping ..."

"Shhhh! Sometimes there are things one can't tell, even to his best friend. So why bring it up?"

"Because it'll make me feel better. *'Geteiltes Leid ist halbes Leid.'* You know the old saying, don't you? It's true!"

"Sure," Ebelshauser replied encouragingly, "I'm listening."

"It was a letter from my sister-in-law, very short, just telling me that Albert, the only brother I had left, was killed in action. Now she is alone with her three small children."

"Oh, Fritz, that's terrible! I'm awfully sorry for you." Ebelshauser extended his arm, reaching for his friend through the mud. They held each other's hand without speaking, shaken with emotion.

"Let's put one more meter between each other before getting on our knees to finish spreading the wire," Apfel again whispered. "No need for the mallet for the stakes. Just hang on to them with all your weight and they'll go deep easy enough, almost like a knife through butter. If we proceed methodically, we'll be through much quicker. Have the outer right man hold the end of the wire and stay where he is, while the outer left unrolls it, and we in between will plant the stakes and fix the wire to them."

The plan was communicated right and left. As soon as the understanding had been reached Apfel gave the signal to begin. They all got on their knees except the left man who began to walk away with the large spool of wire he kept turning and unrolling. Holding his body bent over he presented the figure of an acrobat about to perform a stunt. Each did his share, eager to comply with the order and get through with it as quickly as possible. The distance to cover was comparatively small, but they had to make it on faltering knees, inch by inch, hampered in every move by invisible obstacles. There was no definite course to be followed when trampling or creeping through the shell-torn area of No Man's Land. It might have looked easy from the trench to reach the designated spot, but once the place had been attained one often got caught there, and in no position to return by the same track. The number of men that lost their lives during such excursions was incalculable. It was always with the prospect of death that one left the trench to enter this mortal ground extending between the opposing lines. In a crowd one forgot about one's own danger. But left alone, the dangers seemed to multiply a hundredfold.

"Damn it all, aren't they going to stop playing with those firecrackers?" Schwarz crawled on his stomach toward Ebelshauser who was caught in the old line of barbed wire.

"They're pesting us," he retorted in a whisper. "We won't be able to finish tonight if this keeps up. God, I'm getting fed up with this mud."

"Where is Thaler?" Schwarz inquired.

"Leave it to him, he always finds a hole to creep in. You know what he says, 'A shell never falls twice on the same spot.' You know, he just means to play it safe if he can help it."

"Do you believe in that stuff? It's superstition, because I know of two ..."

"Shhhh! Listen ... a mine!" Ebelshauser brought a finger to his lips. Turning their heads skyward they both tried to catch a glimpse of the flying shell, one of this type being the most feared of projectiles. They both heard the hum and swishing noise passing over them, but could not see a thing.

"It's not meant for us this time. I guess the rear areas like to have their share, too, otherwise they get jealous," joked Schwarz.

"Just watch for the explosion," Ebelshauser said. "It won't land very far from here." He had barely made his prognostication when the loud detonation was heard. The earth shook under them, a clear indication of his correct guess. A rain of shell fragments and pieces of earth, wood and stones came hurtling in their vicinity.

"God, I didn't think that one was so close. They might be after us. We'd better clear the ground before we get it on our heads."

"Two or three more ties and we're through. I'll move toward Apfel as I tie and see what he has to say."

"All right," Schwarz agreed. "I'll stay here and get the cross lines tight. Then I'll wait until you get back."

Ebelshauser set out moving slowly toward the corporal. He was about to reach him when two other mines zoomed overhead simultaneously. He had just enough time to plunge in a hole and bury himself in the mud before the deafening explosions rocked the air. For a short while he remained where he was, fearful to reappear on the surface. When all was quiet again he crept from the hole and continued his course, picking up and tying the wire at various stakes.

"We're finished at our end," he told Apfel. "Aren't we going back now?"

"A few more minutes until this end is done. In the meantime, have Schwarz and Thaler come back here so that we can turn in together."

Still on his knees, Ebelshauser crawled back along the muddy path from which he had just come. He told Schwarz to wait for him until he got back with Thaler.

"Where about is he anyway?" he asked his comrade casually. "Didn't he show up yet?"

"I think he's just a little ways straight ahead, a bit to your right, maybe two or three holes from here. I guess he must have fallen asleep."

"No, not Thaler. He isn't the type to fall asleep. I hope nothing's happened — it looks funny to me. Stay here while I go look for him."

Again Ebelshauser started wandering about. Tired as he was, he could only crawl along very slowly and painfully.

"Thaler! Thaler!" he called, though daring not to raise his voice for fear of being heard on the other side. He paused at every hole, even partly descending into some of them when he couldn't see the bottom. Then, he suddenly became aware of the distance between the rest of the group and himself. A weird apprehension as to his friend's whereabouts began to worry him. "Where can he be?" he kept repeating to himself. Half exhausted, he stopped at the edge of another hole, not knowing what to do or which direction to take. Should he return to Schwarz by the same path or make a small detour in an effort to discover his friend's hiding place? He decided on the latter. Turning back toward the trench he passed two more craters. Puzzled and afraid, he turned once again in the direction of his waiting companion, Schwarz.

At last, inwardly rejoicing, he saw a human form at the bottom of another pit, farther back than he had expected. In the blackness he could not make out whether it was his friend or not; yet, he could not think of anyone else who would be out lying in this hole.

"Poor fellow," he thought, "he fell asleep. The bad news got him this time." He called down to the still form, "Fritz! Wake up! We're through and ready to go back again!"

Receiving no response, he slid down the side of the crater, being careful not to scare the sleeping man should he suddenly awake and think himself facing the enemy. Perspiring, Ebelshauser held his breath. He stared at the form and gradually made out the uniform and recognized the familiar features of his comrade. Thaler was lying on his side in a comfortable sleeping position, his head resting peacefully on the soft slime beneath. His eyes were closed. Both hands were joined together on his neck, partly touching his right shoulder.

"I'm going to hold him by the wrists so he won't be too surprised when he wakes up." Ebelshauser smiled in anticipation of this move. He grabbed Thaler in a tight hold and discovered his hands were ice-cold and immobile. His body had passed the stage of ever awakening again.

Horror-stricken and frightened beyond description, Ebelshauser loosened his grip and released the cold arms. For the next few minutes he stood over the motionless body of his friend, unable to comprehend what had happened. His heart was ready to break. His eyes remained riveted on Thaler's face as if trying to pierce beyond the mystery of death. Hot and cold chills ran down his spine. Beginning to tremble and shake, he was becoming hysterical. How long he stood there he could not tell, though he knew he would never be able to wipe away the memory of his dead friend's face. Twice Thaler had saved his life, but now he could do nothing in return.

Momentarily recovering from the shock, he quickly crept out of the hole to make his way back to Schwarz and the rest of the group. Informed of the news, Apfel directed everyone to follow Ebelshauser. In a short time the seven men picked up Thaler's rigid body and, led by the corporal, reached the safety of their trench after giving the password.

An hour later the Third Company was relieved for three days of rest. With it went the body of Thaler, who was to be buried in a newly made military cemetery. He was one case among hundreds, so there was no need for a special ceremony. After him would follow countless other young men. Who was to blame? Who was the beneficiary of all this human slaughter?

Back at the front, life went on as usual as if nothing had happened.

7

It was nearing the end of August 1916. Time and events moved fast or slow for a soldier depending upon his physical condition, his position and above all, his mood and disposition.

After nearly a month in a field hospital, Ebelshauser was back in the trenches again. His quick readaptation to the rough life of a front soldier was surprising, even to himself. In fact, it did not appear to him that he had been away at all. Everything was so much the same that his absence seemed an illusion, except for a stiff finger bearing witness to the accident. While carrying hurdles a bullet had hit its mark. It had pierced his left hand, splitting a bone at the upper joint of the middle finger. He steadfastly had refused to have the dead appendage amputated and had won his case. The wound still pained him a little and he had to be careful of his movements.

Unconcerned as to his whereabouts, Ebelshauser was following his old habit of taking a walk. He could have found his way with his eyes closed. He made his rounds through the trench alone, thinking of Thaler whose company he sorely missed. A bit of blue sky, a ray of sunshine brought an unspeakable longing to his heart and soul. The day would have been perfect to walk along the shore of Lake Leman. He had a vision of the Alps and the seven peaks of the Dents du Midi whose snow-white slopes always glittered in the sunshine. To his mind surged pictures of Ouchy, Montreux, Vevey, the Mont Pelerin and Les Avants, where he had never failed to visit for the spring picking of narcissuses that grew wild and made the meadows for miles around look white. He would return home with his companions, their bicycles completely covered with the strongly scented flowers. How could he ever forget such sweet memories of not so long ago?

In the beginning, with the game of warfare being new, there always had been excitement and plenty to talk about. Since the advent of the trenches, however, the men had returned to their state of automatism. Casualties — the dead and wounded — were taken for granted, leaving them indifferent. They had lost all feeling. When death struck, the sight of a falling comrade left them cold. Who would be next? The same question always came back. Their spirits were low. There were very few left who still were able to take it on the chin with a smile.

"Boy, what a heat! How are tricks in your family?"

At last Ebelshauser found someone in brighter spirits and in a talkative mood, a man from the adjoining platoon.

"And how!" he replied. "It's a knockout for everybody. I just couldn't stand it down in the dugout. The family is still complete. They're all taking a nap and I seem to be the only one up. I must be going crazy, I guess. How does it look out there?"

Werner Bromberg, a fat peasant lad of 26, turned from his observation post. His large body was encased in a uniform much too small for his size. The company's tailor had been called upon for some adjustment and the entire row of buttons had been moved to the limit. Still, it looked as if the tunic was ready to burst at any moment. The seat of his pants also had been enlarged to a monumental width. The darker shade of the extra patch was quite discernible. Bromberg had tried to reduce but all his efforts had been in vain. After more than three months of a self-imposed diet he had put on three additional pounds. He then blamed it on nature and gave up the struggle.

"Come up here and take a look for yourself," Bromberg said. "I think they have all disappeared and gone back to England. Wouldn't that be swell? We ought to follow suit and do likewise."

"Oh yeah, you think so, heh? How about the Kaiser? I suppose he'll have the last word to say about that."

Ebelshauser stepped up to Bromberg's level on the trench's firestep and found his companion ready with an answer.

"Sure he will. But the old man has said too much already as it is. Believe me, he put the car so deep in the mud he won't be able to get it out again ..."

"Watch out! Don't expose yourself like that," Ebelshauser quickly interrupted when he saw Bromberg protruding his head beyond the safety zone of the post's steel plate.

"Keep your shirt on. I'm no greenhorn just arrived from the hinterland. Besides, it's been peaceful in this sector. The Tommies don't bother us if we don't start any trouble ourselves. They know how to appreciate quiet and ..."

The sudden whizzing of bullets overhead was enough to bring Bromberg to a complete stop in his warbling. He ducked quickly without losing his composure.

"That was just a little mistake. They didn't mean to do any harm, maybe two freshmen practicing target shooting. Just a coincidence. Of course, we shouldn't tempt them by trying to pry into their business. It would be too bad to get knocked over for such an imprudence. Why play with fire?"

"Well," answered Ebelshauser, "I have a different idea about these Tommies. Gentleness, my eye! They don't know anything about that. I don't trust them and wouldn't risk any sightseeing while they're in the neighborhood. It's too dangerous."

"I don't know, Gustav, I believe they are more trustworthy than the French. They're two-faced, like the Italians. They can smile in your face and stab you in the back at the same time, and you don't even know what's happened to you. The English are more open folks, so I've heard."

"Say, you dirty son-of-a-gun, are you trying to insult my race?" Ebelshauser sneered with a frown etched into his forehead. "How dare you openly declare that I am two-faced? I really ought to get mad at you, but on second thought ... oh, what's the use, you wouldn't understand anyway."

"What's wrong with you, Gustav? Are you crazy, talking about your race? What the hell have you got to do with the French or Italians? I certainly don't get the sense of your joke, if it's supposed to be one."

"Didn't I tell you? Have you never heard about the 'dirty Frenchman' we have in the company? Ah, yes, you did! I can see it in your face. Only you didn't know who that Frenchman was. Well, you're now in the presence of that funny guy, so you'd better beware."

"Haha! Haha! Haha!" A burst of wild laughter was all Bromberg could give as an answer. His belly vibrated up and down and his entire face reddened, then turned crimson. He was almost choking. Ebelshauser thought it wise to tap him on the back to help him regain control. Having recovered from the spell, he blew his nose.

"By jove! It's been a long time since I laughed so hard. I hope it's not the last. Where did you get such a story?"

"It's not a story. It's the truth, even if it sounds stranger than fiction."

Ebelshauser went on and told him the whole tale of his young life. "So now won't you behave and be careful when meeting a stranger? I guess the best description of myself would be this: Mother tongue French — my mother was born in Liestal, German Switzerland, but was brought up in Evian, France. I was born and raised in Lausanne, French Switzerland. Personally, I consider myself Swiss. But according to law I'm a German because my father was born in Germany. This is all of it in a nutshell. Simple, isn't it?"

"That's the most unusual case I've ever heard of," Bromberg replied. "Had I been in your shoes I wouldn't be here today. They wouldn't have gotten me out of Switzerland. You were too honest. And what have you got from it now? It's good to be wise, and even a little crookedness is recommended in a game like this."

"Don't remind me, please. When I start to think of it I could just kick myself in the pants. I learned my lesson but it's a little bit too late. I'll know better next time, if there is a next time. Meanwhile, let's forget about it. I'd rather turn in for a stretch before my watch or I'll fall asleep on the job. So long, Bromberg, and take care of yourself. I'll be seeing you sometime tomorrow."

"And good luck to you, Ebelshauser. Come around again for a chat. I'll be relieved in a few minutes. These last two hours have gone by like a flash."

Ebelshauser jumped down into the trench and started on his way back to the dugout. There were still four hours left for him before taking up his duty. He felt somewhat relieved by the conversation. He thought of

Switzerland and his home. It had been a long time since he had news from his parents. Maybe the mail had gone astray.

Rumors had it that the regiment would go to Roubaix. It was to be a three-day outing to give everyone a rest and break the monotony. Official news soon confirmed the rumors and great rejoicing broke out among the soldiers. A change of this kind was always welcome. They probably would be made to pay later for this luxury, but they were prepared.

Happy and carefree, they landed in the small Flemish town amid shouts and hurrahs. For three days the troops went haywire, having the time of their lives. Too soon, and with regret, they had to leave their amusements to return to duty and to war. After a short journey by train to Carvin, not far from Lens, they were loaded into lorries and driven off into the night. Early in the morning of August 26, 1916, they found themselves at a different and unknown place. *

"Aussteigen! Alles 'raus!"

"Antreten! Antreten!"

The orders had to be repeated and yelled many times to get the last man out of the trucks.

"Let's go, boys!"

Apfel suddenly emerged from nowhere. Taking hold of his men he brought them into line. A few minutes later the regiment stood in impeccable form. Tired as they were the men still managed to respond to the commands.

"There is no time to lose," the lieutenant spoke. "We are to relieve another regiment in the front line. They have been in the firing line for more than three weeks in succession. We were to get our meal before leaving but there was a misunderstanding. So, we'll meet the kitchen on our way out to the field. As soon as we are through eating we'll leave immediately. We have to make it before daylight. It'll be a difficult job so take precautions. Don't lose your heads. Give heed to orders and keep marching forward in line. This will greatly insure your safety."

"That's enough," whispered Heimer. "The rest we know by heart."

"Never mind the remark," Rueger admonished him. "Hartmann is all right. He's for the men and means what he says."

"That's true, he can't help it." Pechthold couldn't help butting in. "Don't you think he would rather be at home than here?"

"And now let's form the column and get going," came the lieutenant's

* According to the history of the 17th Bavarian Infantry Regiment, that morning the trucks carrying its troops unloaded behind the Somme front near Bapaume. The 1st Battalion, to which Ebelshauser's company belonged, was billeted in the village of Grevillers. During the night of August 27-28, the regiment relieved the 133rd Infantry Regiment (a Saxon unit belonging to the 24th Division) in the outskirts and immediately south of the village of Martinpuich. The Germans had nicknamed this particular sector "Ferdinand." — R.B.

instruction. "We'll go straight forward. The other companies are converging right and left of us. Let's keep as much as possible to the right side of the road. If anything happens report to me at the head of the column. Understood? Fine, now let's go!"

Like a long, narrow, gray-white ribbon, the road ahead could be seen unrolling into the night. The horizon was a dark impenetrable mass keeping everything beyond its narrow limitations a secret. Here and there lone stars shone bright against an inky sky. There was no moonlight to betray their march to the ever-watchful eyes of the enemy.

How far were they from the line? Tongues of fire flared up periodically but it was hard to figure out the distance. Suddenly, the fields on both sides of the road ceased. They had reached the entrance of what had been a town. The houses were destroyed, some of them completely razed. Only a few walls were left standing and ruins could be seen everywhere. They turned at the first corner and came right up to the field kitchen which was installed behind a brick wall. The whole outfit was lit up by two small candles stuck in two cracked but wind-protected flower pots. No wonder they had not seen the place from afar. The dim light was just enough to permit the cook to fulfill his functions. The men were breathing again at the proximity of a meal. They had come to appreciate "horse goulash" which was better than no meat at all.

Everything was done in haste. "There is no time to lose," the lieutenant once more explained. "This sector has been constantly under fire for the last 10 days. We have to get located and find our positions before daybreak."

After literally gulping down their meager portions, off they went again, still further to the west.

The black shadows of night were beginning to fade, announcing the imminent approach of twilight. Deployed and spread out, the soldiers were still stumbling forward and searching for the first line and men they came to relieve. What a fearful awakening it would be if caught in the open field at daybreak! In no time the entire company could be wiped out.

The advance became more and more hazardous as the enemy's artillery fire grew steadily in intensity. Their own batteries could hardly respond in equal volume. Long streaks of yellow-red fire illuminated the whole countryside intermittently. Sudden flashes followed by formidable detonations became increasingly more frequent as they forged ahead.

"Donnerwetter! There is nothing left but holes," burst out Schwarz as he caught up with Ebelshauser.

"And how! The Tommies are trying to make it easier for us to bury our dead. In fact, they seem anxious to relieve us entirely." He felt a vague fear creep into his heart as he spoke.

"Let them go to it if they please, what the hell. Only it's too bad we can't match them. With one round for every four of theirs how can we expect to win?"

"Win the war? Say, I didn't know you still believed in fairy tales. I don't and the quicker you snap out of it the better." Ebelshauser talked as if he already knew the ultimate outcome of the conflict.

"No, Gustav, I don't believe in fairy tales. Yet, in a way I still have a faint hope. After all, we're still holding out against almost the whole world ..."

"That's just it. That's why we are bound to fail..." His sentence was interrupted by a shell exploding not far away.

"Watch out, my friend. Better look out for yourself. It's raining steel this time, not water."

"What do you expect me to do? No use going out of my way. If my hour has come I'll get it anyway no matter where I stand. You can only run from one trap to another."

"Is that so? Hmmm ... I only wish I had your nerves. I'd be better off and could quit worrying."

"Lie down!" The order ran through the column. Dropped from nowhere came four star shells. Floating down slowly for a minute or so they turned night into daylight. Ebelshauser slightly lifted his head to scan the ground but saw nothing. Apparently they were still far from their goal.

"My God, I'm all in," he said with impatience. "I could just lie down and sleep. Aren't we ever going to get there?"

"We'll be there before you know it," replied Heimer. "The problem is, there probably won't be any trench left. We'll have to be satisfied with holes."

"But soon we ought to find some of the men around whom we're to relieve. They can't all be dead."

The peculiar sound of a flying mine made them keep still and their faces turned skyward.

"Far over our heads," Ebelshauser declared, breaking the tense silence. "We won't even hear or see the explosion. It wasn't meant for us."

"Of course not," a voice nearby said.

"Oh, hello Rueger! How are you getting along? Think we'll make it?"

"Why not? But we'd better spread in line again before we're spotted. It wouldn't take them long to have some of their heavy eggs dropped on our heads. Sneaky like the dickens, these English." With his last words Rueger turned to the right.

"Damn it! Another rain of star shells. They must smell our presence," remarked Schwarz.

The men went down before the limited field of light could reach them. They rose as soon as the danger had passed and resumed their march forward. The holes and gashes in the earth had multiplied. It could not be very far anymore.

"At last!" gasped a man in a tattered uniform when he first caught sight of them. "I thought you'd never come."

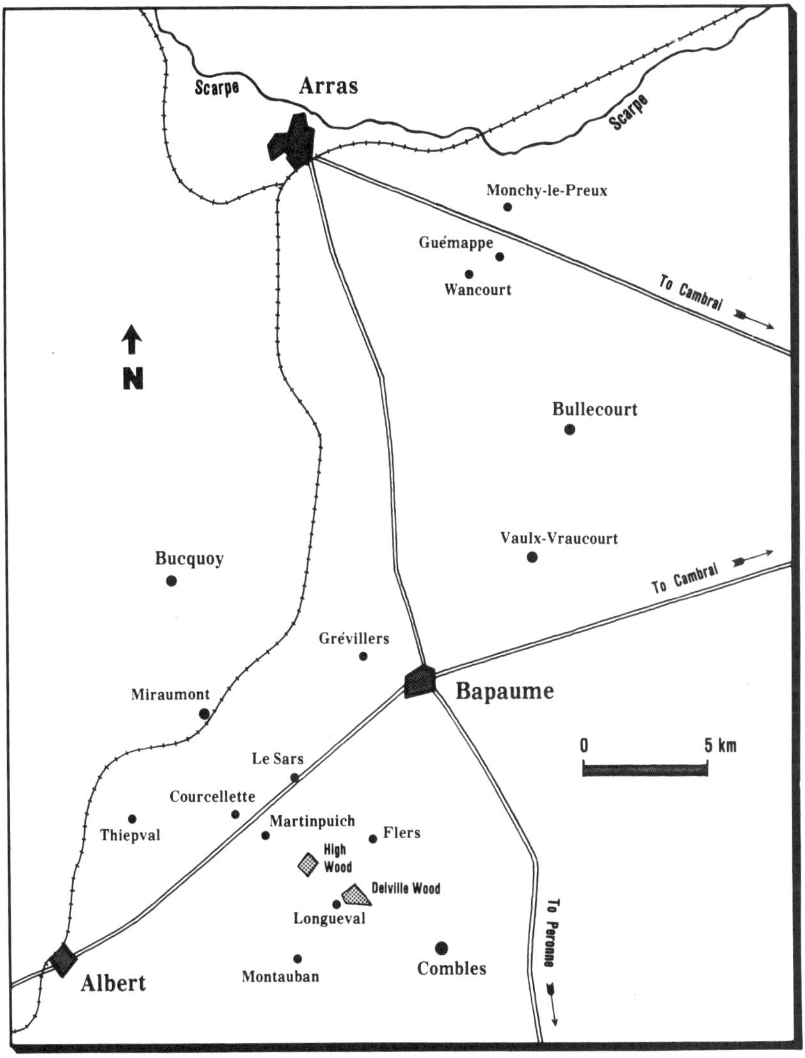

Unexpectedly they had stumbled upon the men they were to relieve.

"I don't know how we made it, but we're here and no one got lost on the way," answered Ebelshauser. "But, where is the trench?"

"You won't find any around this section unless you build your own. All the dugouts, everything has been blown to pieces. I've never seen or heard anything like it. Most of our men must be dead. I don't know how I escaped."

"Going back for a rest, I suppose?"

"Rest, my eye! Nothing like that for us. There are plenty of other places to be taken to now."

"But haven't you been here for three weeks without a break?"

"True, but if you don't you ought to know it by now. Germany needs more soldiers. And where is she going to get them all if you and I were to take a rest?"

"But there's a limit to human endurance. A man can only do so much and no more."

"You'll be surprised how far a man can go."

"Where are the others?"

From the man's group four were missing. In subdued tones they called out the names and looked into a few craters. But there was no time for a search. They soon gave up and left without them to join the rest of their company.

"Good luck to you," were their parting words.

Apfel immediately got hold of his men, divided them and placed each in a hole. They could not think of rebuilding the trench, but tried hard to dig out a new line the following night.

Two and a half weeks passed. Under the magic spell of a pale, watery sun the light of another day on the Somme was breaking through. The battlefield appeared empty. No Man's Land was hiding its dead in unseen and unmarked graves. The steel stakes gleamed among the great patches of barbed wire. So, too, the tops of steel helmets strewn here and there on the death-covered ground. The earth still bled from the terrible onslaught of the preceding days. Few and far apart came the screams of stricken men. Caught between the firing at such a time the many wounded were not only helpless but unreachable.

Ebelshauser and his comrades were overwhelmed by the sights that greeted their eyes. Scattered in their individual holes they followed the fast-shifting scene with apprehension. The enemy's bombardment had suddenly ceased, but what they saw coming was a thousand times worse than the constant roaring of the English batteries. Their hearts almost failed them for fear when a line of machines unlike anything they had ever seen before came into full view, headed straight in their direction.

"They're coming!"

It was a useless shriek of alarm. The whole front was aware of the oncoming steel monsters. "Steel monsters" — the words came out of their mouths in spite of themselves. What were these things? Facing them now they did not know what to do. Could they really offer any opposition? Was it not better to flee? Was it not folly to sacrifice so many lives by trying to hold the position?

The monsters' motors hummed and droned louder as they crawled increasingly nearer. They advanced relentlessly, up, down, closer and closer. Holes, hills, rocks, even barbed wire meant nothing. They pursued their goal in a straight line, leveling everything in their passage.

The men began to shoot, but rifle and machine-gun bullets could do no damage. The iron beasts still were approaching. There seemed to be no possible escape except for a wild retreat.

"Why don't they give the command?" Sonntag was sweating with fear. "What can we do against them? We'll try to beat it when it's too late."

"We'll make it yet, Ernst," Ebelshauser encouraged his friend. "We can run faster than they can crawl."

"But what about their machine-guns? They'll mow us down before we've time to get up out of our holes."

"Just wait, we can't run away without a command."

"Yes, I know. We all die by order ..."

"Throw your hand grenades!" someone nearby shouted.

Those who had not already fled stood and threw from the bottom of their craters.

"Halt! Stop throwing! They'll have to come closer!"

Dozens of explosions obscured the front of the nearest vehicle, but it came on without pause.

"Throw!"

The men were ready, waiting. This time their grenades hit the sides and roof of the steel carcass, but it kept on moving. Then came great confusion and chaos. The defending line broke. Some remained, others rushed forward toward the beast, still others ran in the opposite direction. Machine-guns rattled and screams filled the air. Terror-stricken, Ebelshauser and his comrade seemed nailed to their places. They had wanted to flee before, now their legs trembled, refusing support. They watched the advancing group. Bending forward, one following the other, they reached the monster. They immediately divided, two for each caterpillar. Grenades were thrown through small apertures. Then they took cover running back as fast as they could. Five or six were shot and fell to the ground. But the machine had been brought to a stop. If nothing else this caused one or two others in the vicinity to turn back. Soon they had cleared the field and disappeared behind their own line. Thus ended within an hour an English trial attack with tanks. *

"Hey, Ebelshauser, did you hear that? Both of them are gone."

"Who?"

"Apfel and Hartmann."

"No fooling? That can't be true."

* This attack, the first ever in history utilizing tanks, occurred on September 15, 1916. Thirty-six rhomboidal-shaped Mark I tanks went into action that morning on the front of British Fourth Army, assisting British, Canadian and New Zealand divisions pushing east between Courcelette and Guillemont. Though many of the tanks were knocked out, ditched or broke down, by the afternoon both Courcelette and Martinpuich had been captured, and hundreds of Germans had been taken prisoner. The history of the 17th Bavarian Infantry Regiment flatly states that this day's fighting was the most difficult for the regiment during the entire course of the war. From August 25 to September 25, 1916, losses for the 3rd Bavarian Division (to which Ebelshauser's regiment belonged) amounted to 4,900 men. — R.B.

"But it is. Hartmann died on the way to the hospital. Apfel is still unconscious, or he was when they left him. He was shot in the right eye."

"My God, that's terrible!" gasped Ebelshauser. "When did it happen?"

"Last night."

"Who told you?"

"Heimer. It came all the way down the line. Pass it further."

Another night had passed without mishap. It was twilight and the darkness was slowly receding. The somber gray of a morning mist grew more pale. Soon a broad glimmer of pink-yellow color brightened the sky, bathing the eastern horizon in a magnificent iridescence of light. Nature was awakening, taking on another day of new life. In spite of the picture of desolation that struck the eyes, one could hear the twittering and chirping of birds. As the sun rose they went on with their singing and morning greetings in defiance of the flying bullets.

Sonntag was entirely lost in silent contemplation of the beautiful sunrise. The majesty and radiance of the scene almost made him forget his own plight. He raised himself above the rim of his crater to take a peek at his friend, Ebelshauser, but bullets came whizzing past his head. He quickly ducked and went down again.

Sonntag had been assigned to their group to replace Thaler. Being of a pleasant disposition and only one year his senior, Ebelshauser immediately had felt drawn to him.

"Gustav! Gustav!" Sonntag shouted. He could not stand feeling so lonely. The corners of his mouth curved into a bright smile the moment he heard his comrade.

"What's wrong, Ernst, did you get hit?"

"No, I'm all right, Gustav. How is it with you? Did you take a nap? They seem to be early over on the other side, too."

"I guess I must have. Time passed so quickly. We'll watch to catch them just in time if..." Changing his mind, Ebelshauser continued, "but I don't think they'll come over so quick, unless they know exactly how we stand. If I know my onions about the English they'll have another heavy bombardment, you know, some sort of artillery cleanup before they bubble over. Just wait and see."

"Take a look at the sun and listen to those birds. Isn't it a gorgeous morning? What a day for an outing in the free open spaces! Wouldn't it be grand? What do you say?"

"You know my answer to that. But I'm afraid we'll have to wait a while."

Had it not been for their lamentable surroundings and all it implied, the two could have lost their hearts for joy in admiration of the distant spectacle. As it was, there could be no rejoicing. Nature in all its beauty was being destroyed. Nothing had been left unturned. Where green fields and gardens had been the soil was ripped to shreds and bleeding. There was nothing left except for holes, holes and holes — holes for as far as the eye could see. Gone, too, were the roads which used to bind the villages and towns to each other. Razed were the numerous fruit trees that had flourished in the rich soil a few years before. From a small nearby wood only a few roots and trunks remained. And from their position could be seen half-demolished stone and brick walls which used to be houses and farms — a prosperous community, perhaps — but now pulverized and buried forever. These walls once had been the protection of the inhabitants. Now they were serving the enemy who had turned them into small fortifications. In front of the broken walls and piles of rubble was a long, interminable hedge of barbed wire. Every 10 or 15 yards the edges were cut. These were breaches through which men could pass in case of an attack upon the enemy.

The English continued sending over light and heavy projectiles without doing much damage, though the shooting soon became more steady. It was not unusually heavy fire, but just the same it was enough to cut the front from the rear and thus prevent possible reinforcements. Suddenly and without warning the English guns shifted target. A perfect rain of missiles came falling directly on their position.

"See, didn't I tell you, Ernst?" Ebelshauser shouted. "Now it's our turn. Keep your head down!"

"They would, the bastards! Shooting wouldn't bother me so much if I were sure not to get hit."

"Watch out, duck!"

They both went down. As they reached the bottom of their holes a terrific explosion took place not far away. They had seen it coming — a mine of high caliber. The detonation echoed through the scarred countryside and the earth rocked as if shaken to its foundations. Pieces of steel, mud and wood flew through the air and fell all around them. By sheer luck they were left untouched. The danger barely over, they quickly resumed their positions at the upper rims of their respective holes.

"That's what I call a narrow escape," Ebelshauser called to his friend.

"I got a rock right on the head," Sonntag answered, "but it bounced off my helmet. They have more resistance than I thought."

"Where are the others, anyway? I can't see anyone around. I wouldn't like the idea of being left alone here, would you?"

"Don't scare me. They must be hiding in their pits just like us. One of the bunch is sure to appear any minute now. Just watch! There, what did I tell you? See, over there is Heimer smiling at us. You can see his teeth."

"Yeah, I see him, but just from the nose up. God, I hope they'll soon stop sending over those big babies. Boy, oh boy, they rip some holes!"

"They're getting too tough to suit me. No use taking a chance. We had better get down. Heimer is ducking, too."

"Ah, what's the difference where you are, up or down the hole? They'll get you anyhow, and ..."

Ebelshauser had no time to finish his sentence. As if choking, his face turned as white as a towel. He literally dove to the bottom of his crater. Like a flash of lightning a heavy mine crashed to the ground. It exploded with the loudest detonation he had ever heard. It had landed only a few yards away.

No matter how well trained a soldier was there were times when the war got the best of him. No human being, regardless of his bravery and courage, would have been able to withstand firing of this magnitude with nonchalance and indifference. It was a task beyond human limitations. Ebelshauser, like all the men in his company, was beginning to falter, wondering when the hour of mercy would come for him. In his mind there was no question that he would be struck any minute. He gave up the struggle. What kind of resistance could he offer? The enemy was nowhere to be seen, not yet prepared to go over the top. By the time he did rush forward he would find nothing but death and destruction. It would be easy for him to take possession of the first line without any casualties. To this end the Tommies' batteries sent over their torrential rain of shells and explosives, literally tearing the earth apart.

For Ebelshauser and his comrades the burden had become altogether unbearable. They had been trained and would have been ready to fight an even battle, man against man, but how different from expectations did this war turn out to be. How could men stand against the ferocious onslaughts of modern machines, tanks, machine-guns and airplanes? What chance had flesh and blood against a blinding downpour of iron and steel shot from a safe distance? As soldiers they were not even given an opportunity to defend themselves. Instead, the unseen guns were raising their voices, vomiting their highly perfected explosives and claiming countless victims. The infantry was bleeding to death, but what of it? The English bombardment kept increasing in intensity at the turn of each hour. Even when night settled over the mutilated fields of France there had been no let-up. The fire had gone on. Imprisoned in their treacherous holes, the men dared not risk the slightest move.

To add to their torments, more often than not the food carriers failed to appear. If and when they finally arrived in the early morning hours, half of the rations had been lost en route. Yet, the carriers could not be blamed for the meager supplies. A terrific barrage of fire had cut them off, preventing their advance. Forced to take long detours every step had been a dangerous adventure. They had fallen and stumbled as it had become almost impossible to keep straight and stand on one's legs. The heavy containers, of course, had banged and spilled. And not only did they have to be satisfied with just half their portions, but everything they received was cold. Having no other choice they made the best of it, absorbing the food in the very state it had been brought to them. The effect was predictable. It had not taken long before they started to complain of stomach ache, and the ill-feeling had swept the line. In the twilight, shadows could be seen jumping from one hole to another, responding to the call of nature. Daylight stopped such activity altogether for leaving or changing holes then was to expose one's self to slaughter.

For three more days and nights it was for Ebelshauser and his comrades nothing short of hell on earth. Fire came crashing down from all directions, ceaselessly. It ravaged and destroyed every living corpuscle in its devilish passage, turning shellhole after shellhole into open and silent tombs. How many unknown soldiers lay buried there, soldiers whose bodies would never be found? The earth shook day and night. New, deeper holes constantly were being created by the flying, death-dealing meteors, while those already existing were filled up again or displaced. The air was saturated with explosive fumes. The sun itself, as if ashamed of the human race, sought a hiding place behind dark clouds to escape the sight of so much blood.

The few remaining defenders of this section of the Western Front had become nothing more than crawling animals seeking refuge in ever fresh-made holes. They slid from one crater to another in a vain search for food as well as for protection. But neither could be found.

To top it all, issuing from the sky came the most fearful and damaging of all threats. Without any cover whatsoever they were helpless against the constantly increasing number of attacking fliers. Never had aviation been used so well as in this large scale offensive launched by the English. Reinforced by squadrons of French planes it became apparent from the start how futile and meaningless a defense against these machines would be. There seemed to be magnificent coordination in connecting the planes' operations with those of the enemy's artillery batteries. Not only did the mechanical birds fly low with machine-guns shooting at any moving body in sight, but they dropped signals — star shells of different colors — which were immediately picked up by the batteries. No sooner had such a light touched the ground than the bombardment from the distant heavy guns began.

Heroes sat in these machines — brave men, cold-blooded and sharp-sighted with teeth clenched tightly. They glided here, there, everywhere. Around them, white puffs of smoke marked numerous explosions of shrapnel from anti-aircraft guns. Other fliers surged from out of the clouds, their motors humming and howling. They were soon overtaken and within the flying ships machine-guns rattled. The troops on both sides surveyed the air battle from below, watching intensely the tragedy in the sky. Suddenly, thousands of chests heaved in joy and thousands of eyes sparkled with delight. A plane flipped through the air in a frenzy with a black flag of smoke trailing behind it. A minute later the machine crashed into the earth — its occupants dead, crushed to a pulpy mass. Two men in the prime of their lives had just been killed and thousands were shouting and rejoicing. Thus, systematically the flower of European mankind was being annihilated. Men had become mere numbers — figures to be lined up in ranks, ground into the soil and then replaced by similar figures. The earth was being torn to its bowels, split by shells and grenades, bored by mine excavations, flying up in black fountains and mixed with mangled bodies. The once-smiling countryside was being changed into a vast cemetery that, in turn, was rooted up over and over by never-ending shellfire. In the trenches the shells and bullets screamed. The insane ran through the barbed wire. The wounded moaned. And the dying groaned.

From his crater Ebelshauser watched the inferno, and the picture almost made him lose his balance of mind.

"Gustav! Gustav!"

He vaguely heard his name called. He would have liked to jump up but was hardly able to move. The yell reached him again, more piercing, more insistent than before. Seeing the utter impossibility of taking off his pants, he gave up the idea of cleaning and awkwardly began to crawl.

"Let's stick together here in this hole," Sonntag pleaded the moment Ebelshauser came rolling into his pit. The terrific explosion of a few minutes before had scared Sonntag to death.

"Don't leave me alone," he begged again in a trembling voice. "What kept you so long? I called at least 10 times."

"I came as soon as I heard you, Ernst. But you can't move too fast with those planes overhead. Besides, my pants are full and sticking. I simply couldn't get them down."

"Same here. We'll have to wait for nightfall. Anyway, rather this than get shot."

Sonntag's face was very pale and his eyes were bloodshot red. He needed a good night's sleep. But how? It was a wonder that both of them were still alive.

Night came at last and the airplanes stopped flying. The bombardment alone continued without a second of interruption. In spite of the rumbling artillery, with shells howling and crashing all around, they first helped each other in getting cleaned. Then, in a hurry, they left their hole, creeping on their bellies from one crater to another in search of their comrades. By morning they knew. Those they could find were dead, their bodies lying in the most grotesque positions. Each had died alone, away from his fellow man. And each face wore an abominable mask of awful pain and torture, features reflecting the horrible agonies they had gone through.

During the night the air became very chilly. Relief was due sometime the next day or night, but would the newcomers find them? They felt overcome by the fate of their company. Strangely, they had not yet met with a single one of their comrades. Could they all be dead? Had they gone back without letting them know?

How long had it been since Ebelshauser dozed off? He could not remember. Suddenly, he heard a faint cry. He opened his eyes just in time to see his friend rolling to one side of the pit. Sonntag was moaning incoherently. His eyes, almost bulging from their sockets, looked at him pleadingly. He seemed totally unable to move. At first, Ebelshauser could find nothing wrong with him. Lying as they were he slid his right arm under Sonntag's torso. Instinctively, he then passed his left hand over his chest, throat and back, but felt nothing unusual. A minute later, with an agonizing sigh of pain, Sonntag fainted.

Terror-stricken, Ebelshauser laid his friend on the bottom of the crater to take a good look. He already had opened three or four buttons of his tunic when his eyes fell between Sonntag's legs. There, almost where the thighs joined the trunk, a pool of blood had formed, the origin of which he could not see in his position. He immediately took hold of the left foot. Carefully, he lifted the leg and laid it softly down again, slightly apart from the right. A close examination disclosed the most horrible revelation. For a moment he thought he would faint himself. What he saw was enough to make him lose his senses. A large steel splinter had driven through Sonntag's left thigh, causing a large, deep gash from which blood was streaming. His pants, ripped open, were soaked already. He could not see the extent of the wound for he was afraid to open the torn material and risk further injuring his comrade.

When Sonntag came to he screamed for his mother. Appearing to calm down, he looked at Ebelshauser's face for a moment and in his usual deep voice, said, "Won't you give her my regards when you get back home?" Then he started to rave, groaning like a wild animal in pain. Tears came to his eyes.

"Give me your hand and promise, Gustav. I am dying, I feel it. I am beyond any help."

"Not if I can do something about it," Ebelshauser said, raising his hand in protest.

"It's no use, Gustav," Sonntag retorted in a feebler tone. "You can't do anything for me. I'll soon have peace and rest."

Unable to stand the agony any longer and eager to assist his friend, Ebelshauser decided to look for help. Alone, he realized, he could do nothing. But with two or three others perhaps something could be done. With help he could carry the wounded man to a dressing station.

"Just lie still where you are, Ernst. I'll get some help."

"Gustav, please don't risk your life for me," Sonntag pleaded. "I know ... oh, God! It won't be long. I'll be ... oh my God! The pain is terrible ... I'll be gone ... Please stay here ... with me. Don't go away!"

"I cannot stand to look at you, Ernst, without at least trying to do something. I know I can't do anything myself. I must get somebody. I'm going to look around ... right now. I'll be back soon, don't fear."

Ebelshauser climbed out of the hole but lost no time in diving into the next. A volley of machine-gun bullets came flying in his direction.

Crawling over the shell-torn ground he went through countless contortions in his hurried search for help. In complete defiance of the enemy he went on without a stop, ignoring the shells which continued to fall nearby. His knees and elbows began to ache, and soon his bare skin was scratched and bleeding. Three or four times in succession he dropped into a crater only to find a dead comrade of his company. He knew them by sight if not by name. They formed the most contrasting pictures. One face was distorted in a satanic sneer. The eyes had the most haggard glare one could imagine. The greenish color of the corpse's skin was in itself a repulsive sight. A ghost would have been horrified at such a face.

He had a difficult time pulling himself together after the shock of seeing such a human being. Eventually he found the courage to go on and crawled down into craters farther back. Nearly every one contained a dead man. In one, the victim wore a most contented smile as though he was enjoying a sweet dream. The smile was so natural that he had taken the man by the arm to wake him, only to find the limb rigid.

How far would he have to go yet? Surely he had covered a great distance already. He was completely exhausted and shaken by all he had seen. Moreover, the fear of not finding his way back again almost made him turn around in his tracks. But the vision of his helpless, dying comrade pushed him forward. He resumed crawling with renewed energy and resolution to win the race against death. From now on he did not climb into any more holes. When sighting a human form he called down at the top of his lungs or threw a stone. Receiving no response he pressed on, gliding through the dirt and mud.

It took him and the three men he had found quite some time to get back. It would have taken even longer to find the right crater had not the cries and groans guided their faltering steps. They found Sonntag in horrible pain. His eyes wildly looked at their faces. He was still conscious. His first request at the sight of them was for a drink. They all were thirsty. The water had given out three days before. Not one of them had a drop left in their water bottles, except for Martin, the wonder man, who applied the mouth of his field flask to Sonntag's lips.

They knelt around the inanimate figure and looked at each other in utter helplessness. What could they do? They stared at each other for a long while until Martin asked for a bandage. It was, he knew, a needless question. They had nothing left. Everything had been lost and buried in the earth. Even the rifles had been plowed under by the ceaseless rain of mud and debris. With one purpose in mind they succeeded in unearthing four rifles and were fortunate to find two pieces of canvas taken from the dead. Then, struck by an idea, one of the men took off his tunic and began to rip the lining. They followed his example. In less than 10 minutes they gathered enough material to start the dressing. This was the most difficult operation. Sonntag's thigh had been cut almost clean through and only a small piece of flesh still held the parts together. The flow of blood could not be stopped. There was no time to lose. They worked together in placing the body on the pieces of canvas which were fastened to the rifles to make a stretcher. All through the operation the English batteries were spitting fire without let-up. The whole neighborhood rang with one explosion after another. The succession of blasts caused a terrible, fantastic upheaval of the ground — the shocks could be felt for miles around. As if immune to the storm of steel missiles the four men remained intent upon their serious task.

For a while they considered it too hazardous to risk a straight march over the open fields. But the acute, plaintive cries from their wounded comrade removed any further hesitation from their minds. Besides, in spite of all their sad experiences they counted on human sympathy and mercy. Surely the English would not shoot when they saw the burden they were carrying. But whether they did or not they owed it to their suffering friend to take the risk, even at the price of their own lives. It was a duty of honor, the highest and most unselfish task a soldier could be called upon to perform. They felt responsible for his life.

Ebelshauser, taking the lead with Martin on his left and the two others at the rear, gave the signal to go. They surged forward out of the hole in plain view of the enemy's line. Heaving the body to their shoulders caused Sonntag to shriek with pain. Yells of anguish and agony burst from the stretcher at their first attempt to climb the crater's steep incline. How well they realized what torture it meant for him. But this was the best they could do. If they only could have found a rope to tie and fasten his dangling leg.

For the first 100 feet or so everything went without too much trouble. Just when they thought themselves tolerated by the enemy they had to reckon with their mistake. Shells and bullets came flying their way, bursting overhead and whizzing by on all sides. The frantic, piercing screams from Sonntag acted on them like a whip. They trod forward, blind to their surroundings and the noise of passing missiles. Every now and then they had to halt to adjust the slipping canvas. Painfully weak and hungry, having had nothing in their bellies for the past three days except for what they had been able to find in the breadbags of the dead, Ebelshauser and his comrades themselves were fit for the hospital.

Up and down they went. The earth had long ceased being on an even plane beneath their feet. Every crater, every crevice, every hole unfolded new and more horrible pictures of death. One man they passed had his carcass torn to pieces and was missing his head. Only a helmet lay on top of the open neck as if protecting it. Further on their feet dipped into the belly of another, causing the bowels to burst from the mutilated body. Closing their eyes and sweating, they continued on.

Finally, they landed exhausted in front of a Red Cross dugout somewhere behind the lines. Males nurses helped them to get the body down the stairs. Sonntag immediately was placed on the operating table. His eyes were closed, his face as white as the sheet on which they laid him. His lips kept twisting and he groaned with pain. For a moment he opened his eyes and stared at his friend, lifting his arm feebly. Ebelshauser took his hand and bent over the table.

"Thanks, Gustav ... when you go back ... don't forget ... see ..."

He could say no more for his heart was failing. In another minute he was gone.

Sonntag had breathed his last and joined thousands of others in a more peaceful world. All their efforts had been in vain. They had been too late. He had lost too much blood and was drained by the time they reached the station. Poor Sonntag! Ebelshauser was permitted to look in his pockets under the doctor's supervision. He found the address he was looking for written on the back of a photograph. It showed Sonntag in his best uniform with his mother.

This was as far as his memory went. Ebelshauser still could not account for his presence at the hospital. Search as he might his mind was a blank. Perhaps he had fainted as a result of the tragedy. Martin and the two other men probably had carried him out of the dugout. An ambulance had done the rest. He already had asked the doctor and several nurses, but they all had the same answer, "You came to us the other night."

His ears were still resounding with the noises of flying and exploding shells. He was in a state of utter exhaustion and demoralization. What had happened to him? After the first examination he had been found suffering from a fever and a severe attack of diarrhea. He was ordered to stay in bed and a special diet was prescribed for him. His face was pale and large, blue rings under his eyes intensified his sullen expression. He looked like a ghost just returned from another world. But his mind was still with him and in good working order. Just now, in spite of the terrible pain, he was thankful to Providence for his miraculous escape.

8

After three days of rest and quiet the fever and nervousness left him. Ebelshauser saw his departure from the little hospital drawing closer. He dreaded returning to the battlefield. He would not have minded being seriously sick with a harmless disease requiring a long cure. But one week later he was already rejoining his company at the front. Following the heartbreaking experiences of the Somme, he was relieved to find himself again near the sector the company had occupied before its departure for Roubaix. * He remembered this particular area as rather quiet; at any rate, safer than any other point along the line he had heard of. It surprised him to recognize the surroundings so well. He would not have thought it possible for, in their dismantled state, all places out here looked alike. Yet, things had changed during his absence. He was due for the shock of his life.

When reporting at headquarters he learned about the awful tragedy that had overtaken his company on the Somme. Of nearly 250 men he happened to be one of eight that had survived the terrible holocaust unscathed. He was struck hard and terrified by the news. All his comrades and friends were gone. Heimer, Rueger, Pechthold, Schwarz were names he had known, but now these names were no more. Sonntag's wound, his death even, had probably saved his life. Fate had a strange way of dealing with him. Now, once again, he was going to meet new faces.

"Anything special?"

"Nothing new, everything's under control. Thank God, another quiet night."

"Getting chilly, don't you think?"

"And how! Better put on your overcoat if you don't want to catch a cold. It's a bad time for that and you can't get rid of it so quickly. So why take a chance?"

"I don't. Take a peek at the thick sweater I'm wearing underneath."

* After its mauling near Martinpuich, the 17th Bavarian Infantry Regiment was sent back north to Lille toward the end of September 1916. Its billets were in the Lille suburbs of Lomme, Lambersart and Canteleu. Trenches occupied while in the line were opposite Armentieres. — R.B.

"Say, if you're going back down to the dugout you'll be just in time for a good 'mokka,' and some fresh smokes just arrived."

"How many cigars? They've really begun getting stingy with them. By the way, have you caught any of our subterranean visitors?"

"Not this time. The damned beasts are getting too smart for us. One got its tail cut clean through in its frantic struggle to escape."

"We ought to invent some new way of catching them."

"You said it, big boy. They even get dangerous in the winter. Brrrrr ... it makes me shiver to think of it."

"Well, rats or no rats, I'm going down now. So long, and keep a good lookout."

"Don't worry about that, but tell Kuefer to be on time for once. I hate to be kept waiting. Two hours in the cold is plenty, and don't let the fire go out."

Ebelshauser took up his watch while his comrade disappeared to rejoin the group down in the 17-step-deep dugout. "Time surely flies," he thought while making a rather superficial survey of No Man's Land. The enemy's line already had become invisible in the early evening mist. Far in the background could be seen the flaring of guns. Under the protection of darkness the goings-on over on the opposite side remained shrouded in a veil of mystery spelling danger. Once more his eyes swept across the ground. There was nothing suspicious to hold his attention. Satisfied, he fell back to a resting position. It was pleasant on hot summer nights to cool one's body against the cold moisture of the earth. But in October the touch of the wet sandbags topping the trench wall was unbearable, even repellent.

How fast had the days grown shorter! It was only six o'clock, but already the first shadows of the night were falling. Two months before in the same sector they had almost drowned in the mud. It had rained in torrents for a whole week without a minute of interruption. Veritable lakes had formed and the trenches were nearly impassable with brown water knee deep. Since then he had become a great exponent of fatalism. He believed that if his hour was at hand he would be catapulted into another dark and unknown world, no matter what he did or where he stood. Of course, one had to be careful just the same, otherwise it was not fatalism anymore but premeditated self-destruction. In many cases, however, it was most difficult to pronounce the final judgment between accidental and self-imposed death.

"Did God really know everything, as they say?" he questioned himself. It was one of the many problems he had pondered over for a long time without being able to arrive at a definite solution. "How marvelous!" he then thought as he gazed at the sky in full amazement and admiration. He could not remember a more beautiful scene. In fact, he had never troubled to look heavenward before, except to find out whether it was raining. More and more stars became visible as the clouds began to open like a theater curtain. No, he thought, he had forgotten all about the names of the various constellations and heavenly bodies, with the exception of the moon. There it was, a luminous crescent of soft yellow color, looking down on the blood permeated planet.

A sudden shot — the humming of a rifle bullet past his ears roused Ebelshauser from his nocturnal contemplation. Riding on the wings of memory was his favorite pastime. He saw himself returning to his unit after the short stay in the hospital. What a change had taken place during his absence! At first he believed himself in the wrong place. He had stood speechless when told of the company's great loss, especially about the deaths of everyone he knew intimately. Shown to his quarters he had gotten acquainted with a new set of men, including his new corporal, Otto Stuermer. One after the other he had shaken hands with Kurt Gartner, Alfred Stern, Emil Schultz, Franz Glindemeyer, Gustav Lauber, Friedrich Kuefer and Richard Aldrich. The first five men were much older than himself, while the latter two were boys just finished with high school. The new men were all right, but he could not help remembering and regretting the loss of his departed comrades, some of whom had so endeared themselves to him. Such was life and it could not be helped. Perhaps tomorrow he, too, would be gone.

Suddenly he felt very tired and had a hard time fighting off the drowsiness. His eyes, red with fatigue, refused to stay open in spite of all his efforts. Then, as quickly as he had been overcome, he found himself wide awake.

In 20 minutes his watch would be up, though he felt invaded by a feeling of uneasiness. He could find no reason for the anxiety that had come over him. He liked quietness, but the deep, continued silence permeating the atmosphere roused his attention and suspicion. "If only it was daytime," he wished. It was now too dark to make out what was going on over on the other side and the moon soon lost its light. For the moment he seemed blind to all signs of nature. Pressed against the wall of sandbags Ebelshauser stood motionless, holding his breath. A cold chill shot down his spine. He was not certain at all of his vision. Again his eyes concentrated on the spot, examining the object of his aroused curiosity. He could not make out what, in the space of a few seconds, had given him the scare of his life. He wondered whether he had not been the victim of a hallucination. Or had the furtive apparition out in No Man's Land been the result of his over-active imagination?

"Funny," he grumbled between his teeth, "I could have sworn I saw it move." It resembled a sheaf, and unless it was a dream he had seen it move from one place to another. A very short distance to be sure, but a move just the same. To make certain he laid out his rifle without taking his eyes from the object. After taking time for careful aim, the gun went off. Two frightened crows took to flight from the very spot he had been staring at, making his own observation all the more doubtful. The sheaf still remained, though without the least motion. Smiling, he stopped looking for a while and rubbed his eyes with his handkerchief. "Lucky no one saw me," he thought. "I got frightened for nothing." Resuming his watch he noticed the sheaf at the same spot, but now there was a similar form next to it which he had failed to observe before. Again he doubted himself, but decided not to pay further attention to the matter. "How could anybody go forward in that mud? The Tommies wouldn't risk their lives so lightly," he reflected as if to reassure himself.

He was about to turn away when he suddenly noticed two flashes above the opposite trench. A green light on the left was signalling to a red one on his right. For a full minute, so it seemed, they corresponded with each other by means of long and short flashes. This time he knew he was not mistaken. Something was going on over there after all.

He took another look at his watch. Should he wait for Kuefer to see what would happen or should he go down into the dugout and give the alarm? Perhaps this was only some kind of practice, or even a joke the enemy was playing on them. They had done so on previous occasions. A buzzing noise put him in a trance for the next few moments. His ears had been trained to distinguish this peculiar sound from all the others. It was from a heavy flying mine, the most dreaded of high explosives. At times these fearful projectiles could be seen at night as one would follow the course of a falling star. They emitted a tiny speck of light, though barely visible if one did not happen to look in the right direction. This seemed to be another signal on the part of the English for immediately afterward their batteries began to spit fire all along this section of the line.

"ATTACK! They're coming!"

Ebelshauser shouted in excitement. Running to the dugout to give the alarm he did not trust the power of his lungs and went down the steep steps. Glindemeyer was just enjoying some of a specially brewed concoction.

"How goes it, Glin?" he asked sympathetically. "The Tommies will put you right in a few minutes." Then he yelled at his comrades, going to each cot and yanking off their blankets.

"Come on out, boys! On your guard! They're coming! Attack!"

Preceded by Glindemeyer, Ebelshauser ran out of the dugout and waited on top of the stairs for the rest of the group. Glindemeyer, in the meantime, had taken up his position and was intently peering out into No Man's Land.

"Nothing to be seen yet," he called without taking his eyes from the wasteland out front.

"Keep on the watch. We'll all join you in a second!" Corporal Stuermer gave the order as he reached the trench. Surrounded by his men he discussed the situation. Overhead, the hail of shells and bombs was reaching its climax. All the fire seemed centered on a defined area, falling far back on the second and third lines while leaving their front line trench almost untouched.

"I don't like their strategy," Stuermer said. "It's always their tactic to cut us off from the rear and prevent reinforcements from reaching us."

Lausanne, 1914 — The author, age 16, surrounded by his brothers, Oskar and Albert (seated), and his sister, Elise.

The author, photographed in full marching order at Germersheim on January 12, 1916.

The author, 1916.

German troops marching to the front. (Bundesarchiv Koblenz)

Communication trench behind the front line positions of the 17th Bavarian Infantry Regiment, French Flanders, late 1916.

Heavy-caliber shellfire. (Bundesarchiv Koblenz)

Members of the author's platoon pose in front of a dugout entrance, French Flanders, late 1916.

British troops between Guillemont and Longueval on the Somme, September 1916. (F.P. Caulton)

Battered German trench. (Bruno Schmaeling)

No Man's Land — British dead. (R. Baumgartner)

German prisoners. (R. Baumgartner)

German prisoners. (R. Baumgartner)

Funeral procession for a German prisoner, Bramley, England, June 1919.

The author, age 17, summer 1915.

The author, age 21, December 1919.

"Out With Our Prisoners" — German postcard illustration of 1919 appealing for the release of prisoners held by the Allies. (R. Baumgartner)

There was no reply. The men were in no mood for talking. With worry in their eyes they looked dejectedly at each other. Fear was taking hold of them.

Stuermer, however, had arrived at a decision.

"Ebelshauser, you go up and stick with Glindemeyer. Lauber, you join Gartner at his post. I'm running up to the next group's dugout. Moser and his men can join us here. No use for them to stay where they are. They'd only be in the way if we have to start shooting. In the meantime, Stern, Schultz, Aldrich and Kuefer will get more ammunition out of the supply boxes. Get all you can find there and pile the hand grenades and cartridges next to this post. I'll be right back."

As he rushed off the men got busy making everything ready for the attack which they all felt so near at hand. The whole atmosphere smelled of gunpowder.

"The dirty dogs!" Kuefer said as he and Aldrich turned to fetch the ammunition. "Couldn't they have waited until we were gone?"

"I think it's only fair. They want to give us a chance, too, and bel ..."

Aldrich never finished his sentence. The last word died on his lips. Kuefer was bewildered and horrified. With open mouth and bulging eyes he stood there like a stone as if rooted to the soil or suddenly struck with paralysis. His limbs were stiff. He could not even articulate a sound. With hair standing on end he stared at the form that only a minute before had been a living body. Painful and atrocious as the sight was, Kuefer seemed incapable of detaching his gaze from it. Aldrich had been struck by a large steel splinter that had made a clean cut through flesh and bones slightly beneath the belt, slicing his body in almost two equal halves. A strip of cloth at the back of his uniform had prevented the two pieces from falling apart. Instead it had caused them to open, fully exposing to view their ghastly contents. The splinter hit with such force that Aldrich's head had been forced between his legs. But his face looked as if it were still alive. There was no sign of pain and suffering; on the contrary, a faint smile seemed to linger around his mouth. His eyes were still open, but without expression. The whole form presented one of the most grotesque pictures he had ever seen.

Recovering from the shock, Kuefer called Ebelshauser. Together they straightened out the body, moving it to one side of the trench. They had no time to waste. Even this operation took them longer than expected. In the great excitement Ebelshauser surprised himself by remaining quite calm in the face of this new tragedy.

"Where the devil have you been so long? Where is Aldrich?"

Stuermer had come around the trench bay and was visibly agitated and pale. The situation was becoming serious and more menacing every minute. Tension among the men was great.

"Aldrich got bumped off," Ebelshauser explained. "We just put his body aside."

"My God, that's terrible! If this keeps on there soon will be no one left. Moser and his eight men are gone, too. A shell slipped through at the upper joint and exploded in their dugout. Some of them were terribly mangled." Stuermer gulped a couple of times.

"Then we're only eight, including yourself, for this spot," Kuefer said.

"How about the others on each side of us?" inquired Schultz.

"They might help, but we're too far apart,"Stuermer replied sadly.

"Well, it might still be a false alarm. You know, they get a fit once in a while and start a bombardment without any reason or provocation."

"I hope you're right, Kuefer, although I have a hunch they mean it this time. Are there some more cartridges and grenades in your box? We'll need them. All right, let's get them all."

Three times they went back and forth at full speed, each time carrying armfuls of ammunition. They were about to start on their fourth trip when the warning call was shouted as if from one mouth by Glindemeyer and Ebelshauser.

"They're coming! They're coming!"

It was a cry of anguish, a plea for help. Although it had been anticipated, even expected at any moment, their shouting had the effect of lightning. The men had prepared and were ready to meet the danger. Yet, as they were about to face it, a gamut of human emotions underlying indescribable feelings of fear grabbed hold of them. At the same time they were determined to fight for it to the last man. Comradeship, honor and discipline were the three main factors that held them together. They were going to do battle for the common cause. But above all, as on the opposite side, there was the tie, unique in its strength and power, of self-preservation. They were fighting for their lives. *

Before Stuermer and Kuefer had reached the spot, Glindemeyer and Ebelshauser, without awaiting orders, opened fire. Gripping their rifles tightly they were shooting at the advancing enemy. At a given signal the English surged from under their camouflage and dashed ahead a yard or two, flinging themselves again to the protective ground. A volley of single rifle shots brought down a few during the short rush, but the loss was too small to be noticed. The attack went on.

"Keep cool, men. Don't lose your heads no matter what happens."

Stuermer exhorted his group once the first moment of excitement had passed. He stood in their midst making a general survey.

"Keep on shooting, I'll get the others," he shouted to the three riflemen at his right while jumping to the lower level of the trench. "Get this heap

* The author does not give an exact date for this particular episode, but it most likely occurred during the night of October 12, 1916. According to the history of the 17th Bavarian Infantry Regiment, that night a British patrol/raiding force of 40 to 50 men attacked the Third Company sector after a heavy preparatory artillery and mine bombardment. "Furious man-to-man combat" followed until German stormtroops came to intervene on both flanks of the attacked area. "After half an hour the position was cleared of the enemy and again in our possession." Numerous raids originated on both sides along this section of the front from October 1916 through February 1917, and generally were intended to capture prisoners for information. — R.B.

of ammunition down to the other corner. And you, Gartner and Schultz, come down and give us a hand. They're not close enough yet."

With their corporal helping them, the additional reserve of cartridges and hand grenades was quickly disposed of.

"Now let's line up all together on one spot."

Stuermer, along with the four men he had gone to fetch, established their position on the trench's upper level next to the three already standing there.

"Cease firing!"

The order, unreal and fantastic though it seemed, was followed nevertheless, but the men looked at their leader with consternation. The expressions on their faces left no doubt as to their thoughts. For a fraction of a second Stuermer appeared perfectly satisfied and paid no heed to their reaction. The promptness with which they had obeyed his command had proven his authority, convincing him that discipline was still at hand.

"No use firing when you can't see anyone. Let's go easy with the cartridges. Our supply is too low to waste them. Fire only the minute they get up again. The nearer they come, the better we'll lay them down for good."

The whole group stood in a row with Stuermer in the center, Kuefer farthest to the left, then Ebelshauser and Glindemeyer. Next to the corporal was Stern, followed by Gartner and Schultz while Lauber formed the right wing. They paused as the English had flattened themselves. With one ear they listened to what their leader had to say while the other was attentive to the flying missiles. The bombardment was still falling heavily behind them and on both sides.

A soldier was quick to grasp a situation. Only a few words from Stuermer had been necessary for a full understanding of his plan. The fact of their silence was a simple manifestation of their approval; they were ready to follow him.

"FIRE!"

Eight shots went off at the same time. Two Englishmen fell back of their advancing line. A third went down a moment later. Another volley and three more were laid on the ground. The men in the trench all had eyes to see and knew that the climax was fast approaching. One or two more forward dashes and the foe would reach their barbed wire. If they permitted them to pass this barrier they would be done for.

Stuermer appeared confident that the battle would end in a complete victory for his side. At least this was what he was telling his men. Perhaps he did so to inspire them, to give them courage and drive them to action. His explanation also had given himself a good deal more of much needed self-assurance. Looking over the parapet, he seemed again to be weighing the possibilities.

"FIRE!"

In tense silence the eight figures began firing at top speed, so much so that the rifles were getting hot. With no apparent concern for their falling comrades, the English continued approaching, each time slightly reduced in number.

"Get some water! The guns are starting to burn."

"There is none. You'll have to produce your own."

"All right then, let's get the bucket."

"Cease firing!" came the order once more from Stuermer.

"Just what we wanted," Kuefer said. "I'll go first." He grabbed hold of the pail and let nature take its course.

"Come on, don't take so long," Lauber shouted from his end. "They'll be here before you're through."

Without taking part, Stuermer let the men have their little fun. He knew how futile it would have been to interfere under the circumstances. Besides, the joke was a harmless one creating some merriment and a much needed variation to their thoughts. For a moment they were just like school boys playing innocently at a naughty little game.

"FIRE!" came the order again.

Like madmen close behind their heroic leaders, the Tommies were making the supreme effort. With unexpected rapidity their last dash had swung them right up to the very last obstacle, the cold and rigid fence of barbed wire. They either had to break through or retreat. There was no middle way.

It was the crucial test Stuermer had been waiting for. His hour had come. There was not a minute to lose. If nothing was done then it would be too late. Now was the time to strike.

"READY!" he shouted to his men, raising his voice above the roar of the fire. They all nodded in response, continuing to fire.

"Auf, auf! Sprung auf!" At the raising of his hand they went over the top.

At last, for the first time they were meeting their enemies face to face on the open field. But the meeting lasted no longer than the fraction of a minute. Not a single word was spoken and there were no further commands given. As agreed, every man had his job. Not a single move was lost. Fear seemed non-existent. Their work was swift and precise. It looked as if they had done nothing else all their lives.

In the pandemonium that followed they made use of sign language only, and this in a very limited way because there was nothing to be said. Every shot, every throw of a hand grenade brought destruction of human lives. It was gruesome work, but they had no alternative if they were to survive. They had broken their chains and lost control over themselves. They heard the piercing cries rising above the detonations of their own fire, but they were deaf to the pleading of their enemies whose flesh they were tearing to pieces.

Arrested in their assault, some of the Tommies had become entangled in the barbed wire they had sought to cut through. The wire, suddenly made loose, swung back at them, wrapping itself around their feet, legs and bodies. They were helplessly caught and found themselves unable to retreat, much less move forward. They were trapped in the recoiling wire like flies in the tenacious web of a spider. Before they had time to realize their incapacity, before they could manage to raise their weapons, they were mowed down, one by one, without pity.

Even while raising their hands in surrender the gesture was misunderstood. Bullets brought down their supplicating arms. The English might have called for mercy, but Stuermer and his men spoke another language. For their own salvation the English had to be killed. In the space of a second, Ebelshauser hesitated. A Tommy not much older than himself was staring at him. "Have pity," his gleaming, wide-open eyes seemed to say. Before he could hold back, Ebelshauser's hand had mechanically thrown a grenade. In the midst of the explosion the man's eyes remained fixed on him. Ebelshauser felt relieved when he saw the Englishman drop at last. He could forget himself again and go on with the butchery.

Kuefer, Glindemeyer and Schultz aimed at their own targets made of almost motionless human bodies. Every one of their shots found its mark, bringing an Englishman to his knees with a shriek of pain. They fired without interruption. Their shoulders were aching now at each new shot, but with grinning faces they stuck to their task of destruction. To their right Stuermer was conducting the throwing of hand grenades. His forehead dripped with perspiration as he picked up and passed the missiles after tearing out the fuses. All they had to do was hurl the bombs in the right direction as fast as they could. The damage thus caused to the attackers was beyond repair. Those missed with rifles were being killed or wounded by a rain of grenades.

Suddenly, amid the bleeding, suffering and shouting attackers, Ebelshauser and his comrades became aware of a commotion. At intervals in between the roaring furnace loud commands and whistles were heard. The English were turning back in full flight. As swiftly as they had advanced before they now ran in the opposite direction, leaving their wounded and dead behind. It was a race for their trench, for safety, for their lives. Under the defying and death-dealing fire of their opponents they could hold on no longer. The objective was beyond their power. They had missed their goal.

"Hurrah! Hurrah! We made it!" Stuermer shouted. "Look, they're turning back!"

The men ceased firing. Dumbfounded, as if unable to comprehend what was taking place, Ebelshauser and his comrades stood there in mute contemplation. Tears of emotion filled their eyes. A miracle had happened. They were still alive. It was beyond their understanding.

"We sure got them this time."

Twisting his lips into something resembling a smile, Kuefer uttered the only words, the only thought he could bring forth. With his simple sentence he had just expressed the view of his comrades. It also meant the banishment of the beast and a rebirth to mankind. Above all, it was a suspension of the death sentence that had hung so near above their heads. There was a pathetic note in the sense with which this survival was taken up by those who had fought for it. Kuefer's remark had had the necessary effect. It brought them out of their present state of morbid drowsiness and apathy. The ice of lethargy was broken and the men began to talk.

In the midst of the discussion Stuermer called and led them back to their own trench. He seemed to be the only one who had preserved intact his presence of mind. Replying to Glindemeyer who was pointing in the direction of the English line, he said, "It's all over now. Let them go home again."

"What about the wounded lying out there?" Ebelshauser asked.

"We'll try to get them in tomorrow as soon as it gets dark. The English won't bother us because they'll be out themselves to get those nearest to their line."

"I wish I had something to put in my ears," Gartner said. "I can't bear the sound of those shrieking fellows. We should have finished them."

"You'll get used to it. Those beyond help will die anyway. We'll get the others later."

"Well, I wish I could raise the white flag to get those fellows in. I'll go crazy with this moaning."

"Don't be impatient, Gartner, it won't last. They'll all soon be as silent as the grave, at least some of them."

While they talked, Kuefer and Glindemeyer were back on watch. For fear of reprisal or a renewed attack this duty was taken up with all the seriousness it implied. Contact with the rear was not yet fully established. Glindemeyer faced the open field that only a short while before had been the scene of untold atrocities. A number of bodies could be seen scattered here and there in the darkness, most of them dead. A few moved their heads or hands. They were looking and pleading for help that could not come. They were suffering. Some were probably dying in terrible agony. Some were so badly torn to pieces that no identification would be possible. Their names would later appear among the "missing."

Glindemeyer himself was killed the very next afternoon. His body, together with those of two badly wounded prisoners, was taken in after sunset. He was buried with many other comrades in one of the surrounding cemeteries. His only distinction was that of a soldier who had laid down his life in the service of the fatherland. He had fought bravely the previous night. Face to face with the enemy, he had come out of the blast furnace without a scratch. But in going out to rescue a wounded Englishman a bullet in the head had suddenly brought his career to an end.

Two months later, on Christmas Day of 1916, Stuermer and his men — with Glindemeyer and Aldrich missing — were decorated. With the usual military pomp and circumstance, a roll call of honor was read before the assembled troops of the regiment. Forgotten were the horrors, the cruelties and the suffering endured. Ebelshauser, following the example of Stuermer and the others of his group, stepped out of the ranks, goose-stepping his way to the officer in charge of this solemn commemoration.

"Volunteer Gustav Ebelshauser!

"In view of your splendid behavior and service rendered while facing the enemy, it is my honor to present you, with the approval of his Majesty and on behalf of a thankful fatherland, the Iron Cross Second Class."

While speaking the last words the officer pinned the medal on Ebelshauser's breast. It thus became his everlasting reward and distinction for killing so many of his fellow men. With head lifted high, he turned on his heels and goose-stepped back to his place in the formation. The ceremony was over. The killers had received their just recompense and the troops could now be dismissed until another gathering of this kind.

9

Christmas and New Year passed without much of a celebration. In fact, Ebelshauser could not remember these holidays being so quietly observed before. Despite the obvious display of their medals, sadness prevailed among his comrades. The first day they all exhibited the trophies proudly. Then the Iron Crosses disappeared from their breasts. As was the custom, they only carried the decoration's black and white ribbon in their tunics' second button hole. They did not even care if it showed or not; they were unconcerned about its attraction.

Oskar Schramm, a small, rugged man about 40, was the only one among them without decoration. He had joined the group as a replacement for Aldrich, and came from the low country region of Bavaria — an origin which was revealed when he spoke. Because of his pronunciation he often had difficulty making himself understood. He swallowed half his words on top of owning a most peculiar accent. Schramm seemed to be the only fellow left with some gaiety in his heart. He whistled or hummed his songs all day long and the gloomy state of mind of his comrades simply failed to dampen his animation and spirits.

New contingents had arrived from the interior of the fatherland and were being used to fill the many gaps at the front. The war babies — young boys of Ebelshauser's age, and even younger — kept coming in full swing. The ranks were swelled to full numbers and more. It was a miraculous transfusion, the pouring of new blood into an old and weak body. The fatherland had called on these youthful warriors who had been quick to respond under the law of forced conscription. The heavy losses sustained during the past three years had made this drain imperative. The struggle could not be stopped now. It had to go on. But the young men still would have a chance to undergo a short period of training behind the front before being sent out to the slaughter.

"Next in line are the Boy Scouts, I suppose. Just take a look at these fellows." Turning from the window, Kuefer spat on the floor to accentuate his disgust.

"Oh, be yourself, Friedrich. What else do you expect? Maybe our women will have a chance, too, if it lasts long enough. At least that would teach them how to keep quiet."

Schultz looked up with a frown, ready to start an argument. He was not enjoying his work anyway. Trying to mend a hole in his pants was the most difficult, most absorbing job he could imagine. He was half done with the task, but had stopped while holding the needle, trying to figure out what his next move should be. Gazing a while through the dirty window pane, he was watching for the parade of greenhorns to come by.

"Ouch!" came the sudden, painful cry from Gartner who jumped to his feet as if electrified.

Schultz had not been able to resist the temptation of playing his favorite trick. Sitting next to him, Gartner was caught unaware. Schultz had stuck the needle through the seat of his pants. Gartner turned purple. He was furious and wanted to fight. Barely restraining a smile, Schultz explained that it was purely an accident. Gartner was only half convinced. However, noticing the hilarious response of the others he joined in the merriment by taking the whole thing as a joke.

This little distraction had been sufficient to cause an interruption. The work of cleaning and mending was suspended. All the men went to the window to witness the arrival of the new reinforcements.

"They ought to be going to school instead of being sent out here. What use are they anyway? They're too young to know what it's all about. They're not dry behind the ears yet and will call for their mamas at the sound of the first shot."

"I hope we won't need any of them for a long time."

"Too bad we can't have our say in the matter."

"Look, they all have brand new uniforms and boots. It doesn't look as if we're short of material yet."

"Sure, the stuff they have on may be new, but don't ask me about its quality. Twice in the ditch in the mud and rain and they'll be done for."

"It's a shame."

"And they ask you to raise a family!"

"A couple ought to be wise after that."

"I wish they would, but people are too forgetful. I'll make any bet with you that 20 years from now the new generation will be just as foolish as we were."

"Some of these young fellows look all right."

"Yes, but we need giants and they send us children."

The long column of new uniforms already had disappeared at the end of the road, but the men showed no signs of returning to their unfinished work. Bewildered and confused, hundreds of boyish eyes had looked up in their direction, aware of their presence. Some, less fearful of the iron discipline, had even risked an awkward gesture of greeting with the most pathetic and serious features. It was plain that these boys' thoughts were wandering back home to all the things they had left behind. Few and far apart had been the faces with a smile. Most of them held their lips tightly closed. One did not need to be an expert psychologist to discern the signs of inner pain outwardly etched on their pale faces. Except for the new uniforms there was no brightness, no cheerfulness about them at all.

The young boys who had just passed by were conscripts. Many had been preceded by fathers and brothers, now dead, perhaps, or crippled for the rest of their lives. Who knew and who cared? The monstrous, savage struggle of nations had to go on. They were there to do their share. It was all a huge, perplexing puzzle for them to be caught in the gigantic crushing wheel of modern civilization. Blindly, they were following a road to an unknown destination from which most of them would never return. Was there no one to hold them back, to tell them about the heartbreaking tragedy that loomed ahead? Unfortunately, those who could have spoken out already lay rotting in their premature graves while those still living had to remain silent and impassible at their doom.

The new replacements had come, passed and departed again, noiselessly. A thick carpet of snow had absorbed the sounds of their steps. A streak of grayish-brown dirt stained the otherwise immaculate surface of white and indicated the road which ran through the small town. It was the only trace left behind by the young, unknown warriors who had marched past. Their heavy boots had plowed through the virgin snow with difficulty. Many had lost their balance and slipped, but quickly they regained the ranks and fell into step again. Intemperate weather, they had been taught, should be no cause of impediment or obstruction to a German soldier. Storms, rain, snow, sub-freezing temperatures or excessive heat were all words to be taken out of their vocabulary. Weather itself did not exist when it came to a military objective. When the order was march, it meant march — at any price under any condition or circumstance. Only the dead could be excused for not obeying this high command.

"See, Gartner, you were too quick in your judgment." Lauber took up the subject again while putting the finishing touches to his uniform.

"What do you mean?" Gartner retorted as he carefully inspected the nails on the soles of his boots.

"Well, they didn't even stop. The boys weren't meant for us."

"That's fine. They weren't fit to fall among roughnecks like you and me."

"Wonder where they're going? Is there a depot around here?"

"Not that I know of, but don't bother your head about it. They'll find the place soon enough where they'll be drilled and hardened up. You can count on the staff knowing its business when it comes to that."

"Hey, Gustav, why so quiet?" Lauber interjected.

"Boy, I wish I were in your shoes," Schultz said to Ebelshauser. "If I knew French as well as you do I'd show you a good time."

"The French I learned at school doesn't help me much," Kuefer remarked. "Every time I try it the woman looks at me in utter astonishment, and after a whole lot of tongue twisting, replies, '*Misch nisch spraschen Dutchland.*' Does this sound like encouragement to further the study of a foreign language? I should say not and I give up."

"That looks just like you, Kuefer. You must have picked on the wrong party because I've seen some of these French madams who speak all known and unknown languages ... with their eyes, versteh'?"

A roar of laughter filled the room following the explanation of Stern who accompanied his last words with a wink of the left eye and a "come hither" gesture of the head.

"That shows again the truth of the proverb, 'The less you know the luckier.' "

Schultz's wisecrack, however, did not take effect. Kuefer was not in a mood to let himself be disturbed by it. Besides, the general conversation was so animated that little attention was paid to such a trivial remark.

Men among themselves relish jokes that are fat and juicy, all the more so if they happen to be in uniform. The contest was on. The loudest laughter and most boisterous applause was awarded to the one who brought forth the dirtiest, most lascivious and most lustful tale his imagination could conceive. It was a soldier's most pleasant pastime, during which he found the best opportunity to exercise his wit. Above all, it afforded him a unique occasion of diversion from duty. At such a time sadness, sorrow, bitterness, distress and fear were swept away from his mind. Even death, for a moment, was erased from one's memory.

"Oui, Monsieur, those are my two sons. Nice, aren't they?"

Ebelshauser gazed intently at the two young men in French uniforms posing in the enlarged photograph that he held up against the pale light of an old oil lamp. Two bright faces were looking back at him in silence. It seemed to him that he had seen these faces before, for their features were familiar. But going through the picture gallery of his memory he was unable to place them. He returned the photograph to the woman.

"Charming," he complimented. "One must be about my age."

Madame Chamot took another look before replacing the picture on a dresser. She furtively wiped away a tear that had formed in the corner of her large brown eyes.

"Yes, Monsieur Gustav, I believe so." Pointing to her two daughters, she added, "Jeannette, the youngest, is 18; then Madeleine, 21; Andre is 23 and Henri, the eldest, is 27. May God take care of them."

"Never give up hope, Madame Chamot. The war will soon be over and you will see them again." Ebelshauser did not believe his own words, but felt moved to express his sympathy.

"Thank you, Monsieur Gustav, it's nice of you to say that. After all, it's not your fault. You cannot help it. Come now, do me a favor and take another piece of cake. Madeleine, pour another cup of coffee for Monsieur."

Ebelshauser looked at his watch. The woman had followed his movement.

"Not yet, Monsieur Gustav, it's only six. One more hour to go. Please don't refuse. It would make me feel bad."

"All right, if you insist, madame."

He had found in Madame Chamot's family not only a real spirit of friendship heartily extended to him, but a precious haven of social contact that had put new meaning into the monotony of life. He eagerly looked forward to these visits during the brief spaces of rest the soldiers were allowed when behind the front. In the pleasant atmosphere of this family circle he ceased to be just a machine.

After a delightful evening Ebelshauser rushed out into the night. He was in great haste to rejoin his company. It was marching out at eight. He would have just enough time to get ready. It was cold and the snow did not permit him to go as fast as he would have liked. His thoughts traveled back and forth, every time in a different direction: Lausanne, home, trenches, father, mother, dugouts, sister, brothers, shell holes and barbed wire, Madame Chamot and her daughters, shrapnel, bullets, machine-guns. It was like peering into the mysterious tube of a kaleidoscope, only the pictures and colors would bring grief to the aching heart of an onlooker. Hope of a safe return to his own family in his native land remained the sole inspiration in his drab existence. If he ever got back ... but, would he?

Ebelshauser's group had undergone quite some transformation since he had first joined it. Following the deaths of Glindemeyer, Stern and Schultz — the latter two being killed one day by a single shell burst — three young fellows of high school age, recently drafted, had arrived to fill up the ranks. They were Gustav Spiegelberger, Ludwig Gruenebaum and Hermann Pinkus. The first two were Jews and seemed to belong to a different race altogether. Yet, the eagerness they showed in their duties as well as a tense interest in the common cause proved that they were first of all Germans, a fact they would not deny. At any rate, they did not feel out of place. On the contrary, after their introduction they had been quick to merit the esteem of their comrades by their exemplary deportment and gentle behavior.

"Bang ...!"

Ebelshauser suddenly was interrupted in his meditations by a blow on the table.

"I caught you this time," Kuefer laughed. "Why don't you go under the feathers where you belong. It's late enough anyway."

"I wasn't asleep," he replied with open eyes. "I was just thinking and dreaming."

"Is that so? Then I'm glad I stopped you. Thinking is not healthy for a man in your position."

"You may be right, but can I help it? Don't you ever think?"

"That's just it, I know what it means. It generally gives me the blues."

"But you can't order your brain to stop. There's always so much to think about. If it isn't home it's the trenches and the dog's life we're having out here. Then with all the dead you can't help wondering why you're still alive. And last comes the same unsolvable question. How much longer yet? Will I be next? Doesn't that ever happen to you?"

"Listen, Gustav, when I catch myself in such a mood I either go to sleep or try something else to distract my thoughts. I know exactly how you feel about it, but what's the use. It only makes you disgusted. You know what happens to guys who think too much? They simply go crazy. Come on now, Gustav, it's time to hit the hay. The war will still be going on, even if you sit up thinking the whole night."

"That's just the trouble. Too bad I haven't the power to stop it. I suppose ..."

"There you go again. It's no use, I'm telling you, you're wasting your time. You'd better go to bed. You'll need all the strength you have left to go on for another couple of years, I guess."

Instead of answering, Ebelshauser got up. Recognizing the uselessness of a discussion, he agreed with Kuefer's point of view.

"Good night!"

They both undressed and slipped under the covers.

What hidden secrets would the year 1917 bring to a world whose civilization was about to sink into the bottomless abyss of complete annihilation? Silently bending over a gigantic map of the Western Front, the officers of the German General Staff had come to a supreme decision. Once more the dice of destiny were being rolled by those in authority.

They had just been informed that part of the new defensive line in the neighborhood of Arras — the so-called Siegfried Stellung — had been violently attacked by the enemy. * It had been weakened to such an extent that, if the English renewed their attack, they would find no resistance and could easily break through. It became imperative, therefore, to have the decimated troops in that particular zone replaced immediately by a new contingent. Then followed the actual formal instructions always expected with reports of this nature. Ebelshauser's regiment soon was on its way to the threatened sector.

Filled to capacity, the long train convoy at last came to a final halt in Douai. After assembling in the customary march formation, tired and hungry, they were made to listen to an address delivered in a ringing tone by one of their officers. It was but a repetition of what they always heard each time a dangerous expedition was in the offing. As usual, they submitted with angelic docility.

* On April 9, 1917, the British opened the Battle of Arras in a snowstorm with the Canadian Corps wrestling Vimy Ridge away from the Germans north of Arras. Despite the day's success, the Allied thrust on both sides of the Scarpe River east of the city met with stiff resistance by mid-April as German reserves were rushed to bolster the front from Lens to just south of the Arras-Cambrai Road. — R.B.

"Our company has once more the honor of being selected for the high and supreme task of giving our enemy a lesson in German solidarity and unsurpassed efficiency ..."

Their newly appointed company leader paused for a while after this declaration. Apparently pleased with himself and lifting his right arm to command attention, he continued in a slightly higher pitched voice, but more impetuously than ever.

"Once again the time has come for us to unite for the defense of our dear beloved fatherland. It is needless for me to appeal to your courage, your temerity, your audacity, your bravery and, above all, your splendid spirit of comradeship, because I know that all those qualities are an intangible part of your own bodies. It is written that we will not be deceived in the trust we have placed in our God who dictates our conduct and who will lead us on to the great victory."

The lieutenant had mounted his horse for the occasion and pronounced the last sentence in slow motion, articulating every word with emphatic gestures to impress his audience. In the obscurity of the night the pale light of a distant street lamp made his face appear to be balancing on top of a silhouette, for the dark shade of his uniform was hardly discernible except as a black spot on a slightly lit background. With his orderly holding the horse by the bridle, the officer had had an eye for the proper setting.

"That guy means business all right," Kuefer whispered in Ebelshauser's ear.

"You're telling me? And how! Wish I were him. Boy, what a life!"

"You said it, Gustav. Work up a good patriotic speech and let the men do the dirty work. That's all they do."

Kuefer's voice was full of anger. He had difficulty restraining himself from becoming louder in expressing his opinion.

"A coward trying to tell his men how to behave in battle. Why the hell doesn't he come along? He might change his mind about heroism. Talk, talk, talk, that's all they do."

"Listen, Gustav," Schramm said, "if you were in his position I can see you doing the same thing. The lieutenant alone is not to blame."

"Oh, I know it, but just the same it makes me boil over when I hear these too well prepared speeches. They don't mean a word they say. It's all fake, just to get us ready as cannon fodder, nothing else. They don't give a hang about our lives."

"Now, Ebelshauser, I feel sorry for you. How long have you been in the game? Goodness gracious, you ought to be wise to yourself by this time. We're not all so gullible as we look, but tell me, what can a man do in a situation like this?"

"I guess you're right, Schramm," Ebelshauser admitted, calming down. "Every time it's the same old story, that's the trouble with us all. Why the deuce are we to stick to all these outgrown traditions, like imposing silence and blind obedience on the men of the common rank, while he who commands can do and act just as he pleases? Do you call that fair?"

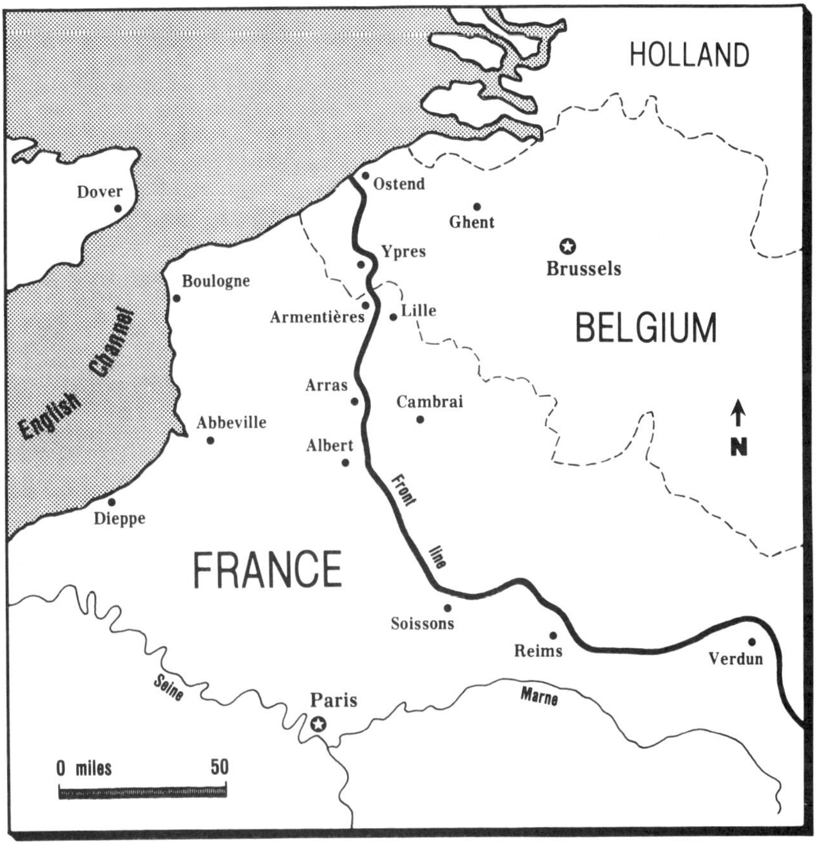

The Western Front April 1917

"Well, old pal of mine, let me tell you something. Once you've reached my age you will have found out that justice exists nowhere in this old world of ours, no matter where you are and what you may be. Whose fault is it? It's a general defect of the human race that has failed in the establishment of its own laws. Whether in or out of the army, rich or poor, men are bound to suffer on this earth. It's only more noticeable in the army, of course, but what's the difference? So just try to forget about it. You'll be much better off if you follow my advice. Believe me, I've had my own experience before."

Nodding his head gravely with a glance of fatherly sympathy, Schramm felt sorry for his young, inexperienced friend. He was about to continue the subject when the order to fall in was shouted. The lieutenant's speech had come to an end and the troops were being called to attention. They would have a four-hour march to reach their destination. As the lieutenant had just explained, the railroad tracks had been damaged by a bomb explosion and, therefore, they would have to go the rest of the distance on foot. Hastily, the long column of men came into formation and following a quick, superficial inspection was on its way five minutes later. At the first crossroad the lieutenant took leave of the company, proceeding in a different direction to his own headquarters.

"You mean it?"

With wide open eyes, Ebelshauser looked up at Schramm who had just brought the startling news. In spite of hearing it again he remained suspicious, simply not believing what he had just been told until it was confirmed officially by their corporal.

"But I'm telling you, Gustav, it's true. Stuermer will be coming along any minute with our new schedules." Schramm sounded very convincing.

"Listen, boys, get this ..."

The men who had just made themselves comfortable for a few minutes of rest did not like being disturbed.

"What's up now?" inquired Spiegelberger. "But don't come with a funny story. I'm not in the mood for a fairy tale. We'd better take a quick nap before we start off again."

"Dish it out and don't make so much fuss about it," Pinkus shouted. "Any good news will do, but don't tell us the war is over." He added the last line with sarcasm, laughing at his own remark.

"Well, boys," resumed Ebelshauser, "I have just learned ..."

At that moment Stuermer rushed up and burst out in a loud voice, "Fellows, this time we made it! We'll keep out of it! We've been selected as food carriers. Isn't that a break for once in a lifetime?"

The news was out. At first the men were stunned. When the reaction came, when they all realized what it meant for them, tongues loosened and a commotion beyond description followed. Each one tried to manifest his own feelings in showing his delight. The thought of not being compelled to take part in the battle this time was indeed a great joy. Food carriers! They looked at the job as an easy one.

Having worked out his program, Stuermer gathered his men to acquaint them with his plan and their duties. At 30 minutes past midnight the Third Company was to march out. If everything went well it would reach the fighting line at about two in the morning. They would be relieving some exhausted Prussian outfit. *

"But," Stuermer added with emphasis as he looked at the smiling faces surrounding him, "this has nothing to do with us. By a stroke of luck we can stay here in the kitchen this time. Of course, we'll have to make up for it later on. Your first run will be at 4:30 sharp. Each one of

* The relieved troops were men from northern Germany belonging to the 2nd Battalion, 162nd Infantry Regiment, 17th Reserve Division. The relief took place just west of the village of Monchy-le-Preux. — R.B.

you will carry two kettles of coffee. There will be no other provisions for the first run.

"You'll proceed together in a group until you reach a signpost marked 'DANGER.' Then you'll separate and go by twos in the four directions I'm showing you. Look here. Lauber and Gartner to the extreme left; Schramm and Kuefer, half left; Ebelshauser and Pinkus, half right; Spiegelberger and Gruenebaum to the extreme right. This way it'll be easier for anyone to get his proper share and you'll be quicker in finishing the job. I've figured you ought to reach the positions in about an hour and a half, and be back here about eight at the latest. The rest of the day is yours to do as you please, but you must be ready for the first run at five. Is everything clear to you?"

There were no questions raised. Instead, Kuefer looked at his watch and said, "Come on, boys, let's see the rest of the company off and give them a farewell, the poor devils."

They stood watching until their comrades faded into the darkness of the night and the sound of their steps could not be heard any more. Tired but happy, Ebelshauser and his companions repaired to their cots. It wasn't long before they were fast asleep.

"Well, that's strange, Pinkus. We had better go back and look for that signpost. It seems to me we're on the wrong track, don't you think?"

"What time have we got now?"

"Damn it, I can't see a thing. But we must have been going for more than an hour now."

"It's funny, we ought to have hit a trench by now."

"I think so, too. As I said before, we should have looked for that signpost before we broke up. We must be going in the wrong direction. Let's get back and find out where we are."

"We can't do that. We wouldn't get there on time and they're waiting for us."

"I know it, but what if we miss them altogether? How are you going to explain that later?"

"Let's try again. Maybe we'll hit the track in another 15 minutes or so. You know, sometimes when they say it takes 30 minutes they really mean two hours."

"All right then, let's go. I hope you're right."

Picking up their heavy kettles, Ebelshauser and Pinkus resumed their march.

"God, couldn't they find something more practical to carry this hot beverage in? My arms are getting limp."

"It isn't as easy as we thought after all. Tonight it's going to be worse."

"It wouldn't be so bad if we were sure of the way. But with this damned fog we don't know where we're going."

"Let's not talk so much and walk faster."

"Not a step further. I'm stopping!"

Ebelshauser halted and carefully placed his two kettles on the ground. Pinkus was undecided. Not wanting to continue alone he also came to a stop, although he still held his kettles as a mute disapproval of Ebelshauser's action.

"Come on, Gustav, it's no use stopping now when we're about there." Pinkus was making a last attempt to urge his comrade to go on. Receiving no reply and realizing that Ebelshauser had made up his mind and would not be budged, he in turn deposited the kettles. Standing close together they looked at each other in complete perplexity. Not a word was spoken for a while as both tried to solve the puzzle in their own minds. At the same time they experienced the odd sensation of a creeping and rapidly growing panic, an oppression of being surrounded by sinister and unknown dangers. They began to shiver and perspire.

Everything had gone fine for the first half hour, until Spiegelberger had seen himself justified to proceed to their dividing. In the early morning hours of April 17, 1917, the fog was so thick that one's own hand placed in front of the eyes could hardly be distinguished. Every step in the open fields was an adventure. Nowhere was there any light to be seen. At a distance of three meters a man appeared like a black shadow whose exact form remained indiscernible. The fog had come down in thick masses and in such volume as to render everyone absolutely blind. It was as if the clouds themselves had forsaken the heavens to settle on the earth's level. There was not the slightest breath of wind. The fog appeared like a dense, watery envelope made up of poisonous fumes ready to swallow any living creature, for even breathing had become a strenuous function.

In such darkness it had been utterly impossible for Ebelshauser and his companions to locate the signpost which Stuermer had told them about. Even the road seemed to have suddenly disappeared from under their feet. Nevertheless, after having walked for another half mile or so, Spiegelberger had decided they part where they stood. Ebelshauser, Schramm and Kuefer, the minority, had been disregarded in their opposition.

"I'm telling you, Pinkus, let's go back and try to find that post instead of going forward so blindly."

Ebelshauser was quite upset about the whole affair. To be lost in open fields was not a matter to be treated lightly. It was high time for them to get their proper bearings and bring this situation to an end.

"Whatever you say, brother," Pinkus said after having taken time for reflection. "I'll stick close to you."

Silently, though breathing hard, they walked side by side for another half hour. Suddenly they found themselves in front of a wooden shed. They approached cautiously, prepared for an emergency.

The building was but an old, half-demolished shanty. Part of the roof had caved in. A strong wind, no doubt, could carry away the badly damaged remains of the superstructure and cause the side and front walls to crumble. Fire and bombs had been the instruments of destruction. The evidence was plainly revealed by the carbonized edges of the fallen timbers. The hut might have been used as a dump for ammunition or perhaps as a storehouse for provisions. They could not say which.

Both put down their kettles at some distance before daring to advance toward the doubtful building. Straining their eyes to search inside they could discover nothing, for here, too, the thick fog hid everything from sight. Not a word passed their lips during the tense moments of close investigation. They dared not speak for fear of being heard. But frightened and oppressed by their own silence they could hold their tongues no longer. Showing audacity, Ebelshauser was the first to liberate himself from this heavy feeling.

"Hello!"

His voice was that of a stranger. He had spoken the word in a low bass, but it had given him courage. He then shouted with boldness.

"Hello, hello, anybody there?"

"Come out of there, whoever you are!" Pinkus yelled, not wanting to be outdone by his comrade.

Receiving no response, they wanted to make absolutely sure. Joining in a duo and louder than before, they repeated the call but with no better result.

"If there is anyone in there he must be dead," Pinkus remarked in a tone indicating the dissipation of all fear.

"Funny, isn't it? We didn't see this house when we passed here first." Ebelshauser spoke more to himself than to his comrade.

"It looks fishy to me, too. Wonder where we'll land by the time it's daylight?"

"We must be running in circles. If only we had something, some landmark to go by."

"The devil is taking us for a ride. I wish I could get hold of his tail."

"That wouldn't help much. What a mess! Damn fog! It's a case of a blind fellow trying to lead another blind man over the edge of a cliff."

"How about going back to where we started?" Pinkus asked after a short pause.

"Don't be silly, man. That's exactly what we've been trying to do all the while. If you haven't any better advice to offer you might as well keep quiet."

"Why don't you show a bit of brain work yourself," Pinkus retorted. "You say we can't stay here. Okay with me. But you don't want to go back either. So just how the dickens are we going to get out of here?"

"I'll tell you what we'll do." Ebelshauser's face was brightening up. He seemed to have a plan.

"No, Pinkus, it's no use trying to retrace our steps. We'll only succeed in getting ourselves lost altogether. Now listen to me ..."

He took a deep breath before resuming in order to command better attention and impress upon Pinkus the grave importance of the scheme he had in mind.

"I think the best thing we can do is this. We'll go right ahead following our noses, BUT ... you'll go on one side of the hut and I'll go around the other. The first one to see something calls the other. If there's nothing we'll meet again on the other side. It's very simple, isn't it? After the building is passed we'll again proceed together. Don't run, just walk. If you're the first to get to the other side, wait for me. If I'm first I'll wait for you. We can't miss each other, get my point?"

"I get your point all right. But suppose we do miss each other, what then?"

"Well, that's out of the question. If we both go as I just told you there's no reason in the world for not meeting each other on the other side, is there?"

"True, it sounds reasonable. But who can tell what is liable to happen while we're separated?"

"Nonsense, Pinkus. A call from you and I run to your side. I expect the same from you. Besides, I don't believe we'll find anything around that shack."

"Since you're so sure about it I don't mind following your idea. But don't you leave me alone on the other side."

"Don't talk foolish! Of course I won't. You can trust me as much as you trust yourself."

"All right, Ebelshauser, it's a go. Shake?"

"I'll see you later," he said, taking Pinkus' extended hand. "The coffee will be cold by the time we get there; that is, what's left of it."

"Better cold than none at all," were Pinkus' last parting words.

Ebelshauser arrived safely at the other side of the house which must have been about 25 meters long, according to his figuring. There had been no obstacles in his way. No call had reached his ears so Pinkus, no doubt, would show up at any moment. He waited, squatting as comfortably as possible on one of the kettles.

"What a slow-poke," he thought. After sitting for more than five minutes he began to grow impatient. He got up and took a few steps, stopping again, undecided. He was visibly distressed at the long absence of his comrade and his anxiety grew more alarming as each minute went by. A faint breath of wind had risen, causing the compact masses of fog to move slowly. Changing directions, they glided and swirled about in circles close to the ground. The gentle breeze was too weak to carry them upward. Yet, their density was diminishing for Ebelshauser noticed a slight improvement in the visibility. This worried him more than anything else and made him feel terribly uneasy. Fifteen more minutes passed and still Pinkus failed to appear. The suspense was intolerable. What on earth could have happened to him?

Perhaps Pinkus had deserted. Though at first he was repulsed at the thought, it rapidly gained momentum, crystalizing during the next few minutes into a firm conviction. The more he debated with himself the more he believed desertion to be the only likely motive for Pinkus suddenly vanishing from sight. Had he not intimated the possibility of getting lost or of missing one another? No doubt he immediately had been struck with the idea of making good this opportunity because, contrary to Pinkus' habit, he had raised no objection to the plan.

Ebelshauser was terror stricken. The battle raging in his brain caused him to despair about himself and to question his own sanity. Desertion? It was inconceivable. Yet, his being alone was mute evidence of the reality. Where was Pinkus otherwise? "I must make sure," came a voice from within. Obeying his instincts, he walked over to the side of the building where his comrade was to have followed. The fog had cleared away somewhat, but his eyes could see nothing beyond a relatively short distance. There was no trace of a human being visible in the whole area. The oppressive silence made him shiver with fearful apprehension.

"Pinkus, Pinkus, PINKUS!"

It was more than a yell. It was a scream of inner agony and terror. Again and again Ebelshauser shrieked in anguish at the top of his lungs.

"Pinkus, Pinkus, PINKUS! WHERE ARE YOU?"

Crushing silence was the reply to his calls. Exhausted in his vain efforts, Ebelshauser relaxed. He lifted his helmet to wipe his forehead which was dripping with sweat. A shudder went down his spine. He leaned against the wall and found his legs shaking beneath him. For a long while he sat there, completely unable to think or make up his mind.

An hour or more had gone by when Ebelshauser remembered his kettles. Rallying all the strength at his command he stepped over to them. Steam had long since ceased escaping from their lids. The coffee was absolutely cold. He took a sip by lying down and tilting one of the containers to his lips. The effect of the cold beverage seemed to work wonders within his body. It unexpectedly helped him to come to a decision. After resting on his stomach for a few minutes he rose to his feet, took hold of one of the kettles and resumed his march alone, relieved to be leaving this lamentable spot.

He was resolved to go on until he knew where he was. In the fog, going forward or backward made no difference. The result would be the same. He was bound to hit upon some point of repair, he thought, no matter which direction he took. While brooding over Pinkus' apparent desertion he had given up the effort of trying to search his way across the swamp of moist clouds. With his head slightly bent he kept walking, having lost all track of time.

His feet were wet for his boots were not as impermeable as they used to be. He was surprised not to have found a single trace of road yet, or at least some sort of evidence showing the passage of troops or artillery. The continuing silence was another puzzle. What time could it be? His watch had stopped. He must have forgotten to wind it up. Suddenly he came to an abrupt stop as if nailed to the ground. With an audible gasp, he beheld a ghastly picture.

Six Tommies, fully dressed and equipped, were lying in a row, dead. One of them still had his eyes open and appeared to be staring at him accusingly. The others, however, simply looked like they were asleep. Ebelshauser was quick to regain his presence of mind after the initial shock. Putting aside his kettle he went over to the first body and looked it over. The first thing to attract his attention was the corpse's stuffed bread bag. Without too much difficulty he succeeded in retrieving it after pushing the dead soldier slightly aside. He opened the bag after sitting down, making ready for a long deserved meal. Inside was enough white bread to still his hunger. A sausage did not look too enticing, so he threw it away. Next came a container of butter, a large dose of jam and finally some hard biscuits on top of a tin can of corned beef in the bottom of the bag. He was having a royal meal thanks to the dead. He got up to fetch the kettle. Undisturbed, he ate and drank with gusto, unmindful of his macabre company.

When the copious meal at last came to an end he rose slowly to his feet. If he had been shocked and afraid when he first sighted these dead men, all traces of fear had now vanished. How well he knew. The cold bodies at his feet were far less terrifying than if they had been alive. The beasts they had been until their last breath were, in death, transformed into harmless carcasses.

Ebelshauser stretched himself a couple of times, taking the moment as easy as if he had been on some picnic ground back home instead of on a battlefield. Rested and refreshed, he began again to ponder what he should do next. He proceeded to examine the bodies more closely. Apparently these soldiers had been killed quite recently, perhaps only the day before. Their features were still fresh and the uniforms almost spotlessly clean. Not desiring to be stared at by the one whose eyes remained open, he passed over to the next body. There his attention immediately was attracted by a rubber coat, rolled and tied to the Tommy's knapsack. Falling to his knees he quickly loosened the three small leather straps holding the coat. Spreading it out he found it to be a brand new trench coat — a long cape such as he always had wished to have. He could not resist the temptation. Such an occasion might only come once so he quickly tied the coat back together and left the place without further delay. He marched off carrying the coat under his left arm and the kettle in his right.

The fog still enveloped him, but visibility was slowly improving. He could see much further compared to an hour ago. He continued on until two other bodies brought him once more to a halt. This time he had no intention of stopping, but an object on the ground caught his eyes. Considering a coming furlough due him sometime next month, he thought it would be a splendid idea if he took the object along. The leather box looked new, but the strap to which it was fastened still hung around the neck of one of the dead Englishmen. Lifting the head he retrieved the box. Inside was a pair of English military field glasses of long range. It certainly looked like a very expensive instrument. He inspected it before bringing it to his eyes. Turning in all directions he searched the horizon, but even the glasses failed to pierce the moist clouds.

Soon he was on his way again, the field glasses dangling on his chest at every step. Confident that he was headed in the right direction and having ceased thinking of his faithless pal's whereabouts, his thoughts wandered back home. The first chance he got this week he would write his parents about his expected furlough. Perhaps they would come to meet him at Mannheim or Pirmasens. It would be an occasion for his father to see his hometown again. Yes, he would ask Stuermer to find out the exact date for him. He could leave his English trophies with his father who would be delighted to take them along on his way back to Switzerland. Ebelshauser's heart was beating fast with anticipation. A smile of preconceived joy parted his lips. He was almost running, as if eager to reach the imaginary place he had in mind. Hope had put wings to his feet. Too bad about this damned fog, but it would help him to explain his long absence.

"Zzzt ... zzzt ..."

The whistling sound of a bullet past his ear brought him to a sudden standstill. At the same time the lone detonation of a rifle could be distinctly heard, indicating the near vicinity of the shooter. The smile and all thoughts of home and his return vanished as he stood riveted to the spot. Gazing intently in the direction from which he believed the shot had come, he watched for a while without discovering anything to guide him.

Although the mist had continued lifting, his field of vision was still limited. With silence again restored he was inclined to take the single shot as a pure coincidence. Believing himself invisible, he did not attribute the firing to his presence. Still, he was not completely convinced. Not wanting to take further risks he began to run in the opposite direction.

"Zzzzzzt ... zzzzzzt ... zzzzzzt!"

A volley of bullets accompanied by the unmistakable rattling of a machine-gun arrested him in his tracks. This time there could be no doubt as to the shooting. One of the bullets passed through the right sleeve of his coat. One more move on his part and he would surely be finished. He knew that. Sensing the great danger of his position he turned around again to face his invisible assailants. He forced himself to stand motionless, awaiting events to come. He dropped the kettle, but held on to the trench coat and the field glasses. Single shots were now being fired from the distant and still obscured line. But he could no longer hear the sound of bullets. They probably just wanted to let him know of their presence in case he felt like darting off again.

Never had he felt so badly. His heart almost stood still under the tremendous pressure. If those shooting at him were his own people, surely they should have recognized his uniform. He must have wandered into the enemy's camp, English or French. He did not know and could not make out their identity by the sounds of the shots. At the same time, a struggle for life was going on within.

"Are they going to shoot me down like a dog?" he thought. Lying flat would be useless. They would simply sweep the ground with their machine-guns. If he could only see them. Standing there like a statue his mind was in a state of violent upheaval. He wanted to flee, but acting purely on instinct he remained rooted to the ground. A sickening feeling began to churn in his stomach. How long would he be able to resist the urgent call of nature? Pressed against each other his legs were shaking, threatening to give way. He pinched them closer together.

Suddenly, like the opening of the curtain at an opera, a breeze came from nowhere, chasing and lifting the fog. In a tumultuous, confused mass it rose to the sky, broken and torn into millions of transparent particles that began to race in all directions. Biding its time, the sun was sending down its partly intercepted pencils of pale light through the little windows which the wind was installing in the turbulent atmosphere.

Ebelshauser had no eyes for this imposing exhibition of nature. He was spellbound by the scene that had been unfolded so unexpectedly before him. The sensation was one of extreme terror. He was facing death with more atrocious internal torture than a terminal patient brought to the operating table. His feet felt like concrete blocks, frozen to the ground. Deep in his soul he was crying and begging for mercy. Would they hear him? Would they spare his life?

The lone traveler that he had been for the past few hours now found himself surrounded by enemies armed to the teeth. He had been caught in the trap in a masterly fashion. Even though he could not see their eyes hidden behind the metallic vizors of their helmets, the Tommies' grinning faces left no doubt as to their intentions. They were ready to kill him if he made one wrong move. There was no escape from the vicious semi-circle. The English line ran straight, as he saw, with the exception of this receding arc inside of which he had walked so blindly. How much longer would he be able to endure this position, for move he must? Never before had a decision been more difficult to make. He hesitated, and finally threw up his hands in despair.

10

With three men in front and three behind, Ebelshauser was dragged through the narrow ditch of the English trench. It took almost acrobatic crawling on all fours to keep below the low walls. At the very moment of falling into their midst he had been relieved of his precious watch. One of the soldiers took it out of his pocket and kept it as a souvenir. Others tore buttons from his tunic. They were all eager to possess something that once had belonged to a German soldier. They would have torn his whole uniform to pieces had it been left to their disposal.

His six escorts had come to the rescue. Marching between the guards he suddenly remembered some horrifying tales about prisoners who were caught wearing the Iron Cross or other medals. Unobserved, he ripped off the black and white ribbon from his button hole, buried it quickly in the sandy soil and stepped on it. "Something less to worry about," he thought.

Pictures continued to swirl around inside his brain. "If they wanted to kill me they could have done it on the spot." But even this argument could not remove all the doubts from his mind. They might have a certain purpose for taking him somewhere else before finishing him off. Their grinning faces, watching his every step, left him perplexed. Whoever they were, these English were certainly not in a joking mood. * They meant business and were very serious about their task. He felt the points of their bayonets following every move he made.

They had gone only a short distance when a flight of rudimentary and muddy steps took them out into the open. Ebelshauser was never to enter a trench again. A new and different life was beginning for him, though he did not know it yet. Bewildered, the reality of his capture still appeared to him like a dream. Prisoner of war, and still alive! Was it possible? Could it be true? Where were they taking him?

"Monchy!"

* It is very likely "these English" were troops of the 50th (Northumbrian) Division whose infantry was composed mostly of Durham Light Infantry and Northumberland Fusilier battalions — men from the extreme north of England. This division was responsible for the sector west of the villages of Guemappe and Monchy-le-Preux (opposite the Bavarians of Ebelshauser's regiment) from 12-20 April 1917. Ebelshauser was captured just southeast of Monchy and north of the Arras-Cambrai Road. — R.B.

"Look ... Monchy ... Boches ... alles kaput ... look!"

Out of danger and masters of themselves, the Tommies had come to a halt in front of the dilapidated village. They had suddenly discovered the use of their tongues and tried to explain to Ebelshauser what they meant to say. Their motions and gestures were far more eloquent than their rattling words. Speaking could not have conveyed their thoughts more precisely than their pantomimes. Nodding as they spoke, Ebelshauser could only approve with a timid and sour smile.

Monchy, once a flourishing little French village, was now completely destroyed. The Boches, said the Tommies, had done it, and he was one of them. He was, yes, but was he responsible for being there and wearing a German uniform?

"Look!" one of them said again.

For a moment they all stood motionless. To Ebelshauser it seemed as if these men were paying a last silent tribute to their departed comrades. In a grotesque pell-mell a large number of men and horses were lying all over the place, dead. Blood still streamed from many of their wounds, and the uniforms and animals were plastered with red. Some of the soldiers lay partially buried beneath the horses. The scene of carnage was indescribable.

Silently, they resumed their march across the village square, jumping a dead man here, a dead horse there. Soon they disappeared behind the village ruins, fleeing its scene of horror and desolation.

"Thank you," Ebelshauser whispered in the ear of his guard.

"Shhhhh!" Placing a finger to his mouth, the man warned him to keep quiet. Steps were heard approaching in the corridor below. It was pitch dark as no light was kept burning in the building. It was impossible to distinguish the lone walker, but as the sound of his heavy steps drew nearer the guard suddenly changed attitude, calling to his prisoner in a loud and rude voice.

"Get up, you! Here is some water ... come on!"

Ebelshauser had some difficulty lifting his stiff body. He managed to get on his feet by sliding down the wooden slab on which he had been trying to sleep the past two nights. The atmosphere was filled with penetrating moisture. His uniform felt heavy with dampness. Of all the places he had visited during his active service in the trenches — including dugouts and mine holes — this was the most uncomfortable. He was cold and shivering. Doubts as to his safety kept creeping back into his mind. How would they ultimately dispose of him?

This marked the beginning of his third day in one of the largest prisons of Arras. From the little Scotsman, his guardian, he learned that the English had taken more than 2,000 prisoners the very same morning that he had been caught. They all had passed through Arras on their way to concentration camps more to the rear. Why had they not sent him along with the others?

What a sight it had been for him while riding in an open lorry on his way here. On anothcr road running almost parallel he had seen columns of soldiers and artillery going in the opposite direction, bound for the front. He had been struck by the powerful array of guns of all sizes and calibers. They were being massed in this particular sector, ready for action. Carefully hidden and camouflaged, they revealed themselves only when passing by. And still more soldiers, guns and shells were being brought up to the same spot. Thinking about all those he had left behind in the trench, a terrible, upsetting feeling took hold of him.

Never had he realized so fully as then the impossibility of Germany winning the war. The conviction of being on the winning side was the mainspring of German tenacity, the very essence of the German soldier's continued stubborn resistance. But after passing from one side to the other he could not help forming a different opinion.

The new guard was much rougher in manner. He had no smile for the prisoner. He wore a stern expression and seemed to take his job as keeper most seriously.The tone of his "Come out here!" command needed no reply.

Ebelshauser knew where he was being taken. He was disgusted at the way they had chosen to spring their questions in an effort to make him confess something he did not know. Even if he did he would stick to his pleas of ignorance. The questioning officers ought to have known better. Could they conceive of an Englishman betraying his fellow countrymen to the enemy? "No, of course not," he could hear them reply indignantly. Then why should they compel and expect him, as a German, to forego his duties?

He was ushered into the large square flooded with daylight. It was the prison yard with a bright blue sky as a ceiling. Standing or seated along one side of a long rectangular table were a number of English and French officers, and one who appeared to wear the uniform of Italy. Their immaculate dress loaned a rather pleasant note of gaiety to an otherwise grave and serious court of inquisition.

Unperturbed, Ebelshauser walked up to the table without the slightest sign of haste or fear. A huge map of Europe was the only change that immediately caught his eyes. But map or no map, he was prepared for the renewed examination. He had made up his mind to show these gentlemen how little he knew about the German positions. He was thankful for one thing, however. A good breath of fresh air was compensation enough for enduring another ordeal.

Standing and facing his unrelenting questioners, he presented the picture of a bewildered young man, though fully aware of the seriousness of his position. His expression was that of a boy, yet his features were hardened as a result of the past year. His eyes stared sadly, first at his inquisitors, then into empty space. His cheeks were hollow and his chin seemed more prominent. His uniform hung loose on his meager body.

His hair was dishevelled; it was so dark in his cell he could not comb it. He looked old, though he was only 19. His shoulders drooped as if carrying too heavy a burden. His lips had long forgotten how to smile. Distress and defiance were in his heart as the questioning began anew.

"Your name is Gustav Ebelshauser, isn't it?"

"Yes, sir."

"How funny," he thought after giving his reply. It was always the same English officer who started the grilling. "This is the third time on the third morning that he is asking me the same question. He ought to know my name by now."

"You said you were born in Lausanne, Switzerland. Is this correct?"

"Yes, sir."

"I understand your mother tongue is French, but you volunteered your services to the German army. Do you still maintain this to be true?"

"Yes, sir."

"Now tell me when, I mean, what year and what month did you join the forces?"

"September 1915."

"If you are of the 1898 class, you were then only 17 years of age?"

"Yes, sir."

"When were you sent to the front?"

"May 1916."

"You mean to say that you have been about one year in the fighting line?"

"Yes, sir."

"With what regiment?"

"Seventeenth Bavarian."

"What company were you in?"

"Third."

"What was your first station when you joined that company?"

"In Flanders."

"This is most exasperating," retorted the English officer as he cast a glance toward his colleagues. Turning again to the prisoner he added angrily, "I'm telling you for the third time, Flanders is big. You understand? What was the name of the town or city nearest to your position? Was it Ypres? Or Lille? Or some other place?"

"I don't remember," Ebelshauser replied, accentuating each of the words.

"Have you always had such a short memory?" the officer asked sarcastically.

"I don't know," came the laconic answer.

The Englishman was visibly annoyed and showed a strong desire to be excused from further proceedings. A French captain or general, Ebelshauser could not tell, came to the rescue and picked up the questioning, this time in French. Everything went smoothly until the query of his exact whereabouts in Flanders was brought up again.

"Come on, young man. Don't tell me you don't remember."

"We were never told the town or city we were in."

"Oh, yes, but you must have seen the name of it at the railway station, no?"

"I don't recall any name."

"If I were you I would give a better answer rather than miss another meal."

"I wish I could, but I swear I don't know."

"Come, come, here is a big map. Let me help you."

Taking hold of a rod he pointed at various spots, asking time and again, "Were you here? Did you pass there?"

"Perhaps I did, but I cannot say for sure."

"Have you been at one place all the time?"

"No, not always."

"Where were you besides Flanders?"

"At the Somme, as I said yesterday."

"How long were you there?"

"About one month."

"Around what time?"

"August or September of last year, I don't know exactly."

"And where did you go next?"

"We returned to Flanders."

"But, my dear young man, as my colleague already has told you, Flanders is the name of a whole region." It was obvious that the Frenchman, too, was becoming tired and impatient.

"Yes, I understand."

"Fine, then!" Once more the officer grabbed the rod and this time pointed at Arras.

"Here is where we are at present, but where did you come from? I mean, from what town if you only arrived the very morning you got caught?"

"If I am not mistaken, we passed Lille on our way down here."

"Now, now," the Frenchman remarked in a most jovial mood, "your memory is not so bad after all. Maybe the prospect of a good meal combined with your appetite will yet loosen your tongue. Just a little bit more information and the reward is yours for the asking."

A short pause ensued during which all the officers crowded together at one end of the table to hold a conference in hushed tones. Ebelshauser guessed they were discussing ways and means to make their prisoner say what they wanted to hear. The French officer rushed back while the others took their time returning to their former places.

"The number 17 you have on your shoulder straps indicates the number of your regiment, doesn't it?"

"Yes, sir."

"Well, tell me how strong is a regiment?"

"Twelve companies."

Ebelshauser was certain that his questioner knew more than he did. He instinctively felt they were probably testing him to take revenge should he make a false statement. He kept a stolid, calm and most innocent face.

"How strong is one of your companies?"

"About 200 or 250 men, I guess."

"What other regiments came along with yours to take up position on the night of your arrival?"

"I don't know."

"What is the location of your artillery in this sector?"

"I couldn't tell. I didn't have a chance to see them."

"Were they alongside your line or more to the rear?"

"I just told you, I don't know anything about the artillery."

"All right, then, but what part of the sector is now occupied by your company?"

"If I knew," Ebelshauser said with a smile, "I wouldn't have gotten lost and would still be there."

"In other words, you insist on keeping your knowledge and secrets to yourself. Perfectly all right, young man, we are not in a hurry. We can wait until tomorrow. In the meantime it's rather regrettable, but we are compelled to leave your diet of bread and water unchanged until further notice. I am warning you for your own good, though, that you'd better come to your senses and change your mind. Let this be my friendly advice to you and I hope that we shall not find you so stubborn tomorrow morning."

Turning to the guard, he commanded, "Take him away!"

When six days of intense grilling brought no other results than disgust and disappointment, the high military dignitaries at last decided to give up their questioning, regarding their prisoner as a hopeless case. That same evening Ebelshauser was served with a decent meal for the first time since his capture. At the suggestion of his faithful guard, he even received a second helping. For the prisoner it was a revelation. They had failed with bread and water, he thought; now they would try to get the best of him with plenty of food. However, so far as he was concerned, food or money would not succeed in making him change his mind. Even if he was "in the know," he would never turn traitor.

At five o'clock the following morning he was awakened from a heavy slumber by the little Scotsman who was eager to present him with a royal breakfast.

"For me? No mistake?"

"Yes, for you," replied the guard with his bright, open smile. Ebelshauser could hardly believe his eyes. The sight of the overloaded tray reminded him of home.

"Get dressed and ready to go when I call you again," the guard said while taking away the tray a short time later. "In about 20 minutes you'll be leaving on a long trip."

After his hearty meal Ebelshauser was marched through the darkened corridors of the old prison for the last time. Outside he once more breathed nature's purifying air. Placed in the custody of two mounted cavalrymen he was ordered to take a position between the two horses. On his way out the prison gate closed behind him.

Riding comfortably across country, the cavalrymen appeared absolutely unconcerned about their prisoner, except when the latter lagged behind. This lingering put them both in a bad mood, especially when compelled to slow up for a while.

"Come on, it's no time for a rest," one of them said while lighting a cigarette. "We are still a long way off."

Bracing up after a brief stop, Ebelshauser rose to his feet with renewed effort to resume the seemingly endless journey. His breakfast had been digested long ago and he was hungry again. There was a hole in his stomach that sorely needed filling. He had been marching for hours now and the short pauses, most unwillingly accorded him, had made him more tired than anything else. Deeply underlined and sunken in their sockets, his eyes had lost their natural glossiness. There was not a sparkle left in them. He was alarmed at his own weakening.

Could he stand it? How he had laughed at this question from one of his guards. Not only had he underestimated the distance, but he had not given a thought to the terrible condition of the path he was to follow. No matter how badly damaged, a real road would have been much better than this track through fields and grassless meadows. Every now and then the thick mud cleaved in a pasty mass to his feet. He was almost unable to lift his heavy boots from the clay-like ground.

For a second time he broke down, falling senseless to the earth. Dismounting, his guards rushed up to him and sponged his pale face with cold water to revive him. They unhooked the safety pins on his tunic for the buttons were all gone. He began to breathe easier, but it took quite a while before he came to.

"Feeling better now?" One of the cavalrymen wanted to show concern.

"Not quite. Please let me rest here for a while yet." He felt like going to sleep.

"But don't you see? It's fast growing dark and we'd better hurry."

"Is it still very far?"

"I don't know for sure, maybe an hour or two depending how fast we can go."

"Come on, man," the other escort said, "get on your feet. It won't do you any good to pass the night here."

Was the guard sympathizing? Ebelshauser did not believe so for his face remained stern. He simply wished to finish the job. With supreme effort and willpower, the prisoner bit his lip and rose again to continue the march. With bruised, swollen feet, he finally reached the camp more dead than alive. And even though the torture of the trek was over, his suffering was only beginning.

For a long while the single line moved slowly toward one corner of the camp in silence. Smoke from a steaming cauldron was like an inspiring beacon to the snake-like parade. Two Tommies in khaki uniforms and trench coats were manipulating the ladles. Hot liquid was poured into containers of all makes and descriptions which each prisoner had the luck to provide himself with. One ladle per man and four hard biscuits constituted a full ration for the time being. Too much to die, not enough to live.

It began to rain again. The ugly weather was enough to bring the already sad spirit of the prisoners to its lowest ebb. The prospect of another long, stormy night made them shiver with apprehension. How would they stand up, so unprotected, against the unchained elements?

Ebelshauser felt miserable. Compared with the countless atrocious pictures that had met his eyes during his career as a soldier, the present scene was but a natural sequence in the various episodes which had preceded. The film of never-to-be-forgotten memories was a faithful reproduction of the war itself. It was a series of illustrations of his actual experience, showing his progressive transformation. But it was evolution of human progress in the reverse sense.

"Where did they get you?" The man behind him was asking the question for the second time.

"What did you say?" Ebelshauser turned absentmindedly toward his companion.

"Are you deaf? I asked where it was you were caught."

"No need to raise your voice, I hear you. At Monchy, near Arras."

"That's funny, they trapped us there, too, but we haven't seen any of your men. When did they put you in?"

"Oh, about 10 days ago. Maybe they're gone now, back to their old positions. How long have you been here?"

"Since yesterday morning. Three full trucks of us came directly from the front."

"How long in this sector?"

"Only three days, but say, how is it that you're the only 17 around here? How did it happen?"

"I don't know what became of the others."

"How did you come alone? Why were you separated from the others?"

"I don't know that either, except perhaps on account of my French."

Ebelshauser thought it wise not to tell the real story. It would have forced him into an endless speech that would have been interrupted with unavoidable questions and long explanations. He was not really in a mood for talking. Tired and hungry, he wanted to be left alone. But his companion kept the conversation going.

"So you're one of those mixtures, what do you know about that! From where? Alsace, I suppose, only they got you on the wrong side. Say, this is interesting. Tell me more about it. You certainly got pinched right and left. My name is Roeder, Karl Roeder, from Dusseldorf in the Rhineland. What's yours?"

"Ebelshauser, Gustav Ebelshauser from Lausanne, Switzerland."

He winced and glanced down at the ground for a moment. "What a pest," he thought. "Just the guy I was looking for." In vain he looked for a chance to step forward and take another place, but it was impossible to move. The food line had come to a dead stop. It was no use stepping aside to fall in the ankle-deep mud. There was no escape and he would have to tolerate this man's flowing babbling.

"Oh, near Geneva, isn't it?" Roeder seemed wound up. "Boy, my uncle has been all over Switzerland. He was a traveling salesman for a big chocolate manufacturing concern in Stuttgart. Some job he had, traveling all around with all expenses paid. Pretty soft, heh? I haven't heard from him for a long time. I guess he had to join the ranks. Switzerland is a lovely place, he told me. Why didn't you stay there? Couldn't you?"

"I suppose so, but I, er ... volunteered." Ebelshauser was becoming more and more annoyed by his neighbor's rattling.

"Haha! You must have been crazy, unless you had it in mind to learn German at the cheapest rate. Only you miscalculated and paid a higher price than you ever anticipated. In fact, you ought to get a refund for the whole course when we get back some day."

"Listen, you!" Ebelshauser turned an angry face to Roeder. "The sooner you stop those silly remarks, the better. Why not shut up altogether? You seem to be the only one enjoying this situation while all the others are sad and heartbroken."

"Come, come, Eselheuzer ..."

"Ebelshauser is the correct name."

"Oh, come on, don't get mad. Can't you take a joke? Don't you think I have feelings, too? But honest, let me tell you something. Making fun of everything is the only thing that keeps me going. If I were to become serious and start to think and worry about all the things that are happening around us, I'd go crazy in no time. Try to laugh this off, it'll do you a lot of good. Why keep brooding when there is nothing you can do to change your position? Am I right or am I right? Push the load off your chest and get wise to yourself. You won't feel half as bad or depressed if you follow my advice and start laughing it off right now."

During the short silence that followed, Ebelshauser had to admit to himself that the man was, after all, applying the best philosophy of common sense under the circumstances. He was a lighthearted chap, but that was his nature. A perpetual and optimistic smile seemed to be glued to his face, and there was not a hint of meanness in his gleaming eyes. Satisfied with his examination, he decided to take a friendlier attitude.

"In a way I must admit you are right," Ebelshauser replied in a softer tone. "But it isn't given to everybody to take it on the chin with a smile. Each of us has a different nature. You ought to be thankful for yours. I have often tried and even succeeded to a certain degree, but tonight I simply can't bring it over myself to be in a pleasant mood. I can't tell you when I felt more depressed, more despairing and more disgusted with life and everything else than just now. If I had eyes that did not see what is going on around me, well, I wouldn't know any better and perhaps I would smile, too, but ..."

"I know how it is, brother," Roeder interrupted. "But my smiling face seems to have misled you. I must confess that my attempt to cheer you up has utterly failed, and why? Because my smile is not genuine, just a disguise to hide what's really going on within. I'm not a bit different from you or the others. I just don't show it, and that's the whole damn difference."

Three more days and nights passed. To the prisoners it seemed an eternity. All of them were in a physical and mental state of utter exhaustion. It was a wonder to find any of them still standing. Fear of a merciless and ugly death in the surrounding mire kept them on their feet. But for three of the prisoners who had collapsed during the second night, the extreme penalty was paid for their weakness. Unable to bear up and carry on under the strain, they had fallen out of the standing line. Had any of their comrades tried to pull them out of the mud? No one could say.

Someone must have stumbled over their feet and kicked them from the narrow path, judging from their peculiar positions. They must have fallen straight down, like freshly cut trees. Not a sound had been heard and no one called for help. They had died noiselessly right where they fell. The bodies still were lying untouched on the same spot. Many of the men had raised their voices to complain, but the English remained impassible, uninterested in their pleas.

If nothing else, these corpses had served as a warning. Their presence in the camp had empowered those still alive with a greater spirit of strength. The sight of their dead comrades brought them closer together, and more than ever they became united in a common effort to resist and hold on to the end.

They stood pressed against each other, body to body, in one compact row. The head man of this giant human serpent seemed to carry the whole load without any support. The last man, forming the tail, rested his back against one of the tall wooden poles holding up the high wall of barbed wire thrown around the camp.

To make sure that no one else fell to the ground unnoticed, they had placed hands on each other's shoulders. The long, curved, single line was thus unbroken. Except for this endless row of men of all shapes and sizes, the vast area appeared absolutely deserted. There was no house, barrack or shelter of any kind, and the men were exposed to the weather which had been anything but good. After the first day the rains had set in and poured down in torrents for hours.

To keep warm and help fight off sleep, the men tramped on the spots where they stood — the only motion they could resort to in safety. They were hungry and tired, wet to the bone and cold. Like drowning men hoping to be saved they were holding out. After being rescued from the bloody carnage of the battlefield and spirited away, they were not willing to die now if they could help it.

At last, shortly before noon on the fourth day, a score of English lorries appeared at the entrance of the camp. Seeing them drive up the men instinctively perceived that the trucks had come for them. The time of their relief had finally come.

Soldiers with fixed bayonets jumped from the trucks the moment they came to a halt. There were about 10 escorts for each lorry. As far as the prisoners were concerned, one guard would have been sufficient. They did not care about their destination. No matter where they were sent the next station could not be worse than the one they were about to leave.

At the sound of a bugle the English, who had been rambling about idly, were brought to order and marched to the southern entrance of the camp. As soon as every sentry had taken his place the gate was opened. An officer signalled to the prisoners to step forward. Keeping formation, the progress of the procession was very slow.

The leading man had some trouble threading his way through the mud. But once a path was made it was easier for the others to follow in his footsteps. Thus the gate was reached. From there the prisoners passed between two lines of troopers. Although loaded to capacity there were not enough lorries to take care of them all. More than a thousand prisoners were left behind. It was a strange and tragic parting.

Ebelshauser and Roeder were among the fortunate ones taken for the ride. In spite of the shape they were in there was a feeling of joy over their transfer. "Where to now?" they asked each other, hoping above everything else for decent quarters and a good square meal.

Like the rest of his companions, Ebelshauser had become used to the drab existence of a prisoner of war. Laboring under the English flag was no special distinction. The French or Italians might have dealt with their own prisoners in different fashion. But on the whole the rough treatment, lack of adequate lodging, poor quality and scarcity of food, and finally, the utter disregard of a prisoner as a human being must have been the same in practically every one of the belligerent nations' camps.

The monotony of his daily tasks was getting on Ebelshauser's nerves. Not a single minute was left for relaxation during the day. After returning to their quarters at night, the prisoners spent evening after evening brooding or pondering over their situation. The most exasperating feeling was being cut off entirely from the outside world, set apart in a sphere of their own. More than ever before the realization came to their idle minds of the complete failure and utter nullity and insignificance of their personalities. Even their names had been erased from the register of men. They were responding to numbers now. Like sheep without wills of their own they were subjected to the whimsical, capricious commands of their masters. Thoughts wandered back home. They all longed for peace.

Despite the boredom, time passed in its relentless course. Days became weeks and weeks became months. Spring was succeeded by summer. Paying no attention to the war, nature pursued its eternal process of regeneration. Even the prisoners were thankful for the return of warmer days.

But during the spring of 1917, Pentecost was the day that would never fade from Ebelshauser's memory. On that day the prisoners were made to work harder and longer than ever before. The English had obviously prepared for it in advance. Contrary to routine, they were roused from their heavy sleep before sunrise and let out of the camp with nothing but a cup of bitter, lukewarm tea. It required more than two hours of fast marching to reach the immense lumber yard where they were put to work. With no lunch and only half an hour's rest, they left the place at sunset and returned to the camp. Because of the late hour they had to turn in without supper. Starved and nearly exhausted to the limit, they fell on their cots that night more dead than alive, searching for a reason for such undeserved punishment.

On a warm sunny day in August, it was Ebelshauser's turn again to take up cleaning duties in the camp, consisting of 20 barracks. Each week a different man, one for each building, was assigned to the cleaning job. Compared to the outside work this was considered a light and restful occupation. Naturally, he was delighted at the opportunity.

For a whole week he could dispose of his time almost as he pleased. But the first morning, much to his disdain, he was called upon to sweep and scrub the wooden stairway at the main entrance of the camp, giving access to the road below. Standing at the top of the stairs he began dusting off the boards. After a while he stopped to stretch his stiff limbs and took a long glance at the surrounding countryside.

The destructive vandalism of war had not reached this far yet. The whole region was still intact and lay before him like an oasis of peace and tranquility. The serenity of the panorama was inspiring. It had the same effect on him as that of a piece of metal drawn to a powerful magnet. He felt irresistibly pulled toward the wide open space that spelled for him the beautiful words of freedom and independence.

For a moment he was almost overcome by the temptation. Had it not been for the guard he would have run away. Surely he could find some sympathetic Frenchman to loan him an old suit of clothes. Once dressed up he would beat it straight through to the Swiss border. Knowing the language as he did ought to make it easy to get there.

With regret he was reminded of his work by a whistle from the sentry. Angrily, he plunged himself back into reality. "Damn it," he murmured. "Disgusting watchdogs, they're all over the place."

As he reached the lower steps a group of five women was coming his way. Interested, he stopped abruptly in his work and turned his attention to them. They were talking loudly, but too fast and swallowing the words. He strained his ears but was unable to guess the subject of their conversation, animated with all sorts of motions and gesticulations. Suddenly, realizing that he was looking at them, the women became silent and stared back at him. As they drew nearer they began to make faces and call him names.

"*Sale Boche!*" said the first.

"*Cochon!*" shouted the next.

"*Tete caree! Chien enrage! Barbare! On devrait vous pendre tous! Bandit! Meurtrier! Salaud! Et cet individu qui a le culot de nous regarder ainsi, il n'a pas honte?*"

Ebelshauser felt the torrential rain of invectives falling on his head. He managed to remain calm without turning his eyes away from them. His nonchalance only served to increase their wrath. Again they began a long series of abusive catcalls. Unperturbed, he held his position without the slightest betrayal of his personal feelings. Brought to exasperation, one of the women stepped forward.

"*Espece d'animal!*" she screamed in his face as if to scare him. "*Une balle dans ta peau d'ours et tu serais liquide, sale Boche que tu es!*"

"But what did I do to you to merit your insults?" Ebelshauser then broke loose in French. "Am I responsible for the war? You hate me, a man you have never seen before in your life. Why? I am only a human being like you. Why pass your hatred and judgment on a poor fellow like me?"

Taking advantage of his mother tongue, he delivered his short speech to the consternation and amazement of his female assailants. The women were reduced to silence, looking at each other as if unable to comprehend. He was enjoying their surprise and about to return to work when one of the camp officers appeared.

"Captain Robson!" The tall and delicately built woman to whom Ebelshauser had spoken rushed up to the officer. "That man annoyed us," she said, pointing at him.

"What's the matter?" asked the captain who did not understand her voluble French.

"This man, bad man, he fresh to us," another in the group explained with a few English words she had picked up since her contact with British soldiers.

"Come to my office," the captain ordered, "and you come along, too."

Without another word he turned, followed by the five women. Ebelshauser, broom in hand, kept a few steps behind. The severe look of the officer was far from reassuring. He would have to do quite some explaining to convince him of his innocence.

"Hurley, hey Hurley!" the captain shouted as he walked through the gate.

The man came running and entered the first barrack which served as an office.

"Hurley, find out what this is all about."

"Yes, sir!" Looking at the women, he asked, "*Qu'est-il arrive?*"

"*Cet homme nous a insultees alors que nous passions.*"

"They say he insulted them."

"What has he to say in his defense?"

Translating faithfully, Hurley addressed Ebelshauser. "*Was haben Sie zu sagen?*" Then remembering that the prisoner spoke French, he started the question over.

"*Qu'avez-vous a dire pour votre dedence?*"

In the same language Ebelshauser began his own explanation of the incident. But he found himself interrupted by the women at the end of each sentence. Hurley could not cope with the situation and began to get mixed up in his translations. For a few minutes Ebelshauser's voice was drowned. The women wanted to speak all at once and started to shout. Losing patience, the officer brought the hearing to a close in the midst of the confusion.

"Stop! That's enough now!" Robson's powerful fist slammed down on his desk and the whole room shook under the mighty stroke. Everyone was brought to instant silence. They awaited the decision.

"Gustav Ebelshauser!" He addressed the prisoner in a most severe and solemn tone. "Your own confession proves that you have violated the law of which you were aware. No prisoner is allowed to speak to a French civilian, male or female. Regardless of the nature of your conversation there was no excuse for you to address these ladies. You'll have to stand the penalty for your transgression with six days of solitary confinement on bread and water."

After a short pause, he added, "Hurley, translate and get the guards."

With smiles of vindication on their lips, the women peered at the prisoner as he was led away by two guards. Triumphantly, they left the camp in a happy mood. Ebelshauser, on the other hand, saw himself the victim of a mean trick.

To his complete amazement, he had barely been placed in the cell when he was recalled to appear before his judge for further questioning. This time Hurley was able to take it easy and give a better translation of the account from the mouth of the defendant. Then followed a long, hushed conversation between the two Englishmen. Hurley cleared his throat a couple of times before he spoke.

"*Pas de punition, comprenez-vous?*"

"Me not going to cell?" Ebelshauser brought forth in English to make sure he had understood correctly.

"Yes, no punishment or jail for you," Hurley repeated. "Captain Robson says you are not to blame. He might have done the same thing in your place. But remember, don't let it happen again."

"Yes, sir, I understand. Thank you."

Surprised and delighted over the first good break he had received since joining the army, Ebelshauser went back to his unfinished job and resumed sweeping.

The prisoners were housed in wooden barracks resting on piles which were designed to keep them dry. There were two symmetrical rows of 10 buildings facing each other. And every entrance had two or three wooden steps leading to the main and sole artery of the camp.

Dead tired from a long, sweltering day, the last group of prisoners was coming back from work. As they passed the main gate the guards counted them. They dragged themselves across the compound and reached their quarters, unable to stand on their feet a minute longer. Those lying in the top bunks barely had the strength to get there.

"I hope they forget the whistle tonight," Ebelshauser remarked. "I'm shot to pieces. God, what a day!"

"It wouldn't be so bad with proper rest and nourishment," Roeder said. But a baby gets more than we do. How the hell can they expect us to work on empty stomachs?"

Everyone was giving way to his grievances. There was no place like the barrack for that. Outside they had to keep quiet. But here among themselves they could unload to their hearts' content. Here, too, their solidarity was each night established anew. After the lights went out their weary and shattered brains began to scheme the most audacious conspiracies and projects of escape. Usually, though, they fell asleep in the middle of their discussions. The next morning they awoke with splitting headaches but without the slightest recollection of their plots, and went off to work more disgusted and discouraged than ever.

Huber's face was white with anger.

"Hang them all, I'm going to take it easy this time, even if it takes me two hours to get there."

Responding to the signal, the prisoners were getting ready. Huber remained lying in his upper bunk. The men of the other barracks already were on their way to the yard. They knew better. Once before they had tried to ignore the call and the result proved deplorable. They had been chased out and for a whole week their daily provisions had been cut down to the bare necessities. They were unwilling to repeat the experiment.

"Come on, Huber. Why get yourself into trouble?" Ebelshauser was urging the recalcitrant, but without success.

"They can go to hell so far as I'm concerned," retorted Huber, turning his back.

"Suit yourself, but I warned you." About to leave, Ebelshauser stopped short of the door when he heard the voice of a guard.

"Hey, you there, come on!" The sentry was shouting from behind the fence. He could see through the back window into the room.

"Say, Huber, the guard is calling you. He sees you lying there."

Huber suddenly seemed to have come to his senses. He jumped down from the bunk and pulled on his pants and shoes. Ebelshauser was still waiting for him, although everyone else was already outside.

"Come on, come on, hurry up!" shrieked the guard again.

"All right, you bloody bastard ..." Huber shouted in return.

The guard looked horrified. He grabbed his whistle and blew the alarm. In the fraction of a minute the entire camp was thrown into an uproar. Out of nowhere a squad of 25 troopers rushed to the spot. Ebelshauser, fortunately, had by now joined his comrades who, for the moment, were left standing in the yard under watch of a reinforced escort.

Sweeping through the camp the guards soon surrounded the barrack. With fixed bayonets they entered the room and fell on the lone prisoner. More surprised than frightened, Huber did not know what was happening to him. An innocent, boyish smile was on his lips as he passed the gate. Lifting his head he glanced at his comrades. It was a pitiful look of utter bewilderment. Like a criminal, he appeared lost amid the horde of soldiers leading him away.

The charge brought against him was unthinkable and he would have to stand chastisement for the insult. Huber was given no chance to defend himself. He could have explained. He did not even know the meaning of the word he had spoken. He had picked it up from the guards without the slightest idea of its significance. In fact, he thought it to be a mere name or surname that was constantly used by the guards when addressing the prisoners. In the end, Huber was taken to the captain's quarters to await further instructions.

Huber was put in a cell for three days. On the morning of the fourth day he made his appearance in the ranks with a face that bore the brutal marks of his jailers. His left eye was entirely closed. The left upper jaw and part of the nose and forehead were so swollen that the eye could not be seen. There were scratches all over his face and a clot of blood behind his right ear. He could hardly speak. Four front teeth, as he showed later on, had been knocked out. The first night in the cell he had been beaten with fists and feet to insensibility. He was physically too weak to ward off the attack of five strong men. Thus had been avenged the honor of a British subject.

"Who was it yesterday?" Ebelshauser asked.

"Georg Siebentritt, the old man," Roeder replied. "It's the second time for him this week."

"Yes, I know. God, they ought to do something about it."

"They might try when it's too late. They don't give a hang about us."

"Disgusting! I hope they get it in the neck someday."

"The same old team song, and what does it mean? Nothing, so long as we remain in their hands. Sometimes I wonder if we wouldn't be better off with the French or Italians."

"No, sir. I certainly wouldn't take a chance on that. If the English are the best, can you imagine the situation in French or Italian captivity?"

"Maybe you're right. Poor fellow, they should have brought him back to the camp."

"Listen, Roeder, these English have no heart. They'd rather let a fellow die than bring him back to his quarters."

Fifty strong that morning, they had left the camp for their work. The usual meager breakfast had helped very little to put them on their feet. There was not much strength in one or two cups of bitter tea and a quarter loaf of white army bread. That's all they had, and they were even supposed to keep half of this small portion for the evening. Every one of them repeatedly had shown the willpower to try it, but hunger had been so great that no one was able to hold out. Consequently, there was nothing left over at night.

For the past 10 or 12 days it had taken them almost two hours to get to the place of work. They were unloading railroad cars filled with freshly cut stones. Provided with long forks they were kept constantly bent over the large heaps of rock that were to be transferred from the seemingly bottomless cars to the ground. Immediately after arriving they were divided into groups of three or four, depending upon the size of the car to be unloaded. Ebelshauser was working in company with Roeder, Albert Wege and Friedrich Weiss. Being from the same barrack they were better acquainted, even though they might not be friends. As prisoners, the tie of brotherhood and their allegiance to the fatherland held them close together. Comradeship loaned them strength.

At 10:30 the customary whistle announced a 10-minute rest. The majority used this short interruption as a breathing spell. Too tired to do anything else, they sat or stretched out with their eyes closed. Others of stronger constitution chatted or smoked cigarettes.

"Why don't you try it once? It really helps. For the moment you don't feel hungry at all." Weiss had been after him for quite some time, but Ebelshauser had steadfastly declined accepting the invitation.

"Not today, thanks. I don't know but I don't see the point yet. How can a smoke stop anyone from getting hungry?"

"But it does," Weiss insisted. "A cigarette always makes me feel swell. By the way, have we enough greens?"

"Well, I picked what I found," answered Wege, "though there isn't much left on this side of the road."

"We have our pockets full, Roeder and I," Ebelshauser said. "I think it'll do for today. See? I got stung this time. The Wolf went after me. He can't stand stepping out of rank, so I had to stop picking."

Every guard had a nickname. Wolf, the tallest of them all, was renowned for his strictness. He never tired in his efforts to maintain discipline. Running back and forth along the column of workers he yelled at the men to stop their loud talking. Seldom did his eagle eyes fail to spot the man out of step. With one mighty jump the Wolf reached him. The prisoner knew the meaning of his sudden appearance and instinctively corrected his gait.

Some of the guards were intolerable. One of these was Pest, the most hated guard in the outfit. Of average height with a tendency toward obesity, he was always picking on someone. No matter how well the work was done he would find cause for criticism. His favorite trick was to catch a man taking a minute's break while work was going on. He delighted in reporting the fellow and then seeing him punished. Whenever Pest was around the men were even afraid to breathe.

Stench, on the other hand, was a nice fellow, but one could smell his presence a mile away. Did the stinking emanations come from his body or from his uniform? It was hard to tell.

Potato was the guard with a nose so large that his face was hardly noticeable. Tomato was the one with purple skin. Oxen had bulging, gloating eyes. The list was a long one, and most of the nicknames fit spendidly the personalities of their bearers.

The signal was given to resume work. Once more the stones began to fly. There seemed to be no end to the task. Perspiration coated foreheads, cheeks and necks. Silence fell over the men and their lips remained tightly closed. They breathed enough dust as it was. The drudgery went on until the next signal which blew at noon sharp. How welcome a substantial lunch would have been at this hour! Instead, they were only permitted again to lie down.

In spite of this, through ingenuity they learned to provide themselves with the raw materials needed for the preparation of something that mimicked a hot meal. However, they were submitting their organisms to a new process of alimentation that was to prove harmful in the long run. But hunger had to be stopped, even at the risk of endangering their lives. On the way to and from the camp, when permitted or unobserved, they would hunt for and gather all kinds of possible and impossible ingredients which, when boiled, might result in the production of some digestible pottage. The odor and taste of such concoctions were most disagreeable. But the so-called soup found its way down to their growling bellies.

A large, dirty metal kettle had been found in a nearby ditch. It had been quite a job to scrub it clean. Brackish yellow water from a puddle helped in finishing the cleansing operation, though some dirt still was left around the kettle's edges. But it would boil down with the rest. Everyone had brought his share of wood. A fire already was burning. All they had to do was prepare the mixture.

Ebelshauser and seven other comrades stood or squatted around the fire. First they had to examine the stuff. Approved ingredients were then placed in the bucket. A few items were rejected as unfit. By contrast, their guards sat comfortably a short distance away, feasting on sandwiches.

"No, Max, don't put that leather in. Come on, throw it away."

Max Blumtritt was holding what appeared to be part of a belt. He had picked it up on the railroad tracks below the car they were unloading. Roeder did not want him adding it to the stew.

"We'll have enough the way it is. See, I told you. The water is now foaming and turning white underneath. Give me a spoon. There, we'll have the cream out in no time."

Standing over the kettle, the steam was blowing in Roeder's face. He waved his hands several times, then plunged in the spoon. He began to skim the boiling surface of the water, throwing out a cream-like mass of yellow-brown color. The water had become clearer, though it was still stained yellow. This was due to the mixture of clay and sand that was part of the ingredients.

"I heard you could get some oil or fat by boiling leather," Blumtritt said, still clutching his find.

"Yes, perhaps, but it might spoil everything else," remarked Wege. "Let's not try something we know nothing about. We haven't got too much the way it is. Let's keep it that way."

"Okay, Max? Don't put it in."

Away flew the leather for Hermann Dingendahl, an expert in the matter, had spoken the last word. He had found a way to make grass look and taste almost like real spinach. He stirred the preparation with a long wooden stick, giving the kettle's contents a careful examination. Roeder stood by, watching.

"It's too late for the leather anyway — the 'lettuce' is already softening. See? The water is turning green. It'll be done in a few minutes, just in time. Get your containers."

This was a superfluous order for everyone already was standing and holding dixies of all kinds and descriptions. They looked anxiously at the boiling pottage.

"No meat this time. That corned beef would be all right today."

Berthold Heinze could not get over Dingendahl's decision of a week ago. He had found an open can next to the heap of stones where he was working. The meat was partly spoiled. Decomposition already had brought a swarm of worms, but in taking off the top he figured the lower part still would have been in good condition. It was a shame to throw the fortune away, but under Dingendahl's final judgment in the case he had done so most unwillingly.

"You'd be pushing up daisies by now," Dingendahl said. "There's nothing more dangerous than rotten meat."

"But we did it once before. Don't you remember, in that trench while wrecking one of those dugouts?"

"I know, Berthold, but it was luck that we didn't get to our graves."

"Say, how about some salt? Here, I brought some along. Got it from the cook this morning."

"Grand idea! Perhaps someone has something else to add?"

Still busy stirring, Dingendahl looked around but nobody moved. What could they have? So far as they were concerned nothing could be added to the overstuffed mixture. The expressions on their drawn faces told the story. They patiently waited for their daily drug, eyes riveted on the mysterious, boiling stew. No matter what the look or taste, it was better than nothing at all. Their bellies were clamoring for food, for satisfaction. They had lived on substitutes of all kinds for so long that they were ready to adapt themselves to the circumstances, absorbing in quantity if not in quality, the diabolical rations put at their disposal.

"Achtung!" ordered Dingendahl. "Who's first? But wait, let me see if the vegetable is done well enough."

With his stick he brought forth a good portion of the green mass from which dirty yellow water dripped back into the pot. Taking hold of a few nettle leaves he put them in his mouth. A grimace came over his face as he chewed. Finally he swallowed the substance, but not without visible effort.

"Swell!" he then declared. "The best we've had for some time. Maybe they were new plants. They're quite soft, almost as tender as spinach. It'll glide down easily. A little broth after it and everything is hunky-dory."

They all lined up behind Heinze. Dingendahl doled out the soup for he was known as a fair divider. Each received his share before squatting back on the ground. Ebelshauser spit out the first spoonful and a few others followed his example. Wege threw his portion away.

"I'd rather starve than eat this rotten stuff. I don't know how you can get it down."

"Do you think we're enjoying it?" Ebelshauser asked. "We just force ourselves. How long we're going to stand it is another question."

They barely had time to finish before the whistle blew and work resumed again. In spite of the rest, most of them were hardly able to stand. The hot sun had sapped their remaining strength. Yet, as if by some sort of miracle, they found themselves on their feet. The shovelling of the stones had to go on.

"You mean it?"

"Of course. What do you think we're waiting here for?"

"My God, look at those sinister and dirty faces. You don't have to be at war to get scared of those black fellows."

"You said it. They're the most dangerous of all, these Senegalese. It's a good thing we won't have to face them."

"But why do they keep them under guard when they're such good fighters for the Allies? It's funny, don't you think?"

"The French don't take any chances with these birds. Perhaps they're afraid they might change sides and start fighting in the wrong line. See, they keep them in camps just as they do with us. They must be evacuating on our account, I guess. Who knows where they're taking them?"

"Look at the last group just coming out. They seem covered with feathers to make them appear white."

"No, don't you see? They get a rubdown at the gate. It's cotton. I heard they sleep in it to keep warm at night. Boy, it's going to be some job cleaning up that mess."

"And watch the vermin. Brrrrr, it makes me shudder at the thought of it. Some luck we have, from one nest into another."

"Delousing is going to be a tough job with all the dirt they're leaving behind."

"And we were just starting to get clean in the old place."

"Wonder what kind of work they'll give us here, any idea?"

"I don't know and I don't care, so long as I don't see those stones anymore. Maybe we'll go back to our old job of dismantling useless dugouts."

"I don't mind that so much. It's less monotonous. You don't have to stand in one spot the whole damn day. And there's always the chance to pick some grub every now and then."

"There they go. Some column of black, white and blue!"

Ebelshauser, Roeder and the rest paused in their conversation to watch the Senegalese march off under heavy French escort. In complete disorder — four, five or six in a row — the black mass moved forward along the highway. The only thing that could be distinguished clearly of their faces were their glittering white, protruding teeth. From a distance one had the impression that they were smiling. The picture became much different up close. It was best, however, for the prisoners to remain where they were. Approaching the marching column might have been dangerous. Forming a close cordon on both sides were French troops in their blue-gray uniforms. Their white faces were a stark contrast against the background of black. Erect, with fixed bayonets, their vigilant eyes swept the column from one end to the other. Ten more minutes and they disappeared at the next turn of the road.

"Didn't I tell you? Here we go!"

It took them more than eight days to get the dirt removed and bring the new camp to a certain degree of cleanliness. But they would never be able to get rid of the regiments of lice inhabiting the place. They had killed them by the thousands, and those put to death were immediately replaced by a new generation eager to go on exploring. The open cotton mattresses were infested and almost moved by themselves. The first morning they were taken and burned outside the camp. It was unbelievable that the former occupants had been living in such filth. To the prisoners the vermin became a source of constant torment and pain. For weeks their skin was covered with scratches. A lack of water added greatly to their general discomfort. But since this camp was to be their home for some time to come, they had to make the best of it.

"Don't throw it out! It's my turn next."

Every morning these words could be heard all over camp. Happy was the man who was first to use the allotted quantity of clean water, for the same water was to serve for the morning washing of 20 others. The last man always found nothing but a dirty brown liquid. In fairness to all, the prisoners had agreed among themselves to give the chance to be first to someone different each day.

"Oh, come on and hurry up. Don't splash so much, it's too precious."

"Say, are you taking a bath?"

"Take it out, you dropped a louse."

"How am I supposed to get clean with that dirty leftover?"

"You'll get your chance someday, be patient."

"Careful, use it sparingly. There are others coming after you."

Morning after morning there was a riot around the wash basins. Everyone dreaded to be the last. Water had become one of the most precious elements, almost as hard to get as substantial food. Delousing was another problem. So contaminated was the camp that riddance of the vermin was imperative.

All their clothing could not be taken care of in a single operation. It took three weeks for enough water to become available to boil every uniform in the camp. Yet, when the work had been done the lice were still there, just as numerous as before. The prisoners could barely get a wink of sleep. In the morning they beheld a frightful sight. Nearly everyone was covered with scratches and ugly-looking blisters. Insatiable in their appetite, the bloodthirsty lice were sucking the very fluid of life from their weakened and defenseless bodies.

"By jove, I got it this time. Look!" Ebelshauser exhibited his capture.

"You ought to send it to the Berlin Zoo," Roeder said. "It's a real monster."

In spite of the hardships, Roeder still kept a sense of humor. His sound philosophy had done a great deal in keeping him fit. He was one of the few who could boast that he had not yet fainted.

Before Roeder finished speaking, Ebelshauser had extracted the life from the insect. He believed in capital punishment in such a case. Death at short notice was the sentence for any of the vermin he caught. There were times when the chase took the form of a real contest, accompanied by all kinds of exclamations, mostly swearing. Everyone became a hunter within the confines of his own territory. The results were dramatic. Hundreds of beasts were captured in the span of an hour. One by one they began to undress. Every garment was scrutinized. Their eyes were trained and there was no difficulty finding the objects of their search. Active fingers picked, pulled and punched. A stranger might have been inclined to laugh at the spectacle, but the actors' faces were most serious. Before long they were stark naked.

"Can you see any on my back? It itches terribly.

"No, further down ... further ...now to the right ... there ... got it!"

"Yes, but wait ... don't move ... hold it ... there it is ... and what an elephant ... look!"

"Donnerwetter! You must have had a regiment. Your back is one big blister. Go and see the doctor tomorrow. He'll put something on it. What an awful sight!"

"The damn beast! It just slipped between my fingers. I had it! Must have fallen on the floor. You can't see it now."

"Wait, here's another one. Damn it, there it goes between your legs. Can't see it anymore. Just feel around, you'll catch it."

So time passed long into the night. The cleansing was completed, but a day later the biting and itching started all over again. They had rid themselves of the old generation to give a chance to the newcomers.

"They should have burned this camp instead of putting us in after those knights of the dark."

"You said it. Never saw a lousier place in all my life."

"Lousy is right! I hope their own troops are put in here some day to find out for themselves how it feels to fall into a nest of vermin."

"Oh, come on. The blasted English wouldn't even know the difference. If they did they wouldn't have stuck us here. Don't you think the guards are getting their share, too?"

The prisoners were in a fighting mood and rebellion was in the air. It seemed the British high command had closed its ears to complaints of this kind. As in Germany, what did they care about a prisoner's plight so long as they were safe and cuddled in their own quarters? They did not take the time and trouble to investigate. It was only a prison camp and they could not be bothered with such trifles. Their minds were concentrated on quite different problems. The war was still going on. They had to apply all of their knowledge and skill to bringing about the complete annihilation of the hated enemy. One of the guards at the camp painted the perfect picture one day when he said, "You prisoners ought to be glad and thankful that your lives have been spared. You wouldn't kick so much if you were six feet under the ground."

•

On March 21, 1918, the change of life they had so long wished for arrived. Awakened earlier than usual, they stood in the camp yard waiting for orders from the new commandant, a Scotsman of giant proportions. His intelligent face and straight military bearing seemed to contrast strangely with the feminine skirt of his uniform. They had seen many of these Scotsmen among their own guards, but never had an officer appeared so ridiculous in their eyes. At the first sight of him they could hardly restrain themselves from laughing out loud.

"Have you ever seen a thing like that?"

"Ah, but you don't understand. At least they can respond to the call of nature without having to pull down their pants. Very practical."

"A soldier should wear trousers. He is either a man or a woman. This is a grotesque mixture, half and half."

"It's all so silly, a leg exhibition."

"It's more than the legs they're showing off sometimes. One inch higher and the whole business would be exposed. You can almost see it when they move or the wind is blowing."

"Remember the 'old fogey?' That guy certainly was immune to temperature. No matter how cold it was he would sit on a stone and watch us work with his shirt open and nothing on underneath. He certainly didn't mind our observing eyes. I don't know how he could stand it. His skin was blue-green as if it was frozen."

"That's nothing for them. They're trained that way. It's not their fault, though. The funny old tradition must be kept up, I suppose."

"Probably, but do the women in Scotland wear pants? Must be a strange sort of people over there."

In spite of the cheerful mood of the prisoners, an atmosphere of tension and agitation prevailed among the English guards and officers. They were pacing up and down the lines and looking about with apprehensive expressions. The weather was heavy. Gray and black clouds hung how and there was no wind. A light drizzle began falling. Flanked on each side by a subaltern, the giant Scotsman appeared unable to make up his mind or reach a decision. The prisoners had been assembled at his request to be sent out to work. Yet, half an hour had elapsed and still they were standing idly on the same spot.

Suddenly, the loud report of an exploding shell not far off caught the ears of the prisoners. They immediately became more attentive to the distant booming which reached them that morning from the battle front. Some of the guards had told them of rumors about a German offensive planned for that day. As they listened they had the impression that the sound of the cannonade was growing louder, that the raging battle was slowly moving toward their camp.

A new light of hope was shining in their eyes. At last their mighty fatherland was coming out of its winter torpor. They could just imagine the new flame of youth and patriotism moving their countrymen to a fresh, challenging start. The steadily approaching noise of the fighting lines was like sweet music to their ears — bells pealing out their metallic voices of victory. If Germany was victorious they would be going home. It meant the end of their suffering. It meant liberation.

Unexpectedly, two motorcycles appeared on the scene like thunderbolts coming from nowhere. At the fantastic speed they were traveling the two news dispatchers could hardly bring their vehicles to a stop without dragging their feet on the slippery ground. The Scottish officer was already upon them before they could ask for him.

He read the two bulletins quickly, glanced at the two messengers and looked at the papers again for a long time. The two cyclists probably came from different points, but the instructions or news they brought were, no doubt, identical in their import.

The officer finally drew out a pencil and signed the two slips. The messengers departed like two torpedoes in the opposite direction from which they had come. A brief conference followed. When the officer and his subordinates had spoken their last words the guards were summoned to take up their stations.

"Go back to your barracks. Pack up everything and be back in your places in half an hour with all your belongings." The order was given in English, but just to make sure it was also translated for them.

"I told you something was wrong," Roeder said.

"Anyone could smell that," replied Ebelshauser.

"Too bad. It looked as if we were to be made prisoners again by our own men."

"Wonder where they'll take us now?"

"By the time we get through roaming around we'll know France like our vest pockets."

"They must be in a hurry all right."

"Why, we don't need half an hour. What we have can be picked up in 10 minutes."

"Give them a chance to get ready, too. They don't want to be left behind."

"Say, wouldn't it be funny if they were overtaken by our men?" Heinze interjected.

"Wait, wait, Berthold, they aren't here yet. You know it's a tough job to push the English back."

"I never saw such a pessimist in my life. Don't you ever have any hope?"

"Sure, but experience has told me different too often. I only begin to believe in something when it actually comes to pass. And even then I'm in doubt sometimes."

"I thought so. You and 10 minutes! The whistle is blowing and you aren't even ready."

The prisoners came nonchalantly, without haste. The past 30 minutes had brought the battle front closer to them. Booming explosions of the artillery were clearer and louder. Perhaps in an hour it would be too late to flee. But five minutes later they left the camp loaded with their canvas bags under heavy escort.

It took two and a half hours of forced marching to arrive at the nearest railroad station. A long row of 40 & 8 cars was waiting for them. They were divided into groups and assigned to various wagons, each with their respective number of guards. It was their first train ride in captivity. Reminiscent of the many rides taken behind their own front, this train also was taking them to an unknown destination.

Tired and hungry after a long journey with many detours, they arrived late that night at the immense concentration camp of Abbeville where they found thousands of other captive comrades waiting for further transfer to other parts of France. In view of all the hasty preparations being made there, the prisoners began to attach more and more credence to the rumors of being sent to England. They became confident of this fact when, after three days, they again entrained for another station.

The train cruised the country for nearly a day. In the evening there was a long stop in the station of Dieppe, during which they were served a meal before the journey continued. After moving at a slow pace through Dieppe the cars stopped again, coming alongside a French freight train that was waiting for the track to clear.

"Hey you, sales Boches!"

The engineer and fireman of the freight train opened hostilities without the slightest provocation on the part of the prisoners. The Frenchmen looked as if they suddenly had gone mad at the sight of them. Seizing the machine's long stoking iron, the fireman lunged forward. The prisoners retreated to a corner of their open car just in time to avoid the heavy weapon falling on their heads. The engineer and his helper were raving maniacs. The fireman tried desperately to reach the prisoners with his iron while the other began to throw large pieces of coal. Three or four times the iron was brought down with force, but fortunately no one was struck. As the train remained stationary the situation threatened to take a serious turn. It prompted Ebelshauser to intervene. He jumped forward to grab hold of the stoking iron.

"What's the matter with you both? Have you gone crazy? What have we done to you?"

His French had performed a miracle. The two railroad men looked at him with startled faces and open mouths. Taken by surprise, they did not know what to say. The coal stopped flying and the fireman retrieved his poker without a word as if ashamed of himself.

"You'd better give us something to eat instead of striking us," Ebelshauser continued. "If we were your enemies, we couldn't help it. But now we're friends."

The two men stared speechlessly at Ebelshauser. It was obvious nothing like this had ever happened to them before. As their train was now about to move, they reached for their boxes and still without a word, threw the rest of their bread and sausages to the prisoners.

"Bon voyage! Bonne chance!" they shouted in a parting gesture as their train rapidly gained speed.

The next morning under a rainy sky the prisoners landed at the port of Le Havre. A steep hill and a small camp made of canvas tents resting on slimy, slippery ground were the only pictures they retained of the town. It rained during their entire three-day stay there and, at the time of their departure, they were barely able to lift and detach their feet from the muddy soil.

On the morning of the fourth day they embarked on a ferry boat. At last they were to see a new country, something that promised to be different from the rest of Europe. Perhaps a new life was about to begin for them. They had heard that the treatment in England was much better. New hope was revived in their hearts. Surely they would not stay long. When peace came they would leave for the great return to the fatherland. It was a relief to see the coast of France — land of suffering and persecution — fade and disappear from sight as the boat ploughed through the water. With anticipation they now turned their eyes toward England.

11

Like a titanic monster the war stretched out its tentacles, not only on the torn and devastated continent of Europe but far out across the seas as well. The narrow Channel was literally a belt of watery fortifications. A huge number of mines had been strewn in this small area for protection of the French and English coasts against the invisible attacks from German submarines.

Under the circumstances, the responsibilities of the skipper were great as he brought his vessel from one shore to the other without mishap. Any miscalculation, the slightest variation from the line marked in red on his map meant danger, explosion and death. Speed had to be reduced. The course set down was not a straight run, but a succession of curves and turns zigzagging through the safety zone — changed periodically in order to delude the implacable enemy.

Although aware of the situation, the prisoners gave no thought to the lurking perils surrounding them. England was the topic of all their conversations. As comfortably installed as possible, they let themselves glide gently and softly. How long they would keep floating around did not matter to them. On the contrary, resting as they were, the sea journey could not be any too long as far as they were concerned. For the first time in many years it really looked as if they were going to be treated like human beings. Since reaching the ship their guards had taken a different attitude. They were not so rough anymore and addressed the prisoners in a friendly tone, making some of them almost unrecognizable. They were also taken by surprise with the great abundance of excellent food. This unexpected but welcome generosity took the appearance of a peacetime banquet. It was a unique opportunity to gorge themselves to satiety and fill their hungry bellies to the point of bursting.

"Boy, oh boy, what a treat!"

"Want some more ham?"

"No, thanks, I had my fill. I can hardly move."

"I don't know but it looks fishy to me. Something tells me we're going to pay for it."

"Oh, quit wailing and lamenting. Enjoy the hour and forget about tomorrow. Must you always see clouds in the sky?"

"Experience, man, experience! It's my second nature. Wait and see!"

"Keep quiet, will you? If you can't, at least let the others have a good time."

"This is what I call a rest. Wish it would take weeks to get there."

"You bet, Max. This is grand! Only too bad they didn't give out any smokes."

"Don't despair, they might still come."

"What a difference a country can make!"

"You said a mouthful. Everything seems to be transformed to our advantage. Wonder what their reaction will be once we get over there? You think they'll keep this up?"

"I don't know, but somebody told me once that an Englishman in England and the same Englishman in Europe are two entirely different persons."

"We can't be very far off the coast now. Too bad we can't go up on the open deck. I'd like to watch our landing."

They were just beginning to enjoy themselves when the order to get ready reached them. They had arrived.

Of the port of Dover they saw very little. From the ship they were hastily hustled onto a waiting train without a chance to peek at the neighborhood. The sun was already on its way down and the first shadows of night were slowly settling over the earth.

The long, spacious passenger cars created a very favorable impression and they were further delighted by the apparent absence of escorts. The seats were most comfortable and in abundance. No one had to stand. They were becoming more human again. An atmosphere of well being generated a spirit of unrestrained cheerfulness and good humor. Merriment and hilarity pervaded the whole convoy and soon they began to sing.

London! There was a long stop during which refreshments were served. There was nothing to be seen of the large metropolis except the underground tunnel where their train had come to a halt. Everywhere were lights — the only signs indicating that this was actually London. A shrill whistle from the locomotive and once more they were on their way to a point unknown. It did not matter much where they went so long as the treatment remained better. With anticipation they were looking forward to new quarters, trying to picture to themselves how they might be. Gradually, they fell asleep in the midst of their conversations.

A rousing gong woke them up the next morning. The sun was up and shining brightly in a spotless blue sky. They were surprised at having slept so long. Where were they? Yawning and stretching, each man took his bag and shuffled lazily toward the exit of the car. Once gathered on the platform they were marched off in an orderly column, four by four. Contrary to their expectations, their passage through the streets of the city created no particular excitement. Some boys and girls on their way to school and a few women stopped a while to look them over. Other civilians paid them no attention whatsoever. They were probably used to this sort of thing.

The prisoners glanced around curiously, only to find a great resem-

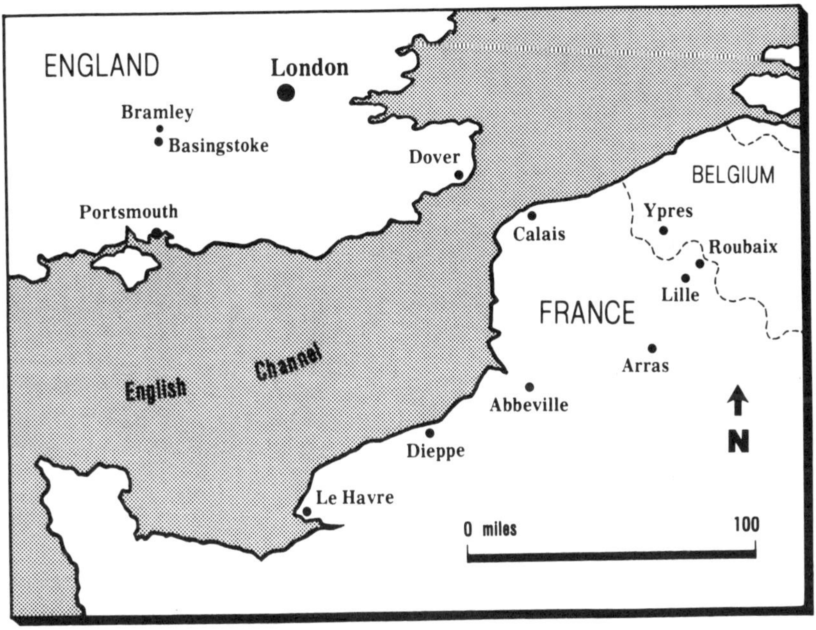

blance between this town and one of their own back home. Were it not for their dirty and ragged uniforms, their bags and the guards marching at their side, they could easily have imagined themselves in Germany.

"Hello, hello! Welcome! A hearty welcome to this wonderful station of rest."

"Where do you come from? But you look like Negroes. You'll need some good scrubbing. One week and you'll feel different."

"How is the treatment here?"

"Swell, nothing to complain about and enough food with no work to do, except resting."

"That's exactly what we need. That'll do us good."

"Don't worry, you'll be well taken care of. Just come in and make yourselves at home."

"For the love of Mike!" Ebelshauser glanced at his friend, Roeder. "Can you beat that? These fellows certainly don't look like prisoners, so fresh and clean and happy. Boy, what a life! It's about time we get our share of the cake. What do you say?"

"I'm telling you I've got to pinch myself to make sure I'm not dreaming," Roeder replied. "It's almost too good to be true. They've thrown themselves into some swell looking outfits. Wonder if we'll get the same stuff?"

If the town had remained quiet, the camp was thrown into wild excitement upon the arrival of this latest batch of prisoners. But with typical

German military efficiency, the apparently disorderly mass of men was rapidly reassembled and brought back to a shapely and flawless formation. To find themselves under a German commander was a fascinating and thrilling sensation. The German soldier was being revived and recreated in them. They could not deny their ancestors. A feeling of pride kindled a new flame in their eyes. German blood still flowed through their veins. Valiant hearts were still beating under now flat and shapeless chests.

They were accorded very little rest that day. For four hours on end they passed from one bathroom and lavatory to another. The cleansing, starting with delousing, came to a conclusion with the so-called purifying act, an ordeal that put them in a state of complete exhaustion. Until then they had not actually realized the deplorable condition of filth in which they had lived for so long. It was hard to believe, much less acknowledge as their own, the amount of dirt and black water they were leaving behind. They were even more amazed at the results this process of rejuvenation had on their bodies and faces. Their skin literally had changed color. It did not look as if they were the same men. Finally came one of the most pleasant surprises. Getting rid of their ragged, dirty and patched uniforms brought a radiance into their faces. They kept looking at each other with great satisfaction and contentment.

Years before, but with quite different feelings, they had passed through the same experience when pulling on an ill-fitting uniform for the first time in their lives. Once again, after an almost incalculable period of time, they were being dressed anew. It was like a dream. Would England really mean the beginning of a new era, a new life?

"The Men in Brown," they called themselves. It was the color of their new suits. No objection could have been raised as to the quality of the material — a Manchester tweed of extra strength and durability. The coat closed at the neck with an inch-high collar, but without stiffness. There was no vest. Pants and coat matched. "Blue moon" was one of the preferred nicknames by which the prisoners designated their suits. A perfect circle had been cut out of the back of each coat. To cover this large round hole a piece of blue fabric of different material and been sewn in. The same procedure had been followed for the making of the pants. Only the blue patch, instead of being round, was shaped oval and appeared on the front of one of the legs. Thanks to this deliberate disfiguring of the suit a prisoner could be recognized both ways, coming and going.

The first six weeks were devoted entirely to a period of much needed rest. To their great astonishment the prisoners found a vast reading room and library placed at their disposal to idle away the hours. However, as they soon discovered, there were too many innocent children's stories in which a hard-boiled soldier could hardly find much interest. Fortunately, since playing cards could be obtained at the English canteen, the majority of the men took to this pastime with an eagerness soon to become a passion. Itching palms would bring down trumps on the tables from morning to night. Future gamblers, adventurers, even gangsters, perhaps, were in the making, unknown yet to themselves.

Bramley was the name of the town next to their working camp and new residence. The British authorities had decided to make use of this extra manpower which was going to waste in pure idleness, if not dangerous laziness.

Then came the change, a reversal back to meager and insufficient rations. As in France, they were again put on a diet. Shortage of food became their chief source of daily complaint, leading to strife and friction between themselves and the guards.

Each morning at eight o'clock the various columns of prisoners proceeded to their respective places of work. The undeniable, ever-present, telltale signs of their captivity pursued them wherever they went. Huge areas, vast estates and an entire net of roads and highways covering countless square miles of ground had been completely bordered and surrounded by strong double fences of barbed wire, altogether impenetrable. Their activities were strictly confined within these limits, beyond which there was no possibility of trespassing. In whichever direction they looked their eyes encountered the wired fortifications. At times the wire enclosures took on the aspect of a gigantic cage into which they had access but from which there was no issue.

Under the guidance of their English masters the prisoners became, in turn, concrete mixers, handymen, brick and track layers, diggers, and road builders.

At noon sharp the sirens of nearby factories blew. It was the signal for lunch. All work stopped and the prisoners gathered at a given point to eat out of their bags whatever meager remnants they had succeeded in keeping from breakfast or the meal the night before. It generally was very little. The majority of the men had trained themselves and grown accustomed to having only two meals a day. Thus they passed the lunch hour lying or resting in all kinds of positions, puffing away at cigarettes made from picked-up stumps. Conversations were infrequent for even talking had lost its meaning. Many squatted together on the ground, looking at each other without a word or staring with wide-open eyes into space.

At one o'clock the shrill whistles of the sirens woke them up. With marked lassitude the prisoners returned to their chores. They performed their duties mechanically with the sole purpose of killing time. Impatient, they waited for the last whistle announcing the end of another day.

Five o'clock found them in a great rush and they assembled under the leadership of their escorts. An hour later they entered the large gate of the camp, a jail within a jail. But there was another meal waiting for them. The barracks had become the homes they longed for at the end of a long day. There they could dispose of their evenings by resting, eating or playing cards.

The rapid development of the camp as a gambling resort simply was ignored. The guards, who were first to be blamed for the situation, kept their eyes closed so long as the prisoners took care not to expose themselves too openly. The prisoners saw no harm in this amusement. It was merely another way of passing time and killing the long hours of impatient waiting until their return home.

In spite of the few distractions, time had become a weighty and serious factor in the minds of the prisoners. They were growing tired and fed up with the continuous monotony of their daily routine. If, at first, the change of coming to England had been welcome, life had by now become old. They craved and longed for something else. Everything was fading away. Time had become an obsession.

Except for a trickle of letters from home, the prisoners were cut off from the rest of the world, completely isolated on an island and living an abnormal life of their own. All they knew was that the war was still going on. There was not the slightest sign of peace to be discerned on the distant horizon. Day in, day out, the men marched to and from their work like herds of sheep. More and more they became conscious of their monotonous and useless existence.

Every now and then, however, some important news item went sweeping through the camp. A few of the English guards always took great delight in deceiving the defenseless prisoners. They would pass on to them fabulous accounts of their own creation with the sole purpose of raising faint hope of glad tidings. With trusting hearts and joyful expressions, the men, craving such outside information, clung to the fabricated tales. But almost all of the reports turned out to be nothing but imaginative stories without foundation.

The men were fed up with falsehoods and thirsted to learn the truth. The whole camp hummed with rumors concerning the end of the war, but the reports were so confusing and contradictory that they were lost in the maze. No one knew what to believe. They had often sworn to themselves not to listen anymore to such invented tales, but the attraction was too great to resist the temptation. Still, as the days went on without a change they became more and more distrustful.

The armistice took them by surprise. Yet, it was not the great day they had expected it to be. The momentous joy soon was overshadowed and drowned by the realization that their state of captivity was to last for quite some time to come. November 11, 1918 — a cause of great rejoicing and happy shouting all over the world. But for these men it was a magnificent rainbow of too short duration. They would never have dreamed that the end of the great conflagration was to be revealed to them in such a pitiful way. They had looked forward to an overwhelming manifestation in which they were to play an important part. Instead, they were greatly disappointed at the sudden coming and going of this "never-to-be-forgotten" occurrence.

Following their regular routine, the prisoners had marched out to work the morning of that eventful day. For the past couple of weeks the camp had been swamped with rumors of all kinds. But in view of their many experiences the prisoners had grown accustomed to regard these news items as pure inventions. No more were they ready to fall for such stories, and they were audacious enough to tell the guards the way they felt about it.

When the whistles and sirens of neighboring factories began to blow, Ebelshauser was in the process of unloading a railroad car. Karl Roeder happened to be his team worker. Together they were shuffling and pushing sand toward the small open side door, standing on top of the load. Instinctively, Ebelshauser's first gesture was to look at his watch, a present from Wege who had two.

"Funny, it's only 11 o'clock on my watch. What time have you got?"

"I haven't got any," Roeder replied, "but it's lunch time for me, so my stomach tells me. You must have forgotten to wind up your onion last night."

In the space of a few seconds, however, the whole atmosphere was suddenly and magically changed. Having stopped working they stood gazing around, amazed at the various scenes taking place before their eyes. The two of them, it seemed, were the only men not taking part in the uproar. They alone kept silent as if stricken dumb. It was only at the sight of girls swarming out of the factories that they began to react to their own feelings. In the distance on the other side of the barbed wire fence, a regiment of English factory girls was singing, calling and whistling at them. Some were jumping and dancing while waving their handkerchiefs and hats.

"Hurrah! Hurrah! Armistice! Peace! Home, home, HOME!"

Ebelshauser and his friend jumped down from the car to join their comrades in the feast. On a first impulse the guards had thrown down their rifles. They came running up to the prisoners, joking and singing in a general spell of jubilation mingled with tears of heartfelt happiness. This spontaneous and boisterous fraternization was, for the prisoners, a moment of complete relaxation and forgetfulness. Each gave way to his natural feelings. Home — a magic word — had taken on new meaning. They would all be there soon, perhaps in time for Christmas. Home — where fathers, mothers, wives and children were so impatiently waiting for them. Home — a place of rest to which they would now return after years of hardship and separation. Home — they felt overcome by the intensity of its closeness, of its terrific magnetic power.

Home! Ebelshauser had the picture of it imprinted deeply in his brain. For him it meant not only his family, but beautiful Lausanne with its majestic lake and the snow-capped Alps in the background. His comrades, too, were thinking of similar picturesque scenes. A little house, a garden, trees, parks and forests at this moment were the only topics of conversation as each one attempted to give some enchanting description of his native town or village, each firmly convinced that his place was the best and most beautiful.

Their awakening to reality took the aspect of a real tragedy. For 15 minutes the whistles and sirens kept blowing their strident message of peace. When they finally stopped the girls, instead of reentering the factories, went home. The guards became more serious again, taking up their weapons and resuming their duties. Even before they had time to recover their senses the prisoners were back at work as if nothing had happened. Recess for lunch was observed in the same old routine. Only in their more animated conversations did they speak of what was most dear to them — home. They wondered how long it would be until they would actually leave. They were cautious not to set a date for the fulfillment of their hopes. Yet, everyone took it secretly for granted that they would be celebrating Christmas within the circle of their families.

But destiny was to prove otherwise. It might have been armistice day for the world, but for them the joyous bells of freedom and liberty were not to ring for a long time. They were in bondage and had to pay their share of the war penalties imposed by their present masters and former enemies.

To alleviate the growing distress and depression, a special meeting hall was allocated to the prisoners to be used as a theater. They were furnished with costumes for the production of stage shows of their own choosing. Musicians and actors by profession, as well as all those interested in appearing as amateurs, quickly responded to the call. Following numerous rehearsals everything was made ready for the first presentation of "Alt Heidelberg," which was pompously announced as a Christmas offering.

In spite of an exclusively male cast, they gave a splendid rendition. The impersonation of the female roles was simply exquisite and beyond reproach or criticism. It brought the men to a frenzy of hand clapping and prolonged applause. Twice the calls went out for the repetition of particular scenes. And each time they produced bursts of laughter and merriment from the attentive audience. There was nothing better than such a show to divert the gangrenous thoughts of incarcerated men. It brought them oblivion, the most welcome tonic under the circumstances.

As the curtain fell after the closing scene of the final act, a commotion went through the spectators. The Scottish commander of the camp mounted the rudimentary stage accompanied by a German interpreter, an indication of a forthcoming speech.

"My dear fellow men," the officer began after having asked for attention. "I am here to tell you, first of all, that I very much regret to have you pass this Christmas holiday here instead of at home where you should be ..."

Loud shouts of approval greeted his first sentence and made it impossible for him to continue. He waited patiently and smiled until silence was resumed.

"I rejoice with you all at the beautiful thought of being able to go home soon ... (more prolonged applause) ... and you can well believe that I sympathize with you in your present predicament. However, we all have great consolation in the knowledge that this terrible war is now over. Let us, therefore, look forward with hope in our hearts to an enduring and long period of genuine universal understanding, as well as a time of reconstruction and prosperity for all nations concerned.

"It is not our desire to have you detained here longer than is absolutely necessary, but you must bear in mind that the vast project of repatriation cannot be achieved and brought to conclusion between today and tomorrow. This problem involves an extraordinary amount of calculation, work and the setting up of a special organization. All these new agencies require a certain length of time in their formation and proper function.

"In the meantime and until then, do not lose courage and patience, but bear up bravely under the stress as you have done so well until now. There is no need for worry on your part because we are not forgetting you. As a sign of your good will and understanding may I request that you now sing for me, in unison, your favorite and beautiful martial tune "Die Wacht am Rhein."

At the first notes of this song, the tall Scottish officer removed his cap and stood at attention. The tune flew like a terrific roar out of hundreds of throats and shook the building to its foundations. Never had a ceremony been more impressive. Tears welled up in the eyes of the singers. They, too, had risen to their feet. The giant male chorus was vibrating under the impulse and charm of the old war melody. Yet, while this song of victory was ringing through the hall, their countrymen at home were already tasting the bitter fruit of defeat.

"Will that day of days ever come?"

"When is the sun going to set on a different horizon?"

"Are we going to pass the rest of our lives in captivity?"

"How long is this situation going to last? How long do we have to wait?"

Work, amusements, the theater, gambling, even food had passed into the realm of unimportant superficialities. There was only one question that really counted for the prisoners. It formed the beginning and end of all conversation. When were they going home? Nothing else mattered. For more than 10 months the war had been over. Spring and summer had come and passed since armistice day. October was fast nearing its end and still there was no prospect of the long awaited return journey. To the prisoners it seemed that they had been forgotten altogether; that, in the quick rush for settlement among the various nations their problem had been completely overlooked.

From letters received from their families they were aware that most of the soldiers had been dismissed. What about them? Would there be no end to their suffering and incarceration? How long would they have to linger in this camp? The endless waiting had become an obsession and worked on their minds day and night. Some were losing weight and sleep over it. They could no longer find enjoyment and pleasure in their few amusements. Their faces reflected stern expressions, revealing inner anxiety and teetering hope.

A state of restlessness had replaced the placid attitude of patience of 10 months before. Even though their bellies craved for food, the little they got was automatically gulped and swallowed without taste or appetite. They attended to their duties like mere machines. They felt defeated in their daily race with time. Every hour became an added torment. Some had even lost their balance of mind beyond all hope of recovery. They had been removed from the camp and placed in hospitals or asylums for observation. None of them had ever come back. What had happened to them? Nobody knew.

In addition to these there were a good number of men who, without becoming violent, had nevertheless lost their senses so as to be unable to distinguish right from wrong. But since they were behaving, as far as outward appearances were concerned, they were considered inoffensive and permitted to stay among their fellow prisoners. Every now and then it became necessary to sound the alarm. The so-called inoffensive patient was suddenly overcome by a spell of fury requiring his immediate removal.

It was shortly after a pale and spiritless New Year's celebration. Snow had fallen during the day which rendered their work most strenuous. They had come back to their quarters at the regular hour and taken a meager supper in an atmosphere of tense silence and grim resignation. Disgust and helplessness could be read on every face.

Ebelshauser well knew how careful he had to be in the distribution of the provisions, a most unthankful task. He had manufactured his own measures of weight as well as a rudimentary scale. He felt himself watched by eager, burning eyes. A fraction of an ounce difference in weight in the portions of cheese and bread meant the start of an argument that quickly could develop into a real battle between the suspicious man and himself. But everything had turned out for the best and everyone appeared satisfied.

The men were in a most serious mood. It seemed difficult for anybody to start a conversation for there was no response. Some had retired immediately after the evening meal, eager to slip under their warm blankets. While two quartets began to play cards, Johann Kissling saw to it that the stove, located in the middle of the long barrack, kept a good fire burning. They all had brought a quantity of wood clandestinely, stuffed into the linings of their coats and pants. Luck had been with the group that night. The guards had let them pass the gates without the customary "touch" examination. So Kissling had his delight in the ample supply of firewood.

"Let's all sit around the stove tonight and tell stories," he proposed while putting some more pieces of wood in the flaming brazier. "How about it?"

"I second the motion," called out Roeder.

Within the next 10 minutes eight of the men were sitting in a circle around the glowing stove — Roeder, Ebelshauser, Altmannsberger, Koch, Kalb, Wege and Weiss. Closing the circle next to the stove sat Kissling on his own box stool. For a long while they remained plunged in private thought. No one seemed willing to be the first to break the silence.

"Let's sing a song," suggested Roeder at last.

"That's a good idea," supported Weiss. "It'll cheer us up a bit.

"What will it be? *'Sah' ein Knab' ein Roeslein stehn'?*" Roeder gave the pitch and began humming the well-known melody.

They all took it up, even the card players and those lying in their bunks. Once more they seemed to have won a victory over themselves. In spite of the inclement weather outside, a wonderful harmony of male voices rose within the room and gloom was on its way out. For the next half hour one song followed another.

Then came a series of jokes as only soldiers can tell among themselves. Eventually, their repertoire being exhausted, they turned from jokes to little stories, anecdotes and recollections of their school days. Each was eager to tell of the worst mischief he could remember.

Finally, Kissling had his word. He recounted to his listeners a trick he once played on a certain teacher, Herr Merzel. In the latter's absence he had slung a string around the bottom of his large inkwell, tying the other end to the lid of his pulpit with a thumbtack. After entering the classroom, it was the teacher's first move to open his desk and put his famous inkwell in full evidence.

"Boy, oh boy! You should have seen that guy," Kissling exploded. "His fine gray suit, coat and pants were full of black stains. There was even ink on his cheeks and nose. Some picture! The whole room burst out laughing, except me. That's how I got caught ..."

"But it wasn't Merzel, it was Richter, don't you remember?"

It was an unexpected as well as unwelcome interruption, for Kissling was a fellow who could not stand any contradictions. As it happened, Weiss, who also came from Ludwigshafen, had been with him at the same school, a fact that Kissling had not thought of in the course of his short tale.

"What do you mean?" he flared up, blushing slightly in anger. "I ought to know the name of the guy on whom I played that trick better than you."

Ebelshauser and the others were laughing, both at the trick and about the little argument the two former schoolmates were having.

"You ought to, of course, but apparently you are mixed up," Weiss replied with a sarcastic smile. "Maybe you played another trick on Merzel."

Before any of the men could foresee the turn this insignificant difference of opinion was to have, Kissling suddenly became a raving maniac. With lightning speed he seized the small hatchet he used for chopping wood. With all his might he brought the cutting edge smashing down on the head of his comrade, cleaving it partly. The blood splashed from the wound. Weiss did not utter a sound. Death was instantaneous.

They all jumped up and grabbed Kissling while another sounded the alarm. The guards came rushing in and called an ambulance. Kissling and the dead body of Weiss were taken away and the evening came to an end. Another tragedy had once more plunged the men into a dark mood of despair. The card players stopped their game and took to their bunks. Tomorrow was another day.

After the armistice, letters from home were the surest sign for the prisoners that peace actually had come. Censorship stations had been liquidated immediately. No longer did the men receive their messages with the contents half erased or completely obliterated. No longer were the envelopes and letters arriving terribly mangled or even torn to pieces. Mail kept coming in more voluminous quantities with up-to-date news left intact. It was the prisoners' only contact with the outside world.

Ebelshauser, Roeder, Baaden and Marberg — the latter two new-made friends — would squat in the open next to the theater hall, bent upon the solution of the world's endless and complicated problems. While their comrades played cards the quartet's interest centered on politics, especially Germany's political situation created by the "Versailles treaty," which the folks back home wrote to them about almost daily.

"Really, I can't see the point why Wilhelm should have been made to abdicate and flee to Holland, do you?"

Marberg was presiding at the meeting as usual. Of tall stature and partly bald, the man looked young for being in his fifties. His steel-blue eyes frowned as he shot the question. Marberg was the personification of the old-school type, having done his share of active military service long before the war.

"The French were scared to death," Roeder said. "It was their stipulation for the signing of peace. Under no condition did they want to deal with the Kaiser. If Germany wanted peace so badly, the Kaiser had to go. So what could we do?"

Roeder seemed to know what he was talking about. He had spoken with rancor and bitterness, disgusted with the old subject that never failed to come up in nearly every one of their debates.

"What's the use of bringing that up all the time?" he continued. "We might as well ask ourselves why we're still here."

"Ach!" Baaden chirped in. "The whole damn business was a mean fraud. It wouldn't have been so bad had the Allies stuck to their promises in keeping with Wilson's 14 points. But the French got the upper hand.

They threw Wilson's plan in the wastebasket because their eyes were bigger than their bellies. They wanted to swallow everything. But they might get an acute case of indigestion some day."

"You said a mouthful," Marberg agreed. "Germany won't stand for it. We have to now but, believe me, some day the French will get it in the neck again. And why? Just because of that silly treaty of theirs which has torn the old map of Europe to pieces."

"Don't get so excited," counselled Roeder. "It's not the time for us to show our teeth. We have to bite the bitter apple. Just the same, I don't see how Germany can remain a republic. That won't last very long. We'll get out of it somehow."

"How did Germany stand in 1806, remember?" Baaden spoke. "When Napoleon drew an iron ring around us he thought he had us licked for good. We certainly taught him a lesson and don't forget, the situation was worse than it is today."

"That's what I say," remarked Marberg convincingly. "Besides, a couple of months more and we would have had them on their knees. Yes, sir, including the big English bull had it not been for the Americans. Even if they came late, they certainly put the last touch to it. As a matter of fact, the Allies owe their victory to the Americans."

"Damn right," echoed Baaden. "But look what they did with Wilson when it came to the final peace settlement. They just pushed him aside and went ahead with their own plans with Clemenceau, the 'tiger,' always leading and imposing his own will."

"Germany a republic? That's a joke," Marberg exclaimed. "I don't think this guy Ebert * is going to be president for long. He's too weak and plays right into the hands of the Allies."

"That Polish corridor was certainly a dirty trick," Roeder said. "East Prussia is now perfectly isolated. If they could have done it they would have cut us to pieces, as they did with Austria. But Germany just couldn't be eradicated from the map altogether. They had to leave some of the parts standing. It's really too bad for the poor Frenchmen. They'd have liked nothing better than to have us constantly at their mercy, just like slaves."

"Don't worry, fellows," Marberg consoled. "France has another guess coming. You just watch. If they don't do away with that shameful peace treaty pretty soon, the Frenchman will have another war on his hands. But this time he'll have to fight alone. America is gone for good and the English and Russians won't bother to come to the rescue. They've had enough the way it is."

"What are Wilson's 14 points you were talking about before," Ebelshauser asked. He always had trouble following their arguments.

* Friedrich Ebert (1871-1925), a Social-Democratic statesman, became chancellor of Germany on November 9, 1918. In February 1919, he was elected provisional president of the Weimar Republic. He died of appendicitis while still in office on February 28, 1925. — R.B.

"I don't know myself," Baaden replied. "My uncle doesn't give me any details in his letter. See here? He just writes that the German delegation agreed to sign the armistice because of Wilson's 14 points. But he says we were tricked because, even while we were signing the documents, Clemenceau and Lloyd George had altogether different plans in mind. And my uncle knows what he is talking about. He was on von Kluck's staff right up to the breakup."

"But why didn't Wilson insist on his 14 points?" retorted Ebelshauser.

"Well, my uncle says that once the agreement had been signed, Wilson was simply sidetracked. France wanted to have it her own way. With the English on her side Wilson was too weak to stand up against the two of them. He lost out and gave up the struggle."

"But just the same, Wilson now has a lasting monument in the League of Nations, hasn't he? That's what my father wrote me a couple of weeks ago," Ebelshauser said.

"Oh, yeah, you don't say!" exclaimed Roeder sardonically. "Too bad they chose Geneva. This is just a masquerade and I feel sorry for Switzerland for having loaned itself to such foul play. They should have put it in Paris. France is the only one doing the real talking. The others just listen, saying yes and amen to everything the French say. That is exactly what the League of Nations amounts to. That's why, in spite of Wilson being its creator, his country is not a member. The Americans were smart enough to smell the fish and stay out of the frying pan."

"I wouldn't be surprised to see them join soon."

"Not on your life — not if they are wise and study the game that's being played there."

"I don't understand," Ebelshauser said. "Why have such a league at all?"

"It's not a league, if you know what I mean," Baaden remarked sarcastically. "It's France and her allies under different camouflage. But they'll be uncovered and sooner or later the famous League of Nations will come crashing down like a house of cards. You mark my words."

"If that happens, it'll surely keep the Americans out of any further European mess."

"Well, now you're talking sense, Gustav. They should have stayed out of the war in the first place. What do you think made them take the last leap across the Atlantic? Nothing but the mighty dollar. They got scared about some investments of theirs, but now what have they got in return? Was it worth the risk?"

"If nothing else, they have the honor of having brought the war to its end. Now they can share in the great victory with their allies."

"Victory? Don't kid yourself, Gustav," Roeder grinned. "In their case 'victory' is just another word for 'defeat.' Instead of saving their investments they literally poured millions of dollars in the field. And how about all the thousands of promising young Americans who died, not for their country but for the sake of France and company? What about all of her wounded and crippled? What is America going to do about them? What kind of a settlement can she claim? You call that victory?"

"You're right," Baaden said. "When it comes to a settlement I can just imagine France and England telling America to go plump to hell, only in a more polite fashion, of course."

"That's exactly what's going to happen. But it will have taught the Americans a good lesson at the price of a great sacrifice. The next time England and France get their hands into another mudpie you can bet your boots that America will be all the wiser to keep out of it. She won't get burned a second time."

"Well, my friend, that would be no more than common sense. What has America to gain in Europe anyway? Absolutely nothing. Its place in the sun is big enough. She should keep to herself and out of foreign entanglements."

"That's probably what she's going to do from now on, if the American people can keep fresh in their minds the lesson they've just learned."

"Why only America?" Ebelshauser vehemently inquired. "Why not every country all over the world? The people should be educated and made to remember the horrors of war. And the public press should be enrolled for such a task ..."

"Because America is the only country that could do that sort of thing," Roeder interrupted. "There they have freedom of the press. Anybody has a chance to speak up. Of course, I don't know how it looks now in our new republic, but under the Kaiser you were simply locked up and put away before you had a chance to say a word against the government."

"But it's going to be different in Germany now," Baaden said.

"Let's live in hope anyway," Roeder replied. "But to my mind nobody won the war. On the contrary, everybody has come out of it a loser. Every country is in a deplorable condition and the whole world needs time to recuperate."

Night after night the four took up their discussions where they had left off the previous evening. Almost always the same question was raised, but each time they found themselves unable to find a solution to the problem. When a letter disclosing some new political event in Germany was received it was read aloud at such improvised meetings. And so time went on as they waited for their ultimate return home.

Two weeks later a great commotion shook the entire camp to its foundations. Unexpected as it was, the official news at first was taken with inborn incredulity. But the report was there, very brief and to the point, and signed by the camp's commander. With hundreds of other prisoners who milled and pushed around the notice board to get a glimpse of it, Ebelshauser read the few lines aloud once more.

> Notice is hereby given that, in accordance with instructions just received from Great Britain's highest military headquarters, all work and activities in connection with the present

> government's projects have come to an end on this day of November 11th, 1919. After breakfast, the men of this camp are to assemble in their regular formations in the camp yard at ten o'clock tomorrow morning to receive further orders and instructions.
>
> Commander-in-chief

"Well, it looks as if something is going to happen," Roeder said in a joyful tone."

"I hope so, but seeing is believing," remarked someone else.

"We must be nearer to home now than we ever have before."

"Funny, just a year to the day after the armistice."

"Well, isn't it time for us to be chased out of here?"

"I don't understand why they've kept us so long in the first place."

"Reparations, my dear. With us they were getting their work done for nothing. They would have had to pay wages to their own men. That's one of the many reasons why we're still here."

In every barrack that evening the prisoners held conferences and discussions far into the night, even after the lights had gone out. The brief notice had worked like magic. Gambling and card playing suddenly were forgotten. In spite of a hard day's work which was to be their last, they were unusually wide awake and no one felt like going to sleep. Had it been within their power and strength to do so they would have passed the whole night talking and waiting. But eventually, overcome by fatigue and emotion, they repaired to the bunks one by one.

Wild acclamations and shouting greeted the speaker the next morning after he delivered his short address. Yelling and whistling could be heard everywhere. The prisoners broke into song and were carried away by happiness and joy. Many of them ran around laughing and jumping into the air in their exuberant state of intoxication. But amid so much pleaure there was also sadness, for a few of the men lost their minds as a result of this sudden and unexpected change.

On November 19, 1919, the prisoners started their return journey home. The "blue moon" suits were replaced by the old field-gray uniforms which had been patched, cleaned and well preserved for this day of days. Faces shined with jubilant anticipation. The men were like schoolboys on the eve of a long-awaited excursion.

After crossing the Channel they endured the long, slow trip through France with challenging patience. A short stop was made at a Belgian station for refreshments. They returned to their "40 and 8" cars just in time to close the sliding doors to protect themselves from a hail of stones and broken glass suddenly let loose upon them. A group of local citizens probably had taken offense at their stopping in the town and had come to chase them out.

Three long blasts from the two locomotives signalled the crossing of the Belgian border and their entry onto German soil. A commotion went through the cars and, as if issuing from one throat, the men roared out their greetings with tears in their eyes by singing "Deutschland, Deutschland ueber alles," the national anthem.

Decorated both inside and outside in their honor, the first German station at Aachen had been well prepared to receive them as returning heroes. A small reception committee led the march to a large refreshment hall. Biting avidly on sandwiches and sipping coffee or beer, the men did not lose a single word of all the impromptu speeches of welcome that each delegate considered his duty to deliver.

At Cologne the train came to a dead stop. After more food and drink they had their first inspection. The men had lost their prison numbers. Names were called and registered. It took another hour to segregate individuals according to their destinations. Then came the parting of Ebelshauser from his friends. They all went in different directions. Together with a small number of men unknown to him, he was sent to Hannover-Muenden, the main camp of all German soldiers whose homes or destinations were in a foreign country.

After a few days in the Hannover installation, set up for a thorough cleansing of human bodies, Ebelshauser emerged from the restoration plant a new and almost unrecognizable person. He had first gone through the delousing process. Then followed showering, bathing and washing — during which his emaciated skin had almost been rubbed from his body. A squad of tough and strong-armed masseurs had given him the works with the idea, apparently, of molding his thin frame into a new shape. He had felt his bones crack under the vigorous massaging, and when he finally was through he felt more dead than alive.

What made him appear so strange to himself, however, was not his body but the new civilian costume with which he had been fitted. After undressing he had never thought of being rid of the old, ragged field-gray uniform for good. It was an unexpected parting. Now everything he had on from head to feet was new. A cap, somewhat large for his head, was alone enough to make him look stupid. He also felt stiff and uncomfortable in the fresh but rough underclothing. The neck of the white shirt choked him, while the collar he had received with it was almost an inch too big and had to be folded in the back to adapt itself to the right size.

The only things he could not kick about were the socks, though he experienced no little trouble with his new shoes. The left was too large and the right so narrow that, for the first two days, he walked through the streets of Hannover with great circumspection, as if stepping on eggs. Finally, his slender body literally disappeared within his oversized black suit. Topped off with a gray overcoat it had the capacity of holding two men his size. But since everything was new and free of charge, and since there was no other choice, Ebelshauser could do no better than declare himself fully satisfied. It was no easy job to transform a soldier into a simple civilian.

A new segregation took place at the end of the first week. Ebelshauser was dispatched to Singen on the Rhine with a batch of other men whose destination also was Switzerland. Singen was no less a concentration camp than that in Hannover or the one he lived in for so long in England. Surrounded by a double fence of barbed wire, this one took on the same appearance as those he had seen in France. True, he was no longer a prisoner of war; yet, there did not seem to be much difference in the situation except for the fact that his prison had been transferred to Germany and that, instead of a uniform, he now wore civilian clothes.

The invisible hand of fate still was holding him back from home and from all those he loved and longed to see after almost five years of separation. Like a poor, frail victim of a shipwreck in a stormy sea, he felt pushed away, then toward the shore, but unable to find a safe place to land. The situation was just the reverse of that in 1915.

Then, Germany had claimed and snatched him for service. He had found himself within Germany's borders, his way to Switzerland suddenly cut out from under his feet. Now that the great struggle had come to an end, Germany had no use for him any longer and was glad to see him go. But this time Switzerland, having enough trouble of her own, did not want him back. There were many people being refused entry into his native country. She could not afford to let them come in and take away work from her citizens. And Germany had no place for them either.

Soon aware of these existing conditions, Ebelshauser, determined to obtain permission to enter Switzerland, decided to take matters into his own hands. From what he had seen happen to the men in Singen he had lost confidence in legal procedures between governments. Soon after arriving there he inquired right and left, and his comrades were eager to furnish him with all the information he was seeking. Within a week he knew of many cases similar to his own. At least 100 men, many of them fathers of large families, had been detained in Singen for a period of a whole year.

Being one of the last to arrive at the camp, it immediately dawned on him that if all these men, whom he considered more eligible than himself, had been refused entry into Switzerland, his own application probably would not be accepted either. If he stayed here and relied on the authorities he might have to wait another year or two before being taken into consideration. There was no doubt in his mind that the best thing to do was to attend personally to the solution of his problem. He had gone to Constance at the end of the first week, but his effort to obtain an interview with the Swiss consul there failed and he returned to the camp the next day. Somewhat discouraged, he wrote to his father for money, telling him of another plan to see the Swiss consul in Mannheim. Upon receipt of the amount requested, he had himself officially discharged from the camp and departed the same day for the city where he hoped to meet with better success.

On the bright but very cold morning of December 20, 1919, Ebelshauser presented himself at the offices of the Swiss consulate in

Mannheim. His heart was beating with a mixture of hope and fear.

"I would like to speak to the consul," he replied in a firm tone to the inquiring clerk.

"What is the purpose of your visit and whom may I announce?" came the clerk's question for which he had not been prepared.

"Well, er, it's very important. Tell the consul I must see him at once."

"What is the name, please?" the clerk insisted.

"Never mind the name. He doesn't know my name but he will know me when he sees me." Ebelshauser surprised himself by this answer.

"But the consul is very busy at present. Would you like to leave a message?"

"Er, no ... thank you, I prefer to wait."

"All right, sir, take a seat. I will see if the consul can see you."

With great relief Ebelshauser watched the clerk disappear behind a door. "Another of his funny questions and I wouldn't have known what to say," he thought to himself.

He did not have to wait long before passing through the same door. At the call of the clerk he was introduced to the man he so urgently wanted to see.

"What can I do for you, young man?"

The consul was a strong fellow who stood well over six feet tall, a real giant. Ebelshauser would have remained speechless had it not been for the bright smile illuminating the consul's friendly and jovial face. He caressed a long flowing gray beard which hid from sight a short neck.

"Have a seat and tell me what brings you here," he added, pointing to a chair next to his large desk at which he installed himself. Reassured by the sympathetic attitude of his host, Ebelshauser lost all of his natural shyness and began the little speech he had prepared and so often rehearsed in his mind. With trust and confidence he told the consul the whole story of his last four years without being interrupted.

"And so, you would like to go back to Switzerland and see your parents, brothers and sister, is that it?" the consul asked with a smile once he had finished relating his tale.

"Yes, sir, very much so. I think the authorities should make an exception when one is born there."

"I don't blame you, young man. They might, eventually, if it could be explained to them in the right manner."

"Could it not be done from here? That's exactly why I came to see you."

"You don't say! Perhaps — I never thought of it," the consul replied whimsically.

"I have nobody here, my whole family is in Lausanne." Ebelshauser was pleading for his cause.

"What is your father doing in Lausanne?"

"We have a shoe business, a large store. We live on the Rue de la Tour, but the store is on the main street below, the Rue d'Halle."

"I can just imagine. I know Lausanne very well for I've been there often."

"Don't you think something could be done for me?"

"You'd like to celebrate Christmas with your folks, wouldn't you?"

"Why, er, of course, but I guess I'm too late for that."

"One can never tell. Anything might happen these days. How would you like me to ask for your visa by telegram?"

"Can it be done? I don't know what to say. Oh, Mr. Consul, that would be wonderful. I don't know how to thank you for so much kindness."

"Nix, nix, you can thank me when you get the visa, not before."

"Do you think you can get it for me even before the holidays?"

"I won't promise anything, but I'm willing to try. Let's see, today is the 20th." He began to count on his fingers. "How about calling here again on the 23rd at noon? Departing the next day you could just make it for Christmas Eve. Wouldn't that be a fine little surprise?"

Ebelshauser was nearly speechless at the prospect of suddenly being so near his goal.

"Here, take this card and present it to the clerk when you call again." The consul gave him a personal visiting card on which he had just written "private, urgent" under his engraved name. He then underlined and signed it with his initials.

"Thank you, Mr. Consul," Ebelshauser repeated on his way out. "I'll be here on the 23rd at noon sharp."

"Auf wiedersehen, young man. But don't count on it, otherwise you'll be much too disappointed if it doesn't show up at the right moment."

"All right, I'll try to forget about it if I possibly can."

As soon as he was out of the building, Ebelshauser hurried to the home of Franz Frech, a brother of his sister's sweetheart. Johanna Frech, Franz's wife, was one of the jolliest persons he had ever met. Always ready to tell a joke, she could laugh so heartily that, no matter how much one tried, he could not remain serious in her presence. He was eager to get to the Frechs' home and tell them the good news. By telling somebody else about it would strengthen his own hope and belief.

How different was his mood when returning from his second interview with the consul! He seemed like a different person altogether. Although he feared and even anticipated such a reply, he nevertheless was terribly disappointed at yet another setback. The hope for an early return to his family was still strong in his heart, but the certainty of having to pass Christmas and New Year away from home when he believed he was so near was more than he could stand. It would be the fifth holiday season he would have to celebrate in strange surroundings all by himself. On such days friends did not count. He knew so little of them. Could they really understand how he felt? Besides, German customs on these holidays were foreign to him. They celebrated, but in a different way and spirit. He felt the lack of sincere gaiety. At the same time he well understood that, under the circumstances, it would have been too much to expect the German people to forget about their own troubles. Could the terrific impression of their gigantic defeat ever be eradicated from their minds? Impossible! And many would carry this indelible scar to their graves.

In the meantime, most of them tried their best to bear up under the burden which the great tragedy had brought upon them. They smiled and laughed, but without conviction. Ebelshauser was really thankful for Johanna. She seemed to be the only one capable of rising above the present conditions and forgetting her plight. But when Christmas and New Year came around he found her no consolation. On Christmas Day he managed to keep his sorrow to himself, but on New Year's Eve, when all the bells of the city began to peal, he could keep his secret no longer. Overcome by emotion and sadness, he retired to his bedroom where he burst into tears and loud sobbing. It was the only action that brought relief and peace.

The melodious voices of the bells eventually stopped, though he continued shedding bitter tears. He thought of the consul's promise to wire him as soon as he received news of his visa. On the 23rd he had been told that the wire was too late. The government offices already had closed in view of the holidays. But surely, the consul had added, his visa would come shortly after New Year's Day. All he had to do was wait with patience.

On January 4, 1920, on the birthday of his father, Ebelshauser received a telegram requesting his presence at the consulate. He immediately responded to the summons and walked as fast as his legs would carry him. He reached the building before noon and found the consul waiting for him.

"Well, young man, I guess I have succeeded in solving the little problem to your satisfaction. It took a little more time than anticipated, but I finally got the visa for you."

"You mean everything is settled and I can go home?"

"That's exactly what I mean."

Ebelshauser felt a lump in his throat, making it impossible for him to articulate a sound. Words failed him. He stared wide-eyed in amazement at the smiling eyes of the consul as if the man had just performed a miracle in front of him. Although he had hoped and waited anxiously for it, he was now stunned at the unbelievably good news. The consul took great delight in studying the various shades of expressions which animated his face.

"Then I can leave today?"

"Certainly, just let me have your passport. Oh, yes, there is one little condition imposed upon your return to Switzerland. You are going with the understanding of paying a visit to your family. Of course, the government will have no objection to your helping your parents in their business, but you are not permitted to take up any kind of job or position in any part of the country."

"That's understood, Mr. Consul. I'm sure my parents will find enough for me to do."

"Perhaps after having taken up your legal residence in Lausanne you will be able to have this condition changed to your advantage."

"Do you think it could be done?"

"I don't know, and I'm not making any promises to that effect. But after a certain time you could take up this matter with the local authorities. You can always try. At least it would not endanger your situation."

"I will as soon as I get a chance. Thank you very much for your advice and for all the kindness you have shown me. I cannot repay you for this great service, but I shall never forget what you have done as long as I live. I'll drop you a few lines from Lausanne after I get there. Goodbye!"

"Auf wiedersehen to you, too, and good luck. I hope you reach home well."

The following day Ebelshauser was on his way home. More than once during the journey along the Rhine he visualized the scene of warm welcome that was awaiting him. Deeply absorbed in his thoughts, he hardly paid any attention to the landscape through which his train rolled at full speed. Many times before he had been eager to secure a seat near a window to watch the countryside of this region. But now all he cared to see were the always-changing panoramas of Switzerland. Besides, he could not forget his last trip in the opposite direction almost five years before. He was still a boy then, full of vigor, strength and youth. Now on his way back, despite the joy in his heart and the rising hopes for a new start in life, he felt like an old man, a creature that had matured and ripened before its time. He might be rich in human experiences, but he had paid too high a price for them. There was nothing but an appalling weakness left in his body. The buoyant fountain of youth within seemed to have dried up.

He was going home. Certainly there would be great rejoicing and a happy reunion. His family would be glad to see him, to have him back again after so many years of separation. But what about later? What would be his next step toward the future? He could not stay at home forever and depend on his parents to take care of him. The best, perhaps, would be to renew his efforts of landing somewhere in the business field. Any kind of line would be good enough for a start. He could not be very particular under the circumstances. He was still pondering over this question when the train suddenly came to a halt.

"Basel, Basel! All luggage and passports ready for inspection!" called out one of the conductors.

It took quite some time before the train could proceed on its last leg from the German to the Swiss station. Having no baggage, Ebelshauser was quick to present his passport. The realization of actually finding himself on Swiss territory sent a shudder through his whole body. He pinched himself a couple of times to make sure he was not dreaming.

Having a little more than a half hour to make the next train to Lausanne, he went straight to the exchange bureau to have a 50 franc banknote reduced to coins of smaller denomination. Standing at the counter in the vast hall, he handed the note to the clerk.

"Change, please."

The man took the paper and gave him 10 fives in silver coins. Trembling with excitement, Ebelshauser dropped the pile of money, sending the silver pieces all over the floor.

"What's the trouble, are you sick?" asked the exchange agent who came running out of his office to help him gather his small fortune. Other people stood around, stooping down to assist in picking up the money.

"Just nervous, I guess. It'll pass," he replied, blushing.

He then walked over to the telephone office. Having found the number in the Lausanne directory he asked the operator for a long-distance call. Five more minutes went by before he got the connection.

"Hello, Monsieur Jomini? This is Gustav Ebelshauser. Would you mind getting my father on the wire, please? Yes, in the shoe store next door. Yes, just arrived in Basel. Thank you."

The next few minutes of silent suspense seemed to him like an hour. Then came the gentle bass voice he recognized immediately.

"Hello, is it you, Gustav?"

"Yes, papa, I'll be in Lausanne at five. Yes, over Berne ..."

He wanted to say more but heard a loud sigh followed by complete silence on the other end of the wire. He then heard the receiver being hung up. He could not imagine what had happened. He had been cut off at his first sentence.

With great impatience he waited for the train to pull out of the station. The signal of departure was given at last, the whistle blew and Basel soon disappeared from sight. He was now traveling on Swiss territory. Wide awake, he surveyed each turn. At every curve new scenery surged forward, more ravishing in beauty than the pictures before. He felt himself in paradise.

Berne, the seat of government and central capital of Switzerland, already was behind. The train was now approaching the famous tunnel of Chexbres and he intently waited for it. For a short stretch before entering the tunnel's entrance the view was even monotonous in its invariability of hills and valleys. Then the cars penetrated the dark hole made through the mountain. He closed the window to avoid the smoke, but held the strap, ready to open it again as soon as the train came out in the open.

Suddenly, darkness changed to light and he was struck by the sight of Lake Leman with the majestic Alps in the background. Meandering along the shore, the train cut its way across a maze of vineyards extending for miles in every direction, until the outskirts of Lausanne finally were reached in another hour.

Uncontrollably excited, Ebelshauser could hardly sit still. His eyes moved first to the right, then to the left, feasting upon the well known scenery of his boyhood days. He knew every nook and corner he was rapidly traveling through, and they brought back recollections which he thought had been lost forever. He was visibly touched by the beauty surrounding the lake and tears crept into the corners of his eyes. He was being borne away on the trusted wings of memory, heaping treasures of joy and happiness on an already overloaded, palpitating heart. Never in his whole life had he realized such a degree of bliss and felicity. When the train entered Lausanne's outskirts his seat could contain him no longer. He sprang to his feet, opened the window and leaned out in expectation of the next moments to come.

"Lausanne! Lausanne! Lausanne!" called the conductor as he passed through the cars.

Slowly decreasing speed, the train rolled into the station. Unable to utter the shout that stuck in his throat, Ebelshauser recognized the tall, bareheaded man standing next to the platform's stairs as his father. He, too, had already seen his son for his eyes were riveted on him and his hand kept waving in his direction. Farther down the platform stood his sister with Theo, both of them waving and waiting to receive him.

"Gustav! Gustav! GUSTAV!"

Responding to the loud shouting of his name, Ebelshauser looked down to see his two brothers running along with the train. The engine finally came to a halt and the passengers left their seats.

"Papa!"

"Gustav!"

Father and son fell in each other's arms in an emotional, close embrace. Neither could speak. Clinging to each other they stood there, oblivious to their surroundings. Tears of joy burst from their eyes and bathed their happy, smiling faces. Reverently, Theo, Elise and his two brothers kept a short distance away, each one waiting for a separate turn to embrace the returning warrior.

"How is mother?" was his first question.

"Fine," his father said in a shaking voice. "She did not feel well enough to come down, but is anxiously waiting at home for you."

"Oh, Gustav, I'm so glad you're back with us." Elise took him in her arms and covered his face with a shower of kisses.

"At last I have come back," he replied, hugging and clasping his sister tightly.

"Better late than never. How are you, Gustav?"

"Glad to see you here, Theo. I'm terribly happy." The two men shook hands vigorously.

"Gustav ..." Before he could go any further in his sentence, his brother Albert fell to the ground in a faint. The sensation had been too much for him. His face had first turned pale, then purple and blue. His father put his arm under his head while Elise ran for some water. Theo, Oskar and Gustav stood by and watched helplessly.

Elise was soon back and began to sprinkle Albert's face with drops of water from her handkerchief. She opened his collar and shirt and rubbed his chest with the moistened cloth. Albert came to his senses and within a few minutes had completely recovered from the sudden attack.

"Hello, Gustav!" Both Albert and Oskar fell around their brother's neck. They could not suffer to be outdone by the rest of the family. Each one having had his fling at him, Gustav took the lead on their way home, walking next to his father. As they neared the front of the house, his mother already was standing at the window.

"Hello, mother," Gustav called out from below. There was no answer. All of them went up the steps. She was waiting for him at the top of the stoop.

"Gustav, my Gustav, my dear, poor son ... how you ..." This was all she could say. With strong, clutching arms she held him by the neck. He bent over her and tenderly patted her back.

"Yes, mother, here I am again ... and ... so happy ..." He, too, was now crying and sobbing aloud. The spell had come over him. Mother and son held fast to each other for a long while before releasing their grip.

"Let me look at you, Gustav," his mother tearfully said. "You'll have to take a good rest now. And hungry, too, aren't you, son? Don't worry, you'll get everything you need."

"Still the same boy," his father piped in, "though he's grown terribly thin. But we'll fix you up and you'll be all right in no time."

"Now we'll be able to get married," mused his sister. "We've been waiting all this time for your return. You know, I want you to be our best man, isn't that so, Theo?"

"Of course, but give him a chance to breathe again. We've waited so long that we can wait another month or two."

Albert and Oskar had nothing to say. They simply kept peering at him as if seeing in him the return of a ghost. Gustav himself was quiet. He looked from one to the other. In doing so he noticed the ornaments and decorations they had arranged for the great occasion. A huge "welcome home" sign surrounded by a garland of paper flowers hung on the wall. Containers of flowers had been placed on every available stand in the small room. An enormous cake bearing the inscription "Welcome home to our soldier son" occupied the middle of the table, and next to it sat another labelled, "To Gustav, our new-found and beloved brother — Elise, Theo, Albert and Oskar."

"What a welcome," he exclaimed at the sight of all these things. "But, it's really too much for me."

During the meal that followed, Gustav was thankful to his family to be given the privilege of silence instead of being bombarded with questions. Without a word he rejoiced quietly at their mutual understanding. They wanted to give him a chance to forget. It was, therefore, with a sense of great relief that he went to bed that night, happy to be home again and grateful for the possession of a father and mother such as he had.

"Good night, son." His mother came to his bed to kiss him and wish him a peaceful rest.

"Good night, mother dear. It's so good, so incomparably good to be back home again. Good night!"